*f*P

Sneaking into
the Flying Circus

HOW THE MEDIA TURN OUR
PRESIDENTIAL CAMPAIGNS
INTO FREAK SHOWS

Alexandra Pelosi

Free Press

NEW YORK   LONDON   TORONTO   SYDNEY

*f*P

FREE PRESS
A Division of Simon & Schuster, Inc.
1230 Avenue of the Americas
New York, NY 10020

FREE PRESS and colophon are trademarks
of Simon & Schuster, Inc.

For information about special discounts for bulk purchases,
please contact Simon & Schuster Special Sales:
1-800-456-6798 or business@simonandschuster.com

Manufactured in the United States of America

1   3   5   7   9   10   8   6   4   2

Library of Congress Cataloging-in-Publication Data

ISBN-13: 978-0-7432-6304-7
ISBN-10: 0-7432-6304-9

Contents

ACT II

ACT III

Introduction

IT ALL STARTED with a phone call in the summer of 1999, when I was sitting at my desk at NBC News in New York City. The voice on the other end of the phone asked, "Do you have any pets?" No, why? "We need you to cover the Bush campaign. Can you be in Austin by Friday?" With that, I packed a bag and moved to Texas. I did not return home until George W. Bush was sworn in as president. Years later my former boss said that the reason he gave me the assignment was because he knew I had no appetite for politics, therefore I could be trusted not to be a partisan hack. When it comes to politics, I am not a junkie. I was drafted into political journalism; it was never my calling.

In my first week on the bus, a CNN producer for whom I had great respect said, "Listen, I've been doing this for twenty years, just do what I do." That was when I figured out that the minute you get assigned to cover a campaign, you become a part of the process, a pawn in the campaign game. The news organizations hand their young over to the campaigns and let the Karl Roves of this world have their way with them.

Every election cycle journalists defy the theory of evolution; living sequestered on a bus with no sleep, few showers, and tons of junk food, going town-to-town listening to the same speech over and over; every day is a repeat of the day before. You're stuck in this dysfunctional relationship between the news organization that has you there to do their bidding and the campaign that is trying to co-opt you. Over time, the relationship gets complicated, and you realize the dirty extent to which corporate media is in bed with the candidates.

Tired of being trapped like a cog in the giant political media enterprise and afraid of becoming a news nun, at the end of my first campaign I quit my network news job and made a movie about my campaign experience that ended up on HBO. When they asked me what I wanted to do next, of course the answer was, "Go back on the campaign trail." Because once you've been there, the only thing worse than covering a campaign is not covering a campaign.

On my second time around, I went out on the road to document the absurd hazing rituals that our presidential candidates have to go through. Whether they are going door-to-door like traveling salesmen to sell themselves on the house party circuit, begging for money from donors, working the union halls for endorsements, or participating in deep-fried food eating contests at the state fairs, every four years, a handful of men (and a few women who never had a chance) jump through these hoops to try to win their party's nomination. As Adlai Stevenson said, "Any boob can run for president." But the winners have to do things that losers won't do. Most decent human beings don't want to be subjected to the indignities of a presidential campaign (they are repelled by how idiotic the process is and all the hangers-on, parasites, and shysters that you have to put up with in public life).

The two-year-long job application process that you have to endure to become president requires a set of skills that have nothing to do with the job description of being president. For example, in 2000, the last election before 9/11, I never heard Bush talk about terrorism, but I sure saw him flip a lot of flapjacks. He made one "major foreign policy address" and his "foreign trip" was an afternoon bus ride across the Mexican border. One of the foreign journalists complained, "The thing that got me most disillusioned with my fellow journalists was that moment during the second debate about foreign policy. It was clear that the people covering it knew nothing about foreign policy because if they did, they would have reported it completely differently. They said 'Bush held his own,' and the test of holding his own was whether he mispronounced a leader's name? He made huge errors about foreign policy. He should have been called on it." By lowering everyone's expectations, Bush managed to overcome the perception that he didn't know anything about foreign policy (and it helped that the press didn't know much either).

Still, years later, no one ever asks me about Bush's positions on any of the issues. It seems the one thing everyone wants to know is, "What is he really like?" Which is a funny question because it implies that everyone knows that the media do not give them an accurate portrait of a person, or that the media filter changes the picture you see. In real life, no one is who they appear to be on TV. Why is that?

This leads us to a conflict that is as old as democracy itself. Ever since the press stopped trusting politicians, the politicians have been suspicious and paranoid of the press. There is a lot of bad blood running in both directions, and that tug of war is undermining our democracy.

Having spent time with all of the men who wanted to be your president in the past two elections, I can report that the only thing they all had in common was their mistrust of (if not disdain for) the "yappy," "elitist," "judgmental" "media wags." (But who has anything nice to say about the profession of journalism? It is common for crowds at political functions to throw things at reporters or to chant "The media sucks"!)

Around the time that the story came out about the *New York Times* reporter who made up stories, I was walking around Capitol Hill and congressmen of both parties were making jokes to each other about how, for once, the newspapers got a story right. I heard a Republican say without irony to a Democrat, "The *New York Times* makes up stories—this is news?" The congressman replied, "Most reporters are liars. They just never get caught." Later, a senator said in the elevator, "What's the big deal? They make stuff up every single day. It's not like anyone here believes what they read in the paper . . . a big media consumer is not a well-informed human being." Politicians accuse reporters of exaggerating to get attention for their story or of being tools who simply print and repeat what they are told.

This makes you wonder: If all the politicians are just spoon-feeding reporters what they want them to report, then how can the press know what is really going on? And if they don't know what is going on, what exactly are they writing and bloviating about on TV? In a presidential campaign, the stories are all about the horse race: the polls, fundraising, and endorsements. By talking about the inside baseball that few outside the Beltway understand, the news media make politics inaccessible to average citizens and drive them away from the process, making elections nothing more than a media event.

You can't blame people for tuning out those made-for-TV political personalities delivering sound bites that have been rehearsed so much they sound suspiciously like propaganda. Having had it drilled into their heads not to ad lib, candidates are so afraid of how their words can and will be used against them in the media that they never dare say anything that was not approved by their Communications Department. (A few, like John McCain, have tried Straight Talk, but it never got him near the nomination because the Republicans anoint their candidates.) This is what it comes down to: If you want to succeed in presidential politics, you have to package yourself as a one-dimensional caricature. You are not allowed to be anything more than that.

Most candidates believe that if we saw them in a raw, human moment it would hurt them. For example, once I saw one of the candidates put a leftover hamburger in his pocket; later, my producer spotted him in the men's room, snacking on that half-eaten hamburger while using the urinal. If reported, this would be an example of the gotcha-style moments that give journalists a bad name.

Or how about this? One of the candidates told me a funny, harmless little story about getting busted in college for stealing a cow and putting it in the elevator in his college dorm. He explained that he can't tell that anecdote to a reporter because they would launch an investigation into his childhood files; the media would exploit it, and his rivals would jump all over it.

When and how did political journalism change? And was that the same time that politics changed? In the olden days, when Teddy White was profiling John Kennedy, the candidate truly was the campaign. Now the campaign is a huge machine, and the candidate is incidental to his own campaign. Backstage, the spinmeisters are feeding him his lines and handing him his marching orders, and a majority of the campaign's time is dedicated to feeding and restraining the insatiable media beast.

Every campaign tries to evade and manipulate the media. Few have done so as successfully as the Bush team. They have waged the most sophisticated campaign to control the press. Bush's strategy of message discipline and restricting press access has turned presidential campaigns into nothing more than a traveling carnival show that rolls into town, throws up the tent, and puts on this elaborate charade, in which the candidate gives the locals "the old razzle-dazzle" and then they load back up and take the show on the road to a new town, where the act begins all over.

In a way, Watergate was the worst thing that happened to American journalism. Or at least Robert Redford and Dustin Hoffman playing Bob Woodward and Carl Bernstein was, because it turned two reporters into celebrities and that made all the politicians afraid of reporters and all kids at home want to be reporters. Today it seems few want to pound the pavement the way they did to get that story—that requires legwork that few reporters are willing to do.

As we all witnessed when the Bush administration got their war on, they knew the only way to win in the court of public opinion was to get the media on board. So they invited all the ambitious young wannabe Scud studs to join in on the fun. Like dogs on the administration's leash, everyone jumped into their flak jackets and ran toward the battlefield excited about the prospect of covering a war. It seemed like the only debate they had at the networks was who will be on the first float.

On cue from the Pentagon, they named their news coverage Operation Iraqi Freedom. How would it be any different if we had a state-owned media?

The media are supposed to be our safeguard, and they are routinely letting us down. Ted Koppel, a self-confessed "adrenaline addict," went live from the battlefield with a tin can on his head doing war zone infomercials. (This is the same man who marched out of the 1996 Republican Convention because it was "more of an infomercial than a news event.") Why wasn't he in Washington, D.C., working his sources, trying to find out if we were going to war on false pretenses? Because that doesn't make good television. Instead, the "embeds" all accepted their bit parts in the Pentagon production of the selling of the Iraq war.

Not all those working in journalism are at fault for sucking the soul out of the institution. We must distinguish between the television personalities who make more money in a day than most beat reporters make in a year and those journalists who work at their craft. For every overpaid celebrity political talk show host (who would disappear if you unplugged every television in America), there are thousands of decent hard-working reporters scribbling away in their notebooks all across this land. My friends in the media believe that what they do is noble and important, and they have encouraged me not to attack the press, but to challenge the methods of political journalism, placing the blame on the spin men for hurting democracy by misleading reporters and telling half-truths. Of course, there are plenty of decent men and women in public office who feel that what they do is noble and important, and they defend their right to withhold information from reporters who are just out to make names for themselves, always looking for that gotcha moment that will sell newspapers. I have come away feeling trapped between the two worlds; I can see it from both perspectives, and I have a grudging admiration for both sides (although I never liked it when those creepy campaign goons lied to me).

In the schizophrenic media culture that we live in, we forget to take the time to reflect on how our history is being made. We are so fickle, we obsess on the candidates until the day after the election, when we instantly discard the losers and tune out the political noise. By now you probably can't even name the dozen who toiled on the campaign trail attempting to become your president. They may be irrelevant today but how we elect our presidents matters and the way in which the media interrupt that process is worth watching, because every four years it is only going to get worse.

As we attempt to export democracy around the world, it couldn't hurt to sneak a peek inside our own system to see how (or if) it is working. During our campaigns, it is the media's job to stalk and scrutinize the candidates. On this trip, I'm going to watch the detectives do their surveillance to see how they interfere with the outcome of our elections. Now I know what you are thinking: Politics is boring. But that is only because you have not had the right guide. I am not going to take you down that same old road. I'll let you eavesdrop on what people *really* say on a presidential road trip. And to those who mind being quoted, remember Billy Crystal's golden rule: Never talk in elevators!

ACT I

"The media has a weird way of, you know, exploiting you sometimes. They really hype you up sometimes, and then sometimes they really tear you down. I mean, that's part of the whole game. So, um, really I've learned, the more you take it personally it's more like, you know, they've won. So you just do your work and do what you love to do and try not to read into it too much."

—BRITNEY SPEARS ON E!

Party Train at the White House

THE NEWSPAPERS SAY that this is the time of the most bitter partisanship in U.S. political history, but you never would have known it if you saw the conga line at the Congressional Christmas Ball. Led by the bandleader wearing a funny snake hat, Democrats grabbed onto Republicans and cha-cha-cha'ed from one side of the White House to the other. On the sidelines, congressmen cheered and high fived the people in the party train.

My boyfriend took one look at the party train and remarked, "This looks like Rome before the fall." When in Rome . . . we jumped in and bunny-hopped our way from the East Room through the Cross Hall to the State Dining Room. Back on the dance floor in the East Room, where seven presidents, including Abe Lincoln and John F. Kennedy, have lain in state, Bill Frist was boogying down next to Barnie Frank and his boyfriend as the band sang Sister Sledge's "We Are Family." The band played on and the lead singer sang, "I can't get no satisfaction" as one of the Supreme Court justices played along on his air guitar.

Trent Lott did not dance, but he was laughing louder than anyone in the joint. A couple of times he laughed so loud that it interrupted my impromptu interview with the hired help. I wanted to spy on John Ashcroft, but I was afraid to. A Republican congressman told me that he saw Ashcroft eating with his hands; apparently, he has the worst table manners. Dennis Hastert was wrestling his way to the front of the line of all the other members of Congress waiting to have their photograph taken with the president, who spent his night playing Santa Claus for his congressional guests.

As we got closer to the president, a member of the Secret Service told me, "You are not allowed to videotape the president." How times have changed since our road trip back in 2000. Now they are treating him like he is the Messiah: His image is sacred and must be protected.

Standing there in the White House looking at the portraits of former presidents of the past two centuries, I tried to imagine what these great presidents would think of the Texas cowboy who moved into their house. Would they wonder what has become of the office? Or were all the great presidents just mere mortals who grew fine with time?

When our turn came, I said, "Hello, Mr. President." He said, "Hello, Pain in the Ass. Where is that stupid camera of yours?" I introduced him to my boyfriend and Bush instructed him to rein me in. "Smiles everyone," the official White House photographer shouted as we all lined up for our photo op. Then I offered the president the starring role in my new movie, which I pitched as *National Lampoon's Political Vacation,* but he declined. (Though the president will not be in my movie, he did make time to star in what he calls "the highly anticipated holiday blockbuster video *Barney Cam,*" which follows his dog Barney on a tour of the White House.)

Now that we had paid our respects to the host, it was time to shoot video of all the white men with no rhythm on the dance floor trying to dance to the disco hits. Isn't it nice to know that white people get high on black music at the White House?

Twice, in the warm spirit of the holidays, a young woman, acting like she had a Christmas tree up her rear end, threatened to take away my camera. But I believe that the White House is the house of the people and the members of Congress are elected to serve us; therefore, the people have a right to see how they behave. Her position was that since the Republican National Committee sponsored this shindig, what happened behind closed doors at Pennsylvania Avenue was private.

Now you tell me! If I had known that the RNC was paying, I would have bellied up to the bar hours ago. It was time to hit the spread. On the menu tonight was caviar, beef sirloin, and lots of items described as Texas-style this or that. In the middle of the table stood an eighty-pound chocolate model of something we could not identify. We walked around to check out the hundreds of wreaths and dozens of Christmas trees (with no gifts under any of them).

Even though all members of both houses of Congress were invited, none of the presidential candidates came, so my sister Christine measured the drapes for them. She stood for a photo in the window with her arms spread out, with a view of the Washington Monument and the U.S. Capitol in the background.

On the way out, we stepped into the library to see what books they had. My boyfriend picked out *Backdoor to War* and started to read it. A partygoer came in and asked, "Are there any words in those books?"

In the White House movie theater, which was being used as the coat check, a congressional wife retrieving her beaver-trim fur coat was talking with her husband about how many movies they had seen there that year.

Living here on the reservation with all the Secret Service and the trappings of power, George has such a tremendous advantage over all the men who want his job. Surrounded by his cultishly loyal diehards, W. seems to be coasting through some of the worst days in our country's history. Being here tonight reminds me that swinging around in the jungle of the Democratic primary is so much more fun than anything that is going on here. When you are covering a president, every moment of the day is scripted. At least when you are chasing the presi-

Tom DeLay getting down with the band.

dential wannabes you get to be a part of the flying circus. It is time to go home and pack my bags. In the morning I am getting back on the bus.

As we snuck out at 11:30, all the lights were off in the residence upstairs. This party went way past the president's bedtime. While the president sleeps soundly in this house where FDR, JFK, and LBJ slept, all of the little dwarves will have lots of sleepless nights in their quest to kick him out of here.

Hello, New Hampshire

Coos Junction, New Hampshire
JANUARY 26, 2003

I HAVE BEEN in New Hampshire for two hours and I haven't seen one presidential candidate yet. That is unusual for this time of year. Even though the primaries are one year from now, the locals are already calling this "silly season." Here is why: There are 167,085 registered Democrats in the State of New Hampshire, and by now most of them have met, at least once, one if not all, of the Democrats who are running for president.

A presidential campaign is divided into three acts. In the first year, the candidates travel the lonely roads of Iowa and New Hampshire collecting endorsements and money; this period is known as the Invisible Primary. If you come here now, you can have a candidate all to yourself. Act II is the horse race: The media arrive in droves and everything changes as the voters go to the polls and decide the candidate's fate. Only one Democrat will make it to Act III: becoming a celebrity as he goes face-to-face with George W. in the general election.

For those of you who slept through your high school history class, let me refresh your memory. New Hampshire is the home of the first primary, which makes it the official location of the media's political soap opera. The networks booked their hotel rooms here years ago because this is the ideal soundstage for good television: It's small, quaint, and has all these quirky New Englanders who know how to give good sound bites.

Since New Hampshirites are the first to go to the polls, as early as two years before the first primary all of the candidates descend on the state to go door-to-door to sell themselves. This is called retail, as opposed to wholesale, politics. The place where most voters go to shop for a candidate is at a house party.

At the beginning of silly season, a friend, neighbor, or total stranger invites you into their home to eat their food, use their bathrooms, look at all of the pictures of their family, and check out a presidential candidate. As one hostess put it, "We get so close to the candidates we can tell you which ones have to clip their nails."

You don't just get close to them; as a house party guest you are entitled to ask or say anything you want to the candidate and he or she has no choice but to hear you out and address your concerns. How the guests treat the candidate is usually based on the relationship between the candidate and the host. If the host is working for the candidate, no one dares to hurl insults. If the host just met the candidate at the door, the guests feel free to be as rude as they want to be. At one house party where the guests were not on their best behavior, I asked the host why she did not intervene when her guests were behaving badly. She said, "I waited because I wanted to see how the senator did under pressure."

There are three kinds of people who host house parties. The first is the politically active person who has a house party for all of the candidates. (It is common to find pictures of the host with each of the candidates on his refrigerator door.) The second kind of host just got drafted: A campaign contacted him and asked him to donate his home for the night. The third kind of host is the one who really believes in the candidate and is working for the campaign. This is rare. More often than not, the host of the house party doesn't even support the candidate in his home.

Usually voters go to see all of the candidates before dedicating themselves to one. As one house partygoer put it, "I don't vote for anyone who doesn't look me in my eyes when he is shaking my hand." Another said, "I have to see all of the candidates in person before I can commit myself to him." What are the house party guests looking for in a candidate? One suggested, "I am looking for that feeling that Clinton made me feel. Clinton made me feel like 'That's the one.' None of the current candidates have made me feel that yet."

Since I have been on the house party circuit, I am starting to recognize all of the people in the room. But at some parties, it looks like the host just grabbed strangers off the street, showered them up, and made them stand there to fill the room. At one party I heard a man ask his wife, "Who will be speaking?" And she said, "It doesn't matter, There will be food." At another I heard the host instructing her two daughters, "He tends to talk on and on and we don't want people to fall asleep, so keep the food rolling."

There is no law that says you must win the New Hampshire primary to become the nominee of the party. But because the media are scheduled to occupy the state for the entire month of January 2004, the voters of New Hampshire have been given a little more power than all the other states.

All of the candidates are working the state from Main Street to addresses that don't even exist on MapQuest, and they have only one year

A reporter gets Howard Dean all to himself in New Hampshire.   *One year from today.*

left. By the time the primary rolls around, it will feel like a nuclear bomb went off. All the locals will hide inside, and the only people left out in the snow will be the candidates and the hundreds of reporters scurrying around after them.

The Early Favorite

"SHE IS DANGEROUS with that camera," declared the Purple Heart Vietnam vet who has been hiding out in the trenches of the U.S. Senate for the past nineteen years. Dangerous? I'm just a kid with a camcorder. "You aren't going to make me look goofy with that thing," John Kerry declaimed the second time we met. The third time was not a charm. He pointed me out to his advisers and warned them, "Watch her, she is going to lampoon me!" This was not what I expected from the guy the Boston politicos nicknamed "Live Shot" for his unrelenting love of the TV cameras.

"Am I going to have to put up with you for the next eighteen months?" he asked. Assuming you last that long, yes. It seems awfully early for Kerry to have already accepted the nomination. Perhaps this is why some think he is arrogant. Of course, every candidate says, "When I'm president . . ." They have to tell voters what they want to hear, and people want to believe they are picking a winner. They all say it, but Kerry is the only one who seems to actually believe it.

If you were smoking cigars with John F. Kerry, he might tell you that he has wanted to be president all of his life. This is his destiny. After all, he has the initials for it. He might even tell you about how he went sailing with President Kennedy and dated Jackie O's half-sister. Surely, you would hear him drop the name of the fellow New England Democrat who is endorsing him, Teddy Kennedy. But you will never hear Kerry mention the name of that other guy from Massachusetts who got the nomination in '88 (even though he served as his lieutenant governor).

Back in November 2002, after he was reelected to the Senate, Kerry made his intentions clear that he would be pursuing a loftier goal. And everyone in Washington predicted that he had a pretty good shot at it. From day one, Kerry has been considered the de facto front-runner in this race. If you made me put down money today, John Kerry is the best bet. He has military experience, a distinguished career in the Senate, and a lot of money. Or at least his wife does.

John Kerry's biggest problem is that right now he is the early favorite, and in places like Iowa and New Hampshire, they like beating the favorite. The word on Kerry is that he is an aloof snob. "That Boston Brahmin won't fare well in Iowa, his blue blood will get cold," a guy with a goatee and a Howard Dean T-shirt said at a Kerry event in Iowa. Yes, they all like to crash each other's rallies.

If you spend a few weeks with John Kerry in places like Iowa and New Hampshire, you will be able to say that he really is getting a bad rap. When he puts on his New Balance sneakers, rolls up his sleeves, and leaves the tie at home, Kerry is a natural when it comes to the hand-to-hand combat of capturing new supporters. Where he falls flat is in the wholesale department (televised national speeches, debates, TV ads, etc.).

Tonight he made a smart move. He showed up at the California Democratic Party State Convention to give the opening night welcome speech. All he had to do was get up on stage and act like a cheerleader at a pep rally. He got out of town before the meeting was officially called to order and the party activists started getting down and dirty with the issues.

Like President Bush, Kerry is a Skull and Bones Yalie. The big question is, Can he come off like a "regular" guy, as Bush did? W. has an amazing ability to make poor folks feel comfortable. After he got W.'s autograph in 2000, the shoe shiner in our hotel said, "I like the guy 'cause he can stand in a room full of people like me and not make us feel like shit." John Kerry doesn't seem to have that gift.

"Not everyone in the party is as in love with him as he is with himself," a California delegate said as she watched Kerry flee the convention hall without working the room. "He is chickenshit. He has shown no leadership. You can't name one thing he has actually ever done in the Senate."

Twenty-five years ago, Richard Nixon wanted to destroy John Kerry for his antiwar activities. A secret White House memo read: "Destroy the young demagogue before he becomes another Ralph Nader." Since then, Kerry has polished himself up, served his time in the Establishment, and now has a good chance of becoming the next Al Gore.

By now everyone will tell you that the one thing they didn't like about Gore was the way he talked down to people. So much so that his own press corps didn't even like him. Will John Kerry make the same mistake that Al Gore made?

Meeting Dr. Dean

New York City
MARCH 15, 2003

OF ALL THE DELEGATES at the Democratic National Committee winter meeting, my sister Christine was the last one Howard Dean should have been asking for support.

This was the first time most of the party loyalists had ever seen Howard Dean. He had just delivered his now infamous speech in which he asked, "What I want to know is, why is the Democratic leadership supporting unilateralism in Iraq?" Which is a legitimate question. However, all of the Democratic leadership did not support the war—the ones running for president did.

After the speech, Dean had to take a lap through the bar to introduce himself to the DNC members. The governor walked up to my sister (who is a superdelegate) and started schmoozing, "Hi, I'm Howard Dean. I am asking for your support." It didn't take long for my sister to cut right into him.

CHRISTINE: I am Christine Pelosi, a DNC delegate for six years, daughter of Nancy, who spoke earlier. I'm sorry you missed her speech because you covered a lot of the same points. I thought it was a bit inappropriate that you said the Democratic leadership supported universal action in Iraq, since she is the Democratic leader and she garnered national and international attention and criticism for opposing that approach and offering instead the Spratt Amendment of multilateralism through the United Nations.

DEAN: Oh, I didn't mean her . . .

CHRISTINE: Well, she's the one who carries the title Democratic leader, so if you meant something else . . .

As Christine and Howard Dean went back and forth clarifying what he wanted to know and from whom, her teacher unionista friends stood next to her, chanting, "Don't dis the mama," and I retreated to the back of the bar, afraid of what Dean might say if he saw my camera capturing the whole scene. This was not an appropriate time for me to meet the candidate. Though I do not share my sister's political convictions, I agreed with her view that Dean was saying something politically popular but not exactly true.

When I watched the DNC's round of standing ovations for Dean it reminded me of something I learned as a teenager at the 1984 Democratic Convention in San Francisco. Mario Cuomo said in his "Tale of Two Cities" speech, "We must get the American public to look past the glitter, beyond the showmanship to reality, to the hard substance of things. And we will do that not so much with speeches that sound good as with speeches that are good and sound. Not so much with speeches that will bring people to their feet as with speeches that bring people to their senses."

Sounding like a Sunday morning talk show evangelist, Howard Dean is bringing people to their feet, but with this crowd, that is easy. They will get knocked to their senses when they start doing the calculus of who has the best shot against this incumbent.

When I got home to New York after the DNC meeting, there was an invitation in the mail for the Women's Campaign Fund event that I had committed to appear at as a special guest. Every year they have an event in Manhattan to raise money to help elect women. In private homes throughout the city they host small dinner parties that feature special guests. It turned out that the other special guests at my dinner were Janet Reno and Howard Dean.

This was the perfect way to meet the man I have been chasing across the country for months now. The dinner was held in a very exclusive home on New York's Upper East Side, across from Central Park. Standing around looking at the Renaissance paintings, an older gentleman confessed to me that the only reason he came was to see the art; he didn't really have any interest in hearing the speakers. We laughed about what a B-level party this was: Janet Reno, who lost the governor's race in Florida; Howard Dean, an unknown former governor from Vermont; and a documentary filmmaker. Who would pay real money for this?

The program was about to begin, so the man who just came to see the art asked if he could walk up to the front of the room with me because he wanted to see if that really was a Giotto on the wall where the host was standing.

Janet Reno told some story, but I can't tell you what it was about because I wasn't paying attention. I could not keep my eyes off her huge shoes. Have you ever seen Janet Reno's feet? They reminded me of Karen Hughes's feet. By the time the host called on me to address the crowd, my thoughts had drifted back to the time during Campaign 2000 when Karen Hughes confided that her feet were so big, she had to buy her shoes at a store for transvestites.

Janet Reno's feet.

Knowing how little the refined uptown crowd cared about details of daily campaign drudgery, I kept it brief. I explained that I have been on the road with all of the men who are running for the highest office in the land and it is a shame that there aren't more qualified women in the pool. I then used the opportunity to pander to Howard Dean by saying that there are good, unknown candidates like Dean who need funding to get their message out.

It was Dean's turn to try to woo the crowd. He took to the top of the steps and delivered his pitch. In a calm, subtle, simple way, this scion of Park Avenue said he wanted to be president of the United States for all the reasons he has already explained so many times out on the campaign trail. Unlike the DNC meeting performance, he was not on a crusade, he did not have that tone, but he said more or less the same thing he has said every day on the campaign trail in Iowa and New Hampshire (which amused me because these rich people paid a lot of money thinking they would be hearing something exclusive).

When Dean finished his remarks the host told us it was time to be seated and we found our way to our tables. At my table, everyone, including a real estate mogul, a famous plastic surgeon, and an aspiring supermodel, wanted to know what I thought of "the little doctor from Vermont." There wasn't much to say, as he was truly a beginner. As one of the socialites declared, "We have to wait and see what the *New York Times* has to say about him."

And that was that. We moved on to small talk among ourselves. "What do you do?" the real estate magnate asked my European boyfriend. "I am working with the Dutch Ministry of Foreign Affairs to teach Americans about Dutch culture," Michiel explained. "Is that a moneymaker?" the mogul asked. Welcome to America, Michiel.

After each course the special guests were asked to rotate to the other tables. When I got up, Howard Dean sat in my seat next to my boyfriend. Later, when I asked how Dean performed at the table, Michiel reported, "He had to fight for attention. The women all wanted to talk about who Mayor Bloomberg is dating!"

After a night full of in-depth discussions about all the issues that plague people in this small tax bracket, we all gathered in the hall to air-kiss our goodbyes and wait for the elevator man to come pick us up and take us back down to the mean streets. After Dr. Dean boarded for his ride, a socialite told him, "I can't wait to see you in the *New York Times*."

The Man of the House

Promise City, Iowa
MARCH 16, 2003

YOU WOULDN'T KNOW it if you watched Fox News, but Congressman Dick Gephardt announced that he is running for president. Fox carried the ceremony live for a few minutes but then interrupted the broadcast for a Fox News Alert about a dog trapped on ice in New Jersey. "Rescue crews are paddling out to get him," the anchor announced, and the drama of the rescue was far too newsworthy to cut away from to listen to one man talk about trading in his twenty-seven years in Congress for his last shot at the White House.

After the announcement in his hometown, Gephardt flew off to Iowa, the only state he won when he ran for president in 1988, and the place where he will be spending a majority of his time campaigning in the next year. Dick has to introduce himself to Iowans all over again. When he asked a schoolteacher in a handmade U.S. flag sweater if she would be coming out to caucus for him, she told him, "I have to see you four or five times before I can make that decision." He replied, "Absolutely."

After he left the room, that woman told me that she does not feel comfortable with Dick for two reasons: "He was for the Iraq war. He didn't just vote for it, he stood with President Bush in the Rose Garden in support of it," and "He has been around for too long."

The distinguished gentleman from the great State of Missouri has served in public life for almost three decades. As the House Democratic leader, he is the only candidate who has campaigned in every state, in every Democratic district in the country. But it is hard to find the right way to sell those years in the trenches fighting for your party. The inner workings of the federal government are complex, and that complexity doesn't fit on a bumper sticker.

Teddy Roosevelt said, "One thing I notice about people who live outside of Washington. They know nothing about Washington." Washington is a byzantine place, and Dick knows the politics and the culture of it thoroughly. But it is cool to hate Washington. Every campaign season the Washington insiders all try to sell themselves as outsiders. In his announcement speech, Dick made it clear that he is not taking that route. "I'm not going to say what's fashionable in our politics—that I'm a Washington outsider, that I couldn't find the nation's capital on a map, that I have no experience in the highest levels of government. I do, and I think experience matters. It's what our nation needs right now. I'm not the political flavor of the month. I'm not the flashiest candidate around. But the fight for working families is in my bones, it's in my gut. It's where I come from; it's been my life's work."

The old-school Washington insider admits that the biggest obstacle he has to overcome in this race is that "people think of me as that guy in a suit standing at the podium talking with other congressmen on C-SPAN." So this is what American politics has come to. After a lifetime in the House of Representatives, having served in the leadership, with the weight of the Democratic Party on his back, Gephardt now has to find a cooler image.

Gephardt's events are full of old people. Really old people. After interviewing a room full of his supporters, you may start to wonder, why is it so hard to find someone with a mouth full of teeth? There is at least one person on an assistive oxygen tank at every Gephardt event. We may even have someone pass out, as one elderly woman did today. They had to bring in an ambulance. Still no word if she will survive to make it to the caucus. At one stop, when Gephardt was promising to give front-row seats to his inauguration to those who join Team Gephardt, one old geezer yelled out, "I'm not going to live that long."

The thing that is so endearing about Gephardt is how this small-town boy rose to such heights in the U.S. Congress and managed to retain his wholesome, all-American, boyish dorkiness. In his heart, he is still that Eagle Scout from the Midwest who wants to listen to people's problems. He is an artifact from the 1950s. He is still that good kid who played by the rules, who cut class only to listen to JFK's speeches. That is where he learned that public office is a higher calling; you can't just take from this country, you have to give something back. He is not in it for his own ego or the fame or the money (there isn't much of that anyway).

After spending time with the congressman in Iowa, it seems strange to see him at fund-raisers in New York City speaking to the stuffy, wealthy New Yorkers. What a contrast this is from the union halls and homes for the elderly he frequents. He seems so much more at home at the In and Out Burger than on the Upper East Side with all the self-important people. At a top-dollar fund-raiser Dick does not look out of place, but at the end of the night, he still prefers to go home to a Super 8 Motel. (There are very few guarantees on the campaign trail. The fact that if you are traveling with Dick Gephardt, you will end up at a Super 8 Motel at the end of the night is one of them.)

Dick Gephardt has served with five presidents, but he says that our current president is by far the worst in U.S. history. Of Bush he says,

"He is nice man, he is a fine man, he is an awful president. He frightens me, and if you had to meet with George Bush weekly you would be running for president, too. Right now the Europeans look at Bush and they question his judgment. If we reelect him, they will question ours."

In his tan Dockers and a comfortable sweater, Dick is hard at work on the trail. In a disciplined delivery, he manages to tell his story, over and over, like it's the first time, with a serial sincerity that makes you believe that this man is for real. When you have been at this as long as Congressman Gephardt has, you can't hide who you are. He has had to vote every single week on every issue in U.S. politics for twenty-seven years. But all that experience is not always a good thing. As one cab-driver sees it, "Dick Gephardt has tried and failed too many times. Every two years he tries to win a majority in the House and he fails. If you are constantly running and losing, you can't get past the label of loser, nobody will be able to think of you as a winner."

Anonymous at Midway with the Great Unwashed

Chicago
APRIL 6, 2003

ONE OF THE WORST PARTS about running for president is that in the early stages you have to spend a lot time in airports. Trailing one of the candidates through Midway Airport on his way to Dubuque, Iowa, I watched him endure the humiliation of modern travel.

Going through security virtually unrecognized, he had to take off his shoes and belt and get the full pat-down, just like the rest of us. The security guard studied his shoes with suspicion: "What is this, a wood sole?" From the looks of it, this was the first pair of leather shoes he had seen in a very long time.

To get to the gate, the senator stopped to take a look at a television and a supersized lady barked at him, "Move it, man, you're blocking the TV." (Far be it from her to move her own fat ass over into the empty seats on either side for a better view.) He instantly jumped out of the way, alerted to the cardinal sin he had committed: standing between a fat lady and the TV.

Walking to the gate was not an option because people were napping, having picnics, or letting their kids spread out all of their toys in the walkways. So there was a huge line just to get onto the moving walkways (which were packed with people who were refusing to walk and were just letting the walkway move them to their gates).

When we arrived at the boarding area, it looked like a campsite with all the people and their huge suitcases and their fast food spewed all over the place. Men and women of all ages were lying all over the furniture in their sweatpants and flip-flops (exposing their toe jam for all the world to see). It looks as if everyone (especially the women) have given up—they are wearing dirty clothes, exposing their unpedicured toes and hairy legs, and sitting with their legs and mouths wide open.

In line to check in for our flight, a barefoot man wrapped in a blanket refused to move from the counter until the agent told him what gate his flight would be moved to. As the agent impatiently explained that she would make an announcement, he complained that the gate change announcements were only made in Spanish "and I only speak English." She promised that they would make an announcement in English for him.

On our left, a white woman with cornrows was eating an entire box of six Cinnabons. On our right, a young mother was feeding her eight-month-old Chicken McNuggets, while her two-year-old shoved an entire Big Mac in his tiny little mouth. In the row across, a skinhead with a U.S. flag tattoo was shouting into his cell phone for all of us to hear, "Don't do my bitch while I'm outta town, dog."

Waiting for our delayed flight, the senator went to answer Mother Nature's call. The line at Mickey D's was blocking the entrance to the men's room and he got pushed out of the way by a teenager calling out her order for a Big Mac, fries, chocolate shake, apple pie, and Egg Mc-Muffin.

Even though it was nighttime, over at the Starbucks, people were waiting for their ridiculously large $5 coffees. A generously proportioned woman was having a fit: "I ordered nonfat milk in my latte." Great, that's just what we need, a bunch of overcaffeinated rude passengers on a long flight with no food.

At the newsstand, it took the cashier at least five minutes to figure out how much to charge us for the *Economist*. First she asked, "What is this?" and then she told us that *People* magazine is the only magazine she ever sells. Which is evident back in the boarding area, where the few who are reading have either *People,* some trashy romance novel, or the latest murder mystery in their hands. Although it was unclear how they could even read with the constant barrage of gate change announcements and the couples shouting at each other on the Maury Povich show on TV.

When it finally came time to board our plane, we lined up behind a woman alone with a large pizza, a mom who was letting her kids scream for no apparent reason, and a man who had obviously spent the night in the airport bar who was hitting on the lady behind him while trying to wheel a suitcase that looked way too big to fit in the overhead bin. The senator remarked, "Isn't this the worst? Flying has become worse than taking the bus." To which I reminded him, "You want to be their president."

These days, the candidates have more time than money, but once they raise it, they will have more money than time. Once the primaries begin, it will be a race against time, and money will not be a factor. When time is not on their side, they will get their own charters, and they will be traveling on the same planes that Pearl Jam, Stevie Nicks, and the Rolling Stones use—that is when they will start to feel like pop stars.

Charters provide the convenience of not having to deal with the airport. Plus, there are other advantages: You get to use your cell phone whenever you want, people wait on you hand and foot, the flight attendants act like your own personal slaves, and they tell you the gossip about the others who have come before you. "Pamela Anderson is really a bitch and she touches her boobs too much" and "The Chicago Bulls sure like to talk about sex a lot" and "The White House Press Corps is our least favorite because they're the rudest, loudest, and most demanding."

But there are disadvantages: Private planes do crash, we have lost candidates—Senator Paul Wellstone, Governor Mel Carnahan, Senator John Heinz were all victims of the campaign curse. So much campaigning to do, so little time.

Meeting Up with the Deansters

New York City
APRIL 14, 2003

So how did this unknown governor from a little New England state become the hottest thing since Napster? They were both the first big organizations of their kind on the Web that became the target of Washington. The only real difference is Napster sold out to stay in business. Will the Deansters?

To understand the Dean crusade, you have to go to a meet-up, a get-together put together through Meetup.com, the Internet party planner that brings together like-minded souls to talk about their obsessions with everything from Dungeons and Dragons to home birthing to boxers (it is unclear whether these are dog lovers or underwear enthusiasts).

At a recent Dean meet-up on the Lower East Side of Manhattan, the Deanies gathered into what had to be the most impressive voluntary workforce ever assembled in a downtown bar. There were all types, young and old, hippies and yuppies, all working together for the cause, writing letters to people in Iowa about why they love Howard. As they worked by candlelight, a bearded man announced to the room, "I think we should all read our letters aloud to each other." He proceeded to read aloud his letter about the pollution of the Hudson River. This freak show clearly displayed the problem that this campaign is having. While there are plenty of perfectly normal-looking Democratic voters who support Howard Dean, the bearded weirdos are the ones who stick out and shape the image of the whole campaign.

A common complaint that you will hear from Dean supporters is that Howard is getting unfairly labeled as angry and liberal. But if you go to a Dean meet-up you will meet a lot of people who call themselves liberal who are angry. They say things like "I'm pissed off, I'm angry, and I think Dean can bring us together" and "I am mad at the Democrats for voting for this war, I am mad at Bush for bombing innocent Iraqis, and I am mad at my fellow countrymen for letting our government do this." Dean has tapped into the huge reservoir of anger toward the Democrats and George Bush. So even if the angry-and-liberal label does not apply to the candidate, it certainly applies to many of his supporters. Perhaps the Deanies are not helping Dean as much as they think they are.

They love to talk about how they blog for Dean. "I blog for Dean," a professional-looking woman in a power suit said, "because I want to talk to all of the other members of the Dean family about everything from how my day was to how I feel about boycotting veal. It is a great release for me." A younger woman wearing an Urban Outfitters Buddha Rocks T-shirt said, "I blog for Dean because it makes me feel a part of something. I am not the only one who hates my president." While the blogging is making all these people feel good, the big question is, "What does it do for Howard Dean?"

As the antidote to the president, Dean is seen as a savior to all those disenfranchised voters, the Bush haters, the antiwar protesters, the activists, and all of those cyber enthusiasts without a voice looking for someone to speak for them, which is why he is attracting groupies. One group of regulars call themselves "the Stalkers"; when they see Dean they holler, "Hey, Howard, look, the Stalkers are here." If you cruise the Internet it is easy to find many who seem to have an unhealthy passion for the man: They sing songs for Dean, say prayers for Dean, there is even a homeless man who writes love poems to Howard Dean on the Internet from the public library.

On April Fools' Day, I went to another Dean meet-up on the Upper West Side. It was packed with enthusiastic young movers and shakers. You could tell by the amount of phone numbers being exchanged at the bar that these meet-ups are getting people's political juices flowing.

It was just another Tuesday night in the city that never sleeps and a couple hundred young swinging singles came out to see Howard Dean give his stump speech. The joint went wild when he went on his rant against Bush and the war. "Give 'em hell, Howard," a college coed screamed out. (Later, she admitted that she did not know the history of that expression, she just picked it up online.)

You have got to give his campaign credit—this night was a huge success (if you ignored the drunk girl at the bar screaming things like "What have we got here, a bunch of stinkin' fuckin' liberals?"). Many well-groomed, sophisticated Manhattanites expressed excitement about hearing a presidential candidate speak for the first time. By the end of the night, all of the seasoned politicos in the room as well as the political virgins were pledging their love to Howard Dean. Despite everything he says about this president and his war, it is now clear that this war is the best thing that ever happened to Howard Dean.

People have been saying that the antiwar activists are on the verge of a revolution: They are using the Internet to bring young people together to meet up in bars to have a beer and talk to each other! From the looks of it, with the 100 million singles in the United States, this is just another excuse for singles to hook up. It is no different from the anti–Vietnam War era, except back then, there was an even better incentive: The women were burning their bras!

Standing over by the bar, a gentleman approached me and asked, "Would you like to celebrate a special occasion with me?" "What's the occasion?" I asked. "Meeting a special lady like you." After mocking him and then letting him buy me an $11 flirtini martini, I asked him what he was doing in a Howard Dean meet-up. He told me that he came to "score with a hot and sexy single girl." A few beers and many rejections later, he confessed that he attends a lot of meet-ups because they are "a great place to meet cuties and a lot cheaper than going to a strip club."

The next gentleman swinger who came to the bar ordered a $12 Big Apple martini and refused to go on camera to talk about his interest in Howard Dean. But he promised, "If I hook up with any of these cuties, you can come and videotape it!"

An attractive, well-informed lesbian (who really likes Dean because he signed the civil union bill) gave me a speech about how she loves Dean but hates all of the single, desperate, horny men who show up at meet-ups. But a man from Queens for Dean, representing both the borough of Queens and the NYC transvestite community, rejoiced, "Dean is sex. This guy is a winner. You know how you can tell? It smells like sex in here."

Well before closing time, Howard Dean left the bar to drive home to Vermont. On his way out, he stopped on the street to take some questions from a few reporters who were hanging around out front, his first impromptu New York City press conference. Nearby, a couple of new acquaintances who met up at the meet-up were making out on the sidewalk. Dean explained, "More than four thousand Dean supporters have been to a meet-up nationwide. You see, we are bringing people together, viral marketing works." From the looks of that couple making it to second base right next to him, it appeared Howard Dean was right: Viral marketing does work.

Dean's first New York City press conference.

Networking and Not Working

AS A COMMANDER IN CHIEF running for reelection, the only thing better than being able to start your own war is being able to get on network television anytime you feel like putting on a pep rally, publicity stunt, or million-dollar Tom Cruise–style *Top Gun* fantasy photo op.

At the same time that our president (who was AWOL from the Air National Guard) interrupted *Friends* on must-see TV night to fly a fighter jet (when he could have taken his helicopter, since it was only thirty miles from shore) onto an aircraft carrier (in a jumpsuit that was a little too tight for prime time) to declare "Mission accomplished" (when in fact we all know the war is far from over), John Kerry supporters gathered downtown in New York City for a meet-up.

Trying to tap into the whole Internet movement, Kerry's people organized this event through Meetup.com, the same group that brings the Deanies together. With everyone standing around "meeting up" with fellow Democrats, the small talk revolved around the usual topics: the hot new bars in the neighborhood, where *Sex and the City* is being shot this week, and whether or not Brooklyn Lager is actually made in Brooklyn. (It is. The Brooklyn Brewery opened in 1996 and every Friday night they have Happy Hour at their Tasting Room in Williamsburg, Brooklyn.)

The small group of single women I talked to admitted that they were not committed to Kerry, they were still shopping for a candidate. We talked about how picking a candidate is a lot like dating. There are plenty of choices out there, but they are all more or less the same, none of them are perfect, and sooner or later you have to pick one. We talked about the pros and cons of each candidate and they seemed to feel that Dean is the easiest one to commit to: He looks good, he sounds good, and he "doesn't have a stick up his ass like all those senators do." But they doubt that relationship has any chance of going anywhere. One of the women explained why she was not falling for Dean: "Everyone is living on instant judgments and instant judgments are always wrong."

The conclusion the day care counselor came to was, "If you took something from each of these men and put them all together, you'd have the perfect candidate." Her friend the aroma therapist added, "I have seen them all. We don't have the right guy, so we are trying to find the one that we can live with." Eternal optimists, they came to work the bar scene and listen to what Kerry loyalists have to say.

John Kerry's New York City meet-up.

Howard Dean's New York City meet-up.

Kerry's old friend Mark Green, the failed mayoral candidate, talked about how his friend of twenty years is the only candidate in the race who has "the charms, the looks, the height, and the combat experience to be president." Kerry's stepson talked about what a cool stepdad John Kerry is because he windsurfs and does other cool stepfather-type activities.

Looking around the empty room, it was obvious that something wasn't right. Thousands of antiwar protesters took to the streets of New York City recently, voicing their anger toward George Bush, and only a dozen people showed up tonight to learn more about the leading Democratic alternative. Since Kerry voted for the war and the whole antiwar movement already has an established network online, this whole meet-up movement may be working for Howard Dean, but it's not going to work for John Kerry. As one Kerry apologist put it, "Kerry attracts a different kind of young professional, the kind with a job who does not hang out in bars."

How to Use Your Family

New York City
JUNE 4, 2003

HOWARD DEAN has no idea what he has gotten himself into. Tonight in his commencement address to the Albert Einstein College of Medicine, he revealed his dirty little secret. He told the graduating class of aspiring new doctors, "Do not make your practice your whole life. Don't ignore your families." Like a lot of things in his stump speech, this is easier said than done.

These days the doctor is in Iowa and New Hampshire making the rounds. While he travels around giving his prescription for the ills of

America with his sterile, impersonal bedside manner, his wife is back home dealing with her own patients and learning why politics is often referred to as a jealous mistress.

While all the other potential first ladies schlep around the country with their husband, Dr. Dean's wife, Dr. Judith Steinberg, insists on staying home to practice medicine. Dean says that if he becomes president, his wife will open a medical practice in Washington, D.C. He has made his wife's lack of involvement in his campaign so clear that a reporter once asked him, "Does your wife even know that you are running?"

Let's give kudos to Dean for liberating his wife from a life of standing by her man. He deserves credit for not exploiting his family for political purposes. And we should congratulate Dr. Steinberg for choosing her patients over her husband's ambition. She is a liberated woman of the new millennium. The question is: Is America ready for a full-time professional woman as first lady?

If Howard wins the nomination, Judith will have to pull a Hillary and adopt her husband's last name. But will she come out for the stump? Election protocol dictates that postconvention the whole ticket (all four of them, nominees and spouses) must all be out on the road. If she doesn't go, you know the public (or at least the media gossipistas) will surely hold this against him.

In 2000, George knew exactly how to use Laura. If you search the video archives, you will find that in three key moments of the 2000 campaign, George had Laura's hand glued to his. The first time was in the heat of the primaries, when it really looked like the $80 million W. juggernaut was on the line. Bush came out to attack McCain. With Laura on his arm to soften the blow he shot out, "John McCain called me an anti-Catholic bigot. That's shameful politics."

The next time Laura made a big showing was after the nomination, when Bush went to Arizona to pose for a kiss-and-make-up photo session with John and Cindy McCain. While McCain looked like he wanted to throw the couple off his land, Laura made it look like the couples were the best of friends by suggesting, "This was fun, let's do it again sometime."

Mrs. Bush's best cameo came on the weekend before the election, when news broke of Bush's 1976 arrest. He came out arm in arm with his wife and admitted, "Twenty-four years ago I was apprehended in Kennebunkport, Maine, for a DUI. That's an accurate story. I am not proud of that." Laura just stood there and smiled like this was just another day at the old ballgame.

A first lady is expected to be a beautiful flower (it is up to her which flower she will be: a delicate little tulip like Laura Bush or a snapdragon like Barbara Bush). America wants its first ladies to be obedient and subservient women who bake cookies and take Barbara Walters on a tour of their immaculate home.

When your wife is too present or when your family comes out too much to stump for you, it can backfire (see Hillary Clinton). When a wife shows up on the trail, reporters ask her all sorts of stupid little questions meant to trick her into sniping at or about her man (see Teresa Heinz Kerry). And if you share some very personal family matter with a town hall meeting full of strangers, you can get accused of exploiting your family for political gain (meet the Gephardts).

It is too early to tell how the family factor will play for Dean. Four out of five cynical reporters sitting on the bus agree that the fact that his own wife doesn't want any part of his presidential pursuits makes him appear like an unlovable loner. (The irony here is, how many of these self-absorbed, careerist reporters have their spouse in tow?) We speculate that she must not have much confidence in his chances of being able to go all the way.

The fact that his children are not appearing anywhere near him suggests that they don't want any part of this either. Whether you are willing to admit it or not, your family has to sacrifice a lot for you to be able to put yourself in public space. Sure, politics can be hateful and hurtful and it must not be easy for those kids to hear all the nasty things people are saying about their daddy, but that has not stopped all the Kerry, Edwards, Lieberman, and Graham kids from hitting the trail on their dad's behalf.

All the candidates have their families out pimping them. Joe Lieberman has his eighty-nine-year-old mother working the retirement home circuit. "My son will make a great president," she pledges in her stump speech. "Joe's always been a good boy. He was born smiling. He never caused any trouble. He watched *Lassie* on TV and kept a clean room; he tutored his classmates in our home; he was the teacher's pet. He was in the choir, he played the clarinet and did lots of sports; he was on the debate team. He was voted the most popular boy in school. He was elected class president and prom king."

POTUS dreaming is an all-consuming pursuit. It requires every ounce of energy you and your whole family have got. If Dr. Dean is out on the road all the time while his family is at home, he is making his presidential campaign his whole life. How involved could he be in their lives if he is out on the road? Evidently, he is not practicing what he preaches.

Putting together a segment about what the candidates do on their days off, I asked all of the candidates if I could hang out with them on their next day off. Of course, the reply from all of the campaigns was, "The candidate doesn't have any days off on his schedule." (Except for Lieberman, who invited me over for Sabbath on Saturday. But I didn't go because what would we do all day if we couldn't eat ice cream and watch TV?)

On the airplane recently I asked the guy sitting next to me who worked on Bob Dole's presidential campaign why he lost in 1988. He explained that Dole wasn't centered. Politics destroyed his first marriage, he didn't have any hobbies, and he had no life outside of politics. "He wasn't a well-balanced guy. In the political game, it is easy to get knocked off your center. After a hit, you have to be able to retain a cool head. Dole could never do that."

This sounds eerily familiar. The big criticism of Dean so far is that he is a hothead. When he gets attacked, he acts defensive. Perhaps if he had a woman by his side, gazing at him lovingly, that would soften that image. All men act better with a woman by their side. If Dean keeps his cool and becomes a serious contender in this election, it will be interesting to see if America wants a man who is just selling himself, not the illusion of Camelot and the perfect First Family.

While some are pining for a little PDA from Howard and Judith just to see the rounded-out version of his personality, no one really needs to relive the Al and Tipper kiss anytime soon. And the appearance of Dr. Judith may or may not change our views of Dean. Remember, Hillary and Tipper were (literally) all over their husbands, but that didn't make Al any more human or Bill any less.

Finding Joey

Merrimack, New Hampshire
JULY 4, 2003

TODAY I INTENDED TO SHADOW Howard Dean on his triumphant march across New Hampshire in a series of Fourth of July parades, but his posse is too big now that his fund-raising numbers are so good. I was forced to find a less popular candidate to roll around with. Hey look, there's John Kerry.

Let's go see what he has to say for himself. Hello there, Senator, looks like Howard Dean is going to be getting all the love today, but I'll be your friend. Want me to keep you company in the parade today? Kerry answered with the same response he has used every time I have seen him in the past few months. "Tell me about your life." By now he must have seen my Bush movie because he was stealing George Bush's material. He, like Bush, is starting to sound like a one-note wonder. I am not in the mood to listen to this broken record, so I let Kerry march on and I waited for the next candidate to come along. It happened to be Joe Lieberman.

Months ago the media concluded that after September 11 and the crisis in the Middle East and Americans' ignorance and intolerance for anyone who is not a solid white Christian, Joe Lieberman has no shot at the nomination. I had no intention of spending any time with "the man who would be vice president if they had counted all the chads," but he comes in first place in all the national polls and his fund-raising numbers are better than expected this quarter, so I decided to see what he was up to.

"Now that you have raised more money, do you feel like more of a man?" I asked. Lieberman declared, "Now that I have more money, I'll finally get some respect." He invited me to tag along with him for the parade under these conditions: "Run ahead of me and blend into the crowd and when you see me coming, ask loudly, 'Isn't that Joe Lieberman?' It will create a buzz." He explained how years ago when he was an unknown candidate that was what he would make his staff do to get attention. But he no longer needs an introduction.

The best part about being Joey Lieberman today is that everybody knows who he is. Because he has already run on the national level, people recognize him and most of them have already formed an opinion of him (for better or for worse). In 2000 we all got to know the "moderate" senator from Connecticut, who, as the first Orthodox Jew to be tapped as a vice presidential candidate, would not campaign on Saturdays in order to observe his religion. As we made our way through the sea of spectators lounging in their beach chairs along the parade route, Joey lovers remarked, "This time, Joey."

Lieberman's threats to put "legal restrictions" on Hollywood and his condemnation of Bill Clinton for his "immorality" in the Lewinsky affair have made Lieberman so popular with Republicans and conservative Democrats that liberals in his own party call him a "Republicrat." It is no secret that it will be almost impossible for Joe Lieberman to win in the Democratic primaries. The voters who turn up to vote in the presidential primaries are the diehard hardcore Democrats, and Joe Lieberman is way too conservative for their taste.

The real reason Joe Lieberman is doing so well in the polls right now is because he is the only candidate anyone can name at this point. The other candidates claim that once people get to know them, they will knock Joey out of the running.

In one day with Joey, you can see everything that most people do not know about him. Essentially, there are two Joe Liebermans. On TV, Senator Joseph Lieberman comes off as a stale, old, boring, sanctimonious speaker. He is the righteous preacher going off on a moralist rant or some grating lecture. Somehow the television filters out his personal charms. You've got to catch him live to see the Joie de Vivre Joey. In person, he is funny and full of life. You can see why he was voted Mr. Personality in high school. He has a goofy, self-deprecating, wry sense of humor and is comfortable enough in his own skin to show it. Who would have guessed it?

He had all kinds of good stories to tell. Like the one about the last time he went to the White House and the president asked him, "How is the campaign going?" And he said, "Great." And then Bush put his hand on his elbow and said, "It's grueling, isn't it? Only someone who has been through it knows." At the end of the first parade, I realized that Joey is worth spending time with because he is great at explaining the humiliation and absurdity of running for high office.

So I jumped in my car and raced off to the starting point of the next parade to meet him. When I got there I asked the local policeman if this was where Lieberman would be arriving. The officer replied, "Who?" I tried again: "Joe Lieberman, you know, he is running for president." He rolled his eyes and gasped, "Oh no, him again? You're kidding, we have to go through all that again?" What does that cop know that Joey doesn't?

Your First Photo Op

The Iowa State Fair
AUGUST 15, 2003

THERE ARE A FEW THINGS you should know if you plan on covering a presidential campaign. The first is that you will be spending a lot of time in Iowa. Grab your sunscreen and pack a parka because you'll be going from Mason City to Davenport and then back to Council Bluffs throughout the dog days of summer and into the ball-freezing cold days of winter.

The candidates must get to the Hawkeye State early and often enough to make friends in every one of the 2000 precincts, so that when caucus night comes, they will have recruited enough caucus-goers to stand up and pledge their allegiance to them.

Their goal here is to "pull a Jimmy Carter," which means they will come out of nowhere and win. That will create the momentum (aka The Big Mo) they'll need to get the buzz going in the states that follow. If they can manage to win the Iowa caucuses, they will attract enough media respect to fill the seats on their press plane for their trip to New Hampshire. If they don't come in second or third in Iowa, they might as well drop out of the race altogether.

But let's not get ahead of ourselves. This week all of the candidates are here for the one event of the year that encapsulates Iowa politics: the Iowa State Fair. Listed in the book of *1000 Places to See Before You Die,* the Iowa State Fair is featured along with Mt. Kilimanjaro, the Taj Mahal, the Sistine Chapel, and the Great Pyramid of Giza.

Presidents Herbert Hoover, Dwight Eisenhower, Gerald Ford, and Jimmy Carter all visited the Iowa State Fair. The State Fair promotional materials boast, "More than just corn dogs and carnivals, the Iowa State Fair is an event that's uniquely Iowan. It exemplifies who and what, as Iowans, we are and where we're going." It goes on to brag, "If all the toi-

34 ~ SNEAKING INTO THE FLYING CIRCUS

let tissue that is stockpiled for the Iowa State Fair were unrolled, it would stretch 1,700 miles from Des Moines to Los Angeles."

Spanning four hundred acres in the heart of downtown Des Moines, the Iowa State Fair is advertised as "one of the world's largest livestock shows," but it is really famous for one thing: It is the home of dead fried everything on a stick: pork-on-a-stick, fried cheese–on-a-stick, they even have salad-on-a-stick.

The fair holds contests for just about anything you can imagine: the chain saw carving contest, the heaviest pigeon contest, the ugliest cake competition, the marble shooting championship, the watermelon seed spitting challenge. But the only reason all of the presidential candidates come through is because this is where all of the cameras are in Iowa! And the only way they are going to get on TV is if they put their mouth (and stomach) to the test.

Howard Dean opened up the food fight on day one by consuming a one-pound hamburger, followed by a pork-chop-on-a-stick, with some deep-fried Oreos for dessert, all on camera. The doctor confessed, "I hate to think what this is doing to my arteries." This was more than enough to make his followers at FoodiesforDean.com proud.

Dick Gephardt came to the fair with his wife, Jane, on the night of their thirty-seventh anniversary. Escorted by a group of local Teamsters, Dick invited us along to the barbecue pits. "This is our anniversary dinner. We want you to have it with us. It is not every day that you are married for thirty-seven years."

Before sitting down for their special meal, Dick had to help flip the pork. Wearing an apron that said THE OTHER WHITE MEAT, he stood over the hot flame fielding questions from the pack with answers like "I like pork" and "I'm having a ball." Then he and Jane ate their pork chops, which were served with a cold red punch.

After dinner, Dick went to throw horseshoes and check out the butter sculptures. This year there was a six-hundred-pound life-size butter cow, next to a Harley-Davidson motorcycle made entirely of butter. (Last year there was a life-size butter *Last Supper*.) Dick took one look at the works of art and it made him want to eat again. He reached into his wallet and got out the money for a corn dog. (This is one of the those rare moments on the campaign trail when a candidate has to buy his own food.) After the corn dog, it was time for the biggest decision of the day: Which deep-fried dessert would he choose, the fried Oreo or the fried Twinkie? He decided to have both. Followed by ice cream. With his third dessert in hand he proceeded to make corny jokes like, "Is this a sweet state or what?" On his way out, he reflected on his trip to the fair, "Only in Iowa."

John Kerry came to the Iowa State Fair right after his episode with a cheesesteak. If you haven't seen the picture, you aren't spending enough time on the Internet. Kerry showed up at Pat's King of Steaks in South Philadelphia, the infamous Philly cheesesteak joint, and ordered a Philly cheesesteak with Swiss cheese! Swiss?

So John Kerry didn't join in the food orgy at the Iowa State Fair. All he dared to eat was a corn dog, and he didn't look too happy having all of the cameras in his face *again* as he was eating it. However, he was pretty pumped up over by the butter art. He seemed to particularly appreciate the butter Harley. As a hawg owner, I think he thought he had a shot at the big endorsement of the fair—I didn't have the guts to tell

The ultimate East Coast food faux pas.

him that the butter cow lady was already taken. "Governor Dean is my guy. He has been an outstanding candidate through this campaign and has talked about the issues I care about in rural America," Mrs. Margarine said in her press release.

As Kerry made the rounds, he made mention of the fact several times that he is "pro–family farms." (That's what they all say. Just once I would love to hear a candidate in Iowa say they are anti–family farms.)

Throughout the week, I was testing the fairgoers' knowledge of the candidates. Even when they were face to face with the man in question, most of them could not name any of them. The best response came when I pointed to a candidate and challenged someone in the crowd, "I'll give you ten bucks if you can tell me who that man is." He responded, "I don't care who that man is. Man isn't going to change the world, God is. You can't put your faith in man."

One guy knew all of the candidates. He was there every day waiting patiently for each of their autographs. In fact, he asked each candidate for his autograph eight times! He is an autograph collector who specializes in politicians and rock stars. He said, "I think of myself as a recorder of history, but I never know if what I am getting will be history. I have to get all the autographs because I never know which one will be valuable."

The same is true of collecting video for a documentary. When I get great video of one candidate, the value is so temporary. Although I spend every day of my life on the road following all of the candidates, people will only be interested in watching a movie about the man who wins; nobody will care about all of the losers. My priceless footage will be worthless the minute that candidate drops out. When I asked the autograph collector which candidate he was most excited to see, he told me that he was still waiting for Joe Lieberman, because today he can get the most money for his autograph.

On the hottest, grossest, stickiest day of summer, Joey Lieberman showed up singing show tunes from Rodgers and Hammerstein's Broadway hit *State Fair* (which the locals say was inspired by this fair). Performing (gastronomically speaking) here would be more of a challenge for Lieberman because this fair does not have much kosher fare.

Joey wandered through the petting zoo, signed lots of autographs, talked to lots of kiddies, made some art in a wheelchair, and stood on a bail of hay to give his stump speech in the lethal humidity in order to avoid participating in the consumption of the sixteen tons of beef all around. Eventually he made his way to the one food that didn't violate his faith: the deep-fried Twinkie.

With all the cameras on him and Twinkie juice oozing out of his mouth, he remarked, "It's a great life, isn't it?" For God's sake, Joe, get a napkin. As the photo mob disbanded, I tried to get Joey to reflect philosophically on the strange tribal nature of running for president.

Why are there so many retarded rituals in American politics? What does this test, going to the State Fair and eating a fried Twinkie? Don't you think it is absurd that you have to eat your way across the fair to impress voters?

Joey burst back into song. As he departed he instructed, "When we get to the White House, knock on the gate, tell them you met me at the Iowa State Fair, and they'll let you right in."

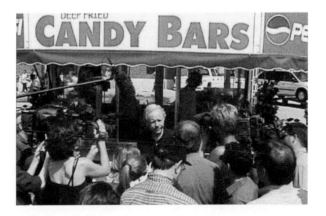

Joey performs for the media.

President of What?

Ottumwa, Iowa
AUGUST 16, 2003

"HAVE YOU SEEN THE SIZE of that bus?" That was the question of the day here in eastern Iowa. Today was day one of the John Edwards "Real People, Real Solutions" bus tour. Iowans came out to meet the junior senator from North Carolina, but all they could talk about was his monster-size bus. "That thing is bigger than our house," the old man in overalls said to his wife. "How on earth is he going to park it?" a shopkeeper wondered as the behemoth rolled into town blasting John Cougar Mellencamp's hit song "Small Town." "We don't have room for that kind of thing in our town."

The megabus, equipped with a fully loaded fridge, satellite TV, DVD, a full sound system, and a computer station with Internet access, delivers the Edwards family to the small towns of Iowa in style. Painted on both sides of the luxury vehicle is "John Edwards, President," which led many of the locals to ask, "President of what?" (In fairness, this is the most frequently asked question on the campaign trail about all the candidates. The first person known to have asked it was Lillian Carter when her son Jimmy told her he was going to run for president.)

At the diner in Independence, Edwards tried to bond with the crowd with a critique of Bush's prorich policies that discriminate against "people like us." But he was having a hard time getting people's attention because many of them were still staring out the window at that larger-than-life-size bus. The U.S. senator continued with his stump speech: "Those people in Washington don't understand . . ." After he made his sales pitch, it was time to move on to the next town.

The senator and his wife, Elizabeth, and their three kids climbed back into their house on wheels and raced through the cornfields to the next event on the schedule: a walk down Main Street.

When we arrived at Main Street, Mr. Edwards got off the bus, walked one block to the ice cream parlor, politely accepted some cookie dough ice cream from the owner, ate two bites in front of her, and then walked out the door and handed the dripping cone to his staffer to throw away. He hit a few more shops, gave his stump speech, and then changed clothes to go for a run on his own.

Meanwhile, the bus sat parked near a church in downtown Dubuque and churchgoers walked by it gawking. One woman walked by explaining to her friends, "Some people think he is a prophet, but I've seen him on TV and it's all smoke and mirrors."

Being near the bus was the only way I got cell service all week, so as I stood there making phone calls, people kept asking me questions like, "Can he really communicate with the dead?" and "Do you think you could get John to talk to my father? He died of colon cancer last year." They obviously thought John Edward, the television psychic from the show *Crossing Over,* was on board.

I explained that this bus belonged to John Edwards. "Who's that?" they all asked. He was a very successful trial lawyer who is serving his first term in the U.S. Senate and he is running for president of the United States. "Oh, when is that?" the woman in the NO WAR T-shirt wanted to know.

A mom who brought her kids over to see the bus asked, "What is it like inside?" I told her I didn't know. I have to drive behind the bus because the campaign told me they didn't have room for me. The woman then stated the obvious: "You mean they don't want you on their bus. Clearly you can see there is room for our whole town on that bus! Why don't they just tell you the truth, why can't they just say 'We don't want you on our bus'?"

It was time for the caravan to move on. First the bus pulled out, then four vans driven by staffers followed. When we got to the house party, two men introduced themselves as Edwards's staff from the Denver office. This is a big organization. At least a dozen people in the room had name tags identifying themselves as staff. This is where all the money goes.

Edwards delivered his stump speech, took some questions, and then said, "We've gotta go." As he rushed out the back door a man said to his wife, "He was the first one out of the room. It's Saturday night in Ottumwa, Iowa. Where in the heck does he have to go?"

On paper, John Edwards has it all: He's a handsome young senator from the South. But when I asked people at the party how the Southern Golden Boy made them feel, a Clinton lover said, "I don't feel anything. He didn't make me feel like I was the most important person in the room. He is slick, but he's too quick. He left without shaking the hostess's hand. He is no Bill Clinton."

Standing between the house and the bus watching the driver try to maneuver his way out of a tight spot, as Edwards's theme song played, "I was born in a small town," one of the guests said, "Why is that his song? So what that he was born in a small town, is that some kind of achievement?" Just then I realized it's true what they've been saying: That bus is actually physically bigger than a house.

John Edwards's bus versus a house.

My Summer Vacation
with the Grahams

Dyersville, Iowa
AUGUST 20, 2003

AS AMERICANS pack their bags and take off on their summer vacations, all the presidential candidates are taking their campaign shows on the road to Iowa. Senator Bob Graham piled his entire family into a caravan of RVs for a two-week trip across the state.

So there I was rolling through the back roads of eastern Iowa with Bob and his wife, their four daughters, four sons-in-law, and ten grandchildren, singing the Graham for President theme song: "You've got a friend in Bob Graham, that's what everybody's saying, all the way across the good old USA, from Atlantic to Pacific, we all say that he's terrific, America needs Bob Graham today . . ." I had never met these people before, but they are not shying away from showing me their cheers, chants, and dance moves to the *Bob Graham for President* CD.

Our first event today was an ice cream social. The door of the RV swung open and the entire family flooded out, all in matching BOB GRAHAM FOR PRESIDENT T-shirts. No more than a dozen locals were there. Bob's wife, Adele, introduced him (as she does at every stop). "If Al Gore had picked my husband we would have a Democrat in the White House right now," Adele testified, "Here he is, the next president of the United States . . ."

Bob started with his stump speech. His wife interjected, "Tell them about your work on the 9/11 report." Bob explained his work on the recently published congressional report about September 11. His daughters clapped loudly, hooted and hollered. The eight people in the audience then clapped along politely. Bob continued with his stump speech. "Don't forget to tell them about veterans' issues," Gwen, his eldest daughter, piped in. Bob explained all he has done for the veterans.

After the speech, the whole family worked the room. His daughters walked around preaching to voters about "Dad's credentials." They were all campaigning so hard it was hard to tell which one was the candidate. A cynical local reporter grumbled, "Who wants to be president more, his oldest daughter, his wife, or him?" Another marveled, "They act like the von Trapp family" (the family of singers in *The Sound of Music*). After a couple of days with the Grahams, I found myself singing along with their entire CD, "Bob will be the forty-third president, an eight-year White House resident . . ."

Tonight, like last night, ended with a family BBQ listed on the schedule as "Grillin' with the Grahams." The sons-in-law manned the grill in their Graham family aprons. The daughters, in matching embroidered GRAHAM FOR PRESIDENT overalls, passed out Bob Graham calendars. The grandchildren sang "Arriba Bob" from the *Graham for President* CD while Doodle (the family's nickname for Bob) welcomed the locals bearing broccoli bread salad and pink pecan pie.

The best part about this RV trip is that it is not a campaign gimmick; this actually is their family vacation. There is no such thing as a day off in the life of a politician, especially if you are running for president. When I asked the senator how the trip was going, he responded, "This is the best family vacation yet." Perhaps he was having so much fun he forgot why they were in Iowa.

The Grahams aren't really going to where the voters are, they are just trying to have a good time. Only once along the way the RV had to make a detour to a candidate forum, which gave Bob an opportunity to invite the other candidates to come grillin'. Unfortunately, none of them took him up on the invitation. While Dick Gephardt was off to Des Moines to receive a big union endorsement, Bob Graham chased his grandkids through the corn maze. For a man who had had open-heart surgery earlier in the year, he is in great shape.

Imagine a whole summer in the bowels and armpits of Iowa. You would be tired, bored, and lonely. Not Bob Graham. He has his own cheering section and team of spinners. And they are not lying. On paper, Bob Graham clearly has great credentials as the two-term governor of Florida and three-term senator. He voted against the war and is the ranking member on the Senate Intelligence Committee. But since he got in the race late due to triple bypass surgery, his poll numbers are at 1 percent and he is polling in seventh place (out of nine candidates). Even though the caucuses are five months away, it is clear this campaign is on the road to nowhere.

Why? That seems to be the million-dollar question. For one, $1 million is about all Doodle has raised so far, and the other Democratic candidates have millions in their war chests. Graham is a seasoned political veteran; he doesn't have any fresh catch phrases like "I want my country back" or "I'm from the Democratic wing of the Democratic Party." As Senator Graham said it, "I cannot offer fire and brimstone." So you will not be reading much about him this year. As Howard Dean celebrates this week with his face on the cover of *Time* and *Newsweek,* Bob Graham doesn't have any national reporters in his RV.

The national newsmen have written off this campaign, and if you ask them why, they inevitably bring up "the notebooks." Bob Graham carries around a little notebook and when someone tells him something he wants to remember, he writes it down. To me, this seems like a highly efficient way to record the issues being discussed on the campaign trail. To the reporters, these notebooks are the butt of many jokes (even though we, too, take notes all day long). They tell me that this habit of note taking, which Bob has been doing for twenty-five years, is the reason Al Gore did not consider Graham for VP in 2000.

It is obvious why Bob Graham's pocket-size notebooks end up in the stories written about him. Reporters go to so many events every day that are all the same; all they are looking for is something, anything unusual that stands out. Bob Graham likes to write stuff down; the reporters think that is odd, so they write it into their stories. And so that is how the media choose to stereotype Bob Graham: as an oddball who likes to takes notes. Unfairly, it is one of those things that people will continue to pick on and it won't go away.

As much as I wanted to stay for the Graham family baseball game at the Field of Dreams in Dyersville, Iowa, I promised Senator Kerry I would meet him over at the hog lots. Then I planned on checking out Howard Dean at a retirement home making his pitch to the senior citizens about how they have to get online and join his Internet movement.

When I went to say goodbye, Adele used the same maternal guilt my own mother would use: "Why are you leaving us? Don't go yet!" All of the Graham daughters offered hugs, and the young grandkids looked as sad as any kid at the end of a good playdate. The senator said, "I don't know how you can leave us," then he broke into a song: "Now on to New Hampshire, it's beautiful there, I'll see you in New Hampshire . . ."

I am really going to miss Senator Graham and his lovely wife, those four wild daughters, ten adorable grandkids, and that one rockin' CD! They won my heart, but I don't think they picked up many votes on their summer vacation. I have got to give Bob Graham credit: The one thing I learned on this trip, which is as close as I'll ever get to a summer vacation, is that to run for president, you need supporters. And if you can't find any, you have to bring your own.

Flying High on the Grassroots Express

Seattle, Washington
AUGUST 23, 2003

AS WE WERE GETTING OFF the bus at the next stop of Howard Dean's Sleepless Summer Tour, a Dean staffer said, "I feel like I am traveling with the Grateful Dead." Maybe it's the tree-hugger selling Dean Head T-shirts (with a listing of the cities and tour dates on the back) or the guys with goatees playing hackey sack on the side of the stage. Somehow this feels more like a Phish concert than a political rally. There is a lot of tie-dye and tattoos, pink hair and piercings.

In front of the media section, the overzealous volunteers are pushing people out of the way so the press can come through. "You are not allowed to stand here—this is for the press only." The press corps is getting VIP treatment. You know that won't last.

Onstage, an ensemble of men with ponytails are singing some song of liberation. This is what is wrong with all political rallies: The music is so polarizing. The crowd is bouncing a bunch of inflatable beach balls over their heads and a woman who must be on ecstasy is doing hippie chick dances in the front row.

You can learn everything you need to know about Howard Dean from the people who introduce him. The first woman onstage screamed, "The government is corrupt and he is going to do something about that!" The crowd roared.

As I walked around talking to only a few of the ten thousand people here, many of them proudly admitted to participating in the World Bank protest. One rallygoer put it this way: "We will protest anything Ashcroftian." Everyone you talk to says this is a "grassroots movement." When asked what the organizing principle of the movement is, here are the first three answers:

1. A self-described Naderite said, "We are against Bush's War."

2. A declared independent said, "I'm against George Bush."

3. A Green Party member declared, "This is about killing the Democrats for acting like Republicans."

Does anyone have anything good to say about Howard Dean? (Or are they all just here to revel in the anti-?) "I have been waiting so long for him to come along. He is not a liar, like the rest of them," a reasonable-looking woman replies. "Can you tell me one lie any of his competitors told?" After a few mumbles she says, "Well, they just lie about everything."

I don't believe in any of the candidates, but I believe what some of them say, even if I don't agree with them. They are not all liars, they are all politicians who parse their words to please everyone. If Dean really wants the nomination, he, too, is going to have to start talking Washingtonese like the rest of them in order to appeal to a national audience. Howard Dean is just as much a politician as the rest of them, but he has a better sales pitch than his competitors because he doesn't have a day job, so he has the luxury of being able to say whatever he wants without consequences. It is easy to say that you are against the war if you never had to vote on it.

As Dean took to the stage, it hit me: It's not him, it's them. Look at all the desperate faces in the crowd. Better yet, look at all the women with hairy armpits and white men with dreadlocks. You can see it in their eyes. They are hungry for something, someone, anyone to fill their void. Howard Dean gives them their red meat, although it looks as though very few in this crowd even eat meat. In fairness, there are a lot of L.L. Bean–style, Average Joe, suburbanites in the crowd, but the gypsies were screaming louder than the rest, so they are the ones we ended up focusing our attention on.

Pointing to the crowd, Dean yelled out, "George Bush needs to be sent home to Crawford, Texas. You have the power to take this country back . . ." Tears of joy are now rolling down the face of the middle-aged woman in the front row. Next to her, a guy has his middle finger in the air.

Dean seems to bring out the sixteen-year-old in everyone—he is fulfilling their adolescent frustrations. But all this finger-pointing rhetoric is going to repel future potential supporters and scare the housewives in suburbia. I want to get up on stage and tell these people that if they really want to help Dean, they will tone down their anger. But that would be sacrilegious and Howard Dean is their new religion. As the guy who introduced Dean in Boise, Idaho, said, "The last time I was this excited about someone was when I heard about a man called Jesus."

Many in Howard's cult admit to being "obsessed with Dean." These are true believers; they drive from state to state, Grateful Dead style, to support their man, and anytime anyone attacks their guy (à la Tim Russert asking him tough questions that he can't answer), they send him more money.

On the plane, Dean told the reporters that as he looked out in the crowds, "For the first time I realized the fate of the country might be in my hands. Not just because I might become president of the United States of America, but because there were a very, very large number of people depending on me to change the course of this country." To which one of the reporters reacted, "It's so naïve and arrogant for him to assume that he can change the course of this country." This comment reveals the fundamental difference between the way reporters and politicians view the world.

Politicians are optimists who believe in their ability to effect change; they often quote Margaret Mead: "Never doubt that a small group of thoughtful committed citizens can change the world. Indeed it's the only thing that ever has." Reporters are much more skeptical; they say things like one did today: "Welcome to Fantasy Island. This guy has delusions of grandeur. Realistically, he is going to end up as roadkill outside the Beltway."

There is a Pollyannaish quality to his campaign: If the people come together we can take on Washington. We wish it could be true, but those of us who have seen it all before know it will never happen. I suspect it is a lot harder to change the system than Dean and his supporters think it is. Howard Dean seems to have a naïveté about how this game is played. He has absolutely no concept of how far off the election is and how dirty the road ahead will be. Yes, his crowd sizes are impressive, but that means nothing a year before the general election even starts.

In 2000, when George Bush lost the first few primaries, he always used to say that running for president is a marathon and you have to pace yourself. On the bus, Dean's all substance–no style, Internet junkie campaign manager Joe Trippi repeated that sentiment but added his own twist: "Running for president of the United States is a marathon. We decided we were going to run the first four miles at a 100-yard-dash pace. We decided we're going to run the second four miles at a 100-yard-dash pace." But the thing you need to know about Joe is, he's the unconventional one that none of the boys inside the Beltway want to have around. Trippi comes from the Jerry Brown school of grassroots campaigning, and his contempt for the rules and the other candidates is not a secret. (If you went to Dean headquarters, he would have his dog perform a trick for you. "Would you rather work for John Kerry or be dead?" The puppy rolls over and plays dead.)

Trippi is crafting an image of Dean that is not as pure as many think. Dean tells his crowds that he is the top fund-raiser in the field because he raised all his money on the Internet from people who have never participated in politics before. True, but . . . He just had a fund-raiser at one of the wealthiest homes in San Francisco. When I called the hosts to ask if I could come to the party, they said, "The campaign does not want the media here." He lambastes Bush for fund-raising in secret, but time and time again he is shutting reporters out of his top-dollar fund-raisers, while inviting us to the coffeehouse $25-per-person affairs. All the campaign wants us to see is that Dean is a man of the people, putting pennies together to make a movement.

Riding on some hippie bus to the Portland, Oregon, gig, a woman got up and introduced herself. She is from the New Progressive Movement, a grassroots organization that dedicates their hearts and souls to helping grassroots candidates get elected. They should be helping Dennis Kucinich, he is the vegan in the race.

When we arrive, there is a huge sign behind Dean that says what the crowd is chanting: THIS IS DEAN COUNTRY. This is Dean country? Dean is a fiscally conservative, blue-blooded, Park Avenue Yalie. Why is he the one they have anointed to carry their torch? When asked this question, one of his staffers explains that Dean has spent most of his life in Vermont; he has an image of himself as a Vermont outdoorsman. He is known in Vermont as L.L. Dean because of his official portrait in the capital, where alongside all the other uptight portraits of former governors in dark suits, Dean is seen in short sleeves, khakis, and boots with a paddle in his hand and his canoe by his side.

While reporters were writing their stories in the filing center, the campaign paraded in a dozen Dean Heads to give their testimonials about why they love Howard Dean. Showing us their scars from the 2000 election, they all confessed that they felt alienated by politics and they were still bitter and demoralized post-Florida. All agreed to being antiwar; many had voted for Nader. When asked "Why Dean?" the death rocker who claimed to be "heavily involved in the progressive political movement" said, "He just seems to genuinely care about the people. It's just the fact that he cares." A young man who defined his political affiliation as independent explained why he has been living abroad: "The government lies." This was starting to feel like a Bush-hating anger management therapy session.

A registered Green Party member said she was out all week flyering at coffeehouses for today's rally because "Howard Dean is the coffeehouse candidate." Now here is the problem with that. Very few people in America have wasted more time in coffee shops than I have. And let me tell you one thing: In the seventeen years that I have been sipping on those foamy lattes, I have not talked to one person who has ever voted for a winning candidate.

He is bringing new people into the system, but I suspect that the inevitable rise and fall of Howard Dean will make people hate politics more than they do already. Just like falling in love, you have to wait for the right person to come along, instead of just jumping in bed with the first guy who tells you what you want to hear. I want to stage an intervention with the Deanies: Don't give your life to this man. As one senator told me, "He would be a good candidate for the Senate." He is not The One; he will break your heart. He is your first; how many of those last? After him you will be heartbroken and jaded. For their passion, I salute them, but as someone who has to attend the events, it is so tiresome watching all these political virgins who are oblivious to the fact that they are about to get deflowered.

"Here is how we are going to win: Go to our Web site and sign up and we are going to e-mail you and then you send that e-mail to the one hundred friends on your e-mail list," Dean explains. It's a pyramid scheme, like Amway. Why would anyone on my e-mail list want me to spam them? Are any of your friends going to support him just because you told them to? Why does Howard Dean assume we all have one hundred friends on our e-mail list?

There is a new phenomenon that just came over from Europe called "flash mobs." Strangers e-mail each other and plan to meet in public, for no purpose whatsoever, just for the fun of it. The Dean rallies feel like a flash mob. The guy onstage tells the crowd to wave their signs and they do.

At every rally there is a guy shooting the video on his robotic cameras and putting it all up live on the Internet. If you go on the Internet to Dean TV you can see video of any event that Dean ever did, from twenty different angles. There are so many people shooting video on their camcorders that when you are looking at him you can't help but think, is it Dean or is it digital?

You can't talk to a Dean Head without hearing about The Blog. Throughout the Summer Tour, the Dean campaign invited bloggers to ride on the press bus. Or was it that the press were invited to sit on the bloggers' bus? When a grown woman squealed, "The bloggers are going to die when they find out I met you," the *LA Times* reporter sitting next to me said, "I feel like I am at a Star Trek convention."

The blogger sitting in front of us on the way from Austin to San Antonio said she spent four to five hours a day on The Blog. "I was religiously devoted to eBay until The Blog came along." She admitted to being obsessed with checking "the bat" to see how much money Dean has raised. So let me get this straight: You spend hours of your day fixated on how much money a presidential candidate is raising? She then said something that explained the psychology of every political campaign: "I work in the health care industry with people who die because they cannot afford health insurance. If you work with people who are dying, you either give in and collapse or become an optimist." She then pledged herself to Howard Dean. "I'm not going to say Howard Dean is the Messiah, but I think he is the only one telling the truth."

The funny thing is Dean is now a *Newsweek* cover boy, but in spite of all the media attention that he has been getting, real people still do not seem to know who he is. Standing in Bryant Park in New York City one week after Dean had ten thousand people at a rally during the Sleepless Summer Tour, I took a poll. Only one person said that he had heard of Howard Dean. "I don't know who Howard Dean is, but I know that he has been getting a lot of media attention." What does that tell you about the power of the media? Most of America still is not paying attention to any of the stories about this election, and despite what *Newsweek* and the boys at the networks tell you, Howard Dean is not the nominee. And if he is going to be the nominee, he has a lot to learn about how the media function.

This is what a Deaniac looks like!

Alert the Media

JFK Airport, New York
SEPTEMBER 1, 2003

ALERT THE MEDIA: John Kerry has an announcement to make. You know how he's been taking those trips to Iowa and New Hampshire for the past nine months telling the people how much better off the world would be if John Kerry were president? Well, tomorrow morning he's going to, get this, announce that he is running for president!

This is news? How could any member of the media show up for that? Summoning the press to your charter to parade them around from state to state so that you can get up onstage to state the obvious is not news. It is a gimmick to get your face on TV. And no legitimate news organization should pay to participate in this sham. But they must, for taking what is fed to you now is the key to access in the future, when actual news is being committed. Reporters looking to make a name for themselves have to pay to play because access is the only real currency in political journalism.

Although I am philosophically opposed to the whole idea of an announcement tour a year after the candidate actually started campaigning, I signed on because there are only so many good moments in a campaign and you never know when you are going to miss one of them. In other words, you don't go because you want to be there or because you think you will actually learn anything about the candidate. You go just in case he does something embarrassing or says something stupid that will be used against him throughout the campaign.

So I'm sitting at Chili's at JFK Airport waiting for my flight to D.C., where the Kerry charter departs on a swing through the early primary states. Of all the days this year for Kerry to stage his announcement, he could not have picked a more inconvenient day. My boyfriend's grandfather just died, so instead of being a decent human being and attending the funeral in The Hague, I'm sitting at JFK Airport ("where America greets the world") on my way back to the campaign trail. My name was even on the invitation to the funeral and I am missing it to go to Iowa—again?

To make matters worse, after the funeral, our friends are getting married in Italy. How is he going to explain to his friends and family that I couldn't be there because I had to sit on the bus with a pack of reporters watching John Kerry tell the world he is running for president? Even the Europeans already know that!

My Dutchman does not understand the whole American work ethic thing. In Europe they believe in prioritizing quality of life, and events like funerals and weddings are important. As I kissed him goodbye I reminded him of what Rummie and the Bushies have been saying: Old Europe doesn't get it.

But deep down I know he's right. The thing I hated about my year and a half on the road with George Bush is that as reporters, we are all just voyeurs, living on someone else's airplane, watching him achieve his life's goal, while we're just along for the ride. We are the dogs that bark as the caravan passes by. Sure, we got a front-row seat while history was being made, but all we had to show for it was a few good war stories that only our fellow journalists would want to hear. I had to work every Christmas, Thanksgiving, birthday—basically every important day of my life. I missed my friends' weddings, baby showers, graduations, and grandparents' funerals. Though there were some fine moments in 2000, overall the experience was intellectually, emotionally, and morally bankrupt.

I remember the actual moment when I realized that I didn't want to be a news nun. We were rolling along somewhere in the middle of nowhere, waiting for the campaign to hand out our box lunches, and I asked one of my fellow traveling press corps members, who was twice my age, "How is life outside of work?" She replied, "What else is there?" A hungry scribe started shouting, "Feed me," and that was when it hit me: We are pigeons, pecking around for our next feed. As the most famous former journalist Tom Wolfe said, "Being a reporter is very unglamorous work. You are essentially a beggar holding out a cup, begging 'Please tell me something.' "

Who would choose a trip to Iowa and New Hampshire with a pack full of surly reporters over a week in Holland and Italy with the love of their life? What is more important: shooting staged photo ops or standing by your man in important moments in his life? Campaigns are addictive, and like a recovering junkie, I was going back for more.

So there I was again, sitting in the airport bar waiting for my flight, when I ordered a "presidente" margarita. The old drunk guy sitting next to me started talking to himself. "She had it all." Excuse me? "I always knew she had it all, you know." I took the bait. Who?

"Margarita," he declared proudly, happy to have a sucker on the line to listen to his drunken babble. "Margarita was an American woman in her fifties who had a vacation home in Mexico. She served this drink regularly and her guests chugged it down. Then they went home and told their friends about it, and everyone tried to copy her in their own homes. That's how her drink got popular."

When the bartender delivered my frozen fluorescent pink chick drink, he said, "She would not have wanted it that way. It had to be on the rocks with salt on the rim. That thing ain't a margarita. She would be ashamed to have her name on it. You ought to try the real thing. It comes close to magical. When I was down there across the border back in the sixties, Margarita gave me her secret recipe. You ought to try it, nothing approaches it."

And then he shared with me the secret of the magical margarita. Here is the recipe:

> 1 part fresh-squeezed lime juice (don't pour it from a bottle, squeeze it yourself)
>
> 1 part silver tequila (none of the gold stuff)
>
> 1 part Cointreau, a French liqueur (it tastes the same as Gran Marnier, but it's white)
>
> Mix in sugar to taste so that you get the lime juice not to taste so bitter. Then shake it.

"It comes out a nice color. It's so pretty, prettier than a teenager spread-eagle on my lap. No other margarita comes close," he promised, and then he went on with his rant. "She earned her reputation the old-fashioned way. She earned it by gaining the respect of her friends. That's the only important thing I know."

With that, I left my barfly Yoda with my Slurpee margarita and headed for the ticket counter to book the next flight to Italy. Something told me that John Kerry would have enough cameras in his face this weekend and he would not miss me.

The next night, while the pack sat in the press filing center eating lukewarm Sterno meat gone bad, I was at Alfredo's in Rome (the place fettuccine Alfredo was created). There in the Eternal City, where my boyfriend later asked me to marry him, I knew that few would care to watch the movie I was supposed to be making, but everyone would ask to see the ring!

My New Last Name Best Friend

New York City
SEPTEMBER 25, 2003

TONIGHT AT THE DEMOCRATIC DEBATE, candidate number ten, General Wesley Clark, the former supreme allied commander and Rhodes scholar from the South, made his prime-time debut. When asked if he enjoyed being in the spotlight, he blushed. "I enjoy it." That will change.

For those of us who have been out in the field for the past year tiring of the Democratic wannabes, we could not have been more excited to meet our new subject. We were all fighting to get a piece (of video) of him, and tonight I had the honor of meeting General Clark not once, but twice.

The first time we met was in the elevator at Pace University. I turned my camera off and formally introduced myself. He gave me a blank, uncomfortable stare while his wife feigned interest in the stranger they were stuck in the elevator with. "Pelosi, how do you spell it?" she asked. I spelled out my last name. "That's funny, I have a cousin named Peluzzu," she explained. As the general tried to look away (which is hard to do in the small confines of an elevator), there was a nice long bit of silence. He made no attempt at small talk, but why should he? He is a four-star general and I am a media buzzard.

Relief came when the elevator doors opened and the general made his way to "the Wes Wing," the college classroom that served as his dressing room, where donors and staffers were celebrating his performance in his first debate.

As the debate after-party got rockin', I waited sheepishly outside in the hallway talking with the perky young woman from NBC who just got promoted from being embedded with the Moseley Braun campaign to being embedded in the Clark campaign.

Every so often, a campaign staffer would enter or exit the Wes Wing, deliberately trying to avoid opening the door wide enough for us to see the secret soiree inside. A Pace University officer guarded the door in a military stance to ensure that I, and my innocent-looking embed friend, did not bum-rush the door to shoot video of the general standing around in his dressing room with his staff. Panic struck the rent-a-cop on duty when one couple took a little too long to say their goodbyes at the door. I am almost sure I actually heard the woman say "You *really* did a *great* job tonight." This must have been a major security breach, because we were asked to take a step back.

The other candidates came and went, but I ignored them and waited in position for the Clark entourage to charge out of the dressing room for his victory lap through the Spin Room, where three hundred reporters were waiting to see and hear the general up close and personal for the very first time.

Mr. Perma-grin, Terry McAuliffe, head of the DNC, was working the hallway, gripping and grinning with anyone who would take it. You have to hand it to that guy: He sure is a total cheese ball, but he doesn't take any chances. He extends his bear hugs to everyone just to be safe. Hey, you never know whom he might offend if he held back!

An hour later, the general emerged, but his staff assistant (whom I met on a ski lift at Sundance last year) told me there would be no Spin Room. As the general stood waiting for the elevator, the stranger I skied with introduced me to Clark as my mother's daughter. Clark's whole demeanor changed, he even apologized for ignoring me earlier: "I didn't know who you were." On the way out, the NBC embed asked me, "Didn't it bother you how rude he was until he found out who your mother is?" I couldn't care less if he talked to me, but this was the moment I realized what a tremendous disadvantage a military man has in the political world. He does not carry himself like a politician—he does not have a smooth glad hand, he is not a fine craftsman at the art of bullshit, his political skills are unrefined and everyone can see it.

My sister Christine lives in Washington, works on Capitol Hill, and has lots of friends. But she always says that in the political world, there are two kinds of friends: first-name friends and last-name friends. First-name friends are people who are interested in you from the minute they meet you. Bob and Adele Graham are first-name friends. If you walk up and start talking with them, they will instantly take an interest in you, no matter who you are. Last-name friends are the people who want to be your friend once they hear your last name. When I was an average ordinary everyday citizen standing in the elevator, I was of no use to Wes Clark. But when he found out who my mother is, he gave me the time of day. This goes with the territory, but you have to be a little more subtle about it, Wes! God bless him for being so honest, but this is the business of double-talking, poker-faced, friendship salesmen and he should be showing the love to every man, woman, and child right now.

There are a lot of voters in America that Wes Clark needs to make friends with. As he learns the ropes from the advisers who worked with the other Rhodes scholar from Arkansas, we will all be watching to see whether Clark learns something (which our Arkansas president never seemed to learn): You need friends in this business and you better remember the people who got you where you are today, whatever their names may be.

"Rock on, Senator"

Boston
SEPTEMBER 28, 2003

JOHN KERRY IS WORKING HARD to overcome that stuck-up Senate stigma. That's why his schedule is packed with trips to go hunting, windsurfing, motorcycle riding, playing hockey, and gigging with a rock star!

While Howard Dean issues press releases daily announcing his latest endorsement from this Rent Board commissioner and that former town administrator, John Kerry has chosen the perfect way to show off that he has picked up the coolest endorsement of the political season, by having a jam session with him!

Moby, the pop star and king of rave, has not only endorsed Kerry, he has volunteered his musical services to the campaign. In the ballroom of Boston's historic Park Plaza Hotel (the most unlikely spot to find the king of New York techno underground nightlife), Moby made his debut appearance with the senator for fund-raising purposes. Unlike a regular Moby show, no one was standing outside selling ecstasy.

As the senator walked through the posh lobby (built in 1927), wearing a formal white collared dress shirt and business suit pants, I asked him if this was his first rave and he said, "No," but he did not provide any further details about his rave experiences.

This is so much more rock and roll than walking through hog lots like we did last month in Iowa! When Kerry emerged into the lavish Imperial Ballroom, Moby announced, "And now, the next president of the United States," and the crowd went wild. As he made his way to the stage, a white-collar rocker shouted, "Rock on, Senator." Another screamed, "Senator, are you ready to rock?" He responded, "You be the judge."

He climbed up onto the podium and grabbed the mic to address the crowd. "Are we ready to beat George Bush?" They audience roared. "Let's rock and roll!" Under the hot lights of three crystal chandeliers, a pack of sweating photographers pushed and shoved to get the money shot of John Kerry strumming along to a decent cover of the Boss's "Tenth Avenue Freeze Out." When the song ended, Kerry promised, "I won't be giving up my day job." He encouraged the crowd to stick around because "I want a chance to hang."

Over at the cash bar, the well-dressed young professionals who had already paid one hundred bucks to see the *John Kerry Unplugged* show were lining up to buy white wine and whiskey sours. This is how you knew that you were at a Kerry event: The guests were tipping at least a dollar per drink.

After the show, I made my way over to Moby to ask him the one question I came all the way to Boston to ask: "Why John Kerry?" He explained that he had researched the candidates on the Internet and Kerry was "on the mark." Follow-up: "But you seem so Howard Dean." Moby, the DJ known as a god in the world of Electronica, said, "Dean is too extreme, and he has no experience in foreign policy."

At that point we changed subjects and moved on to the battle of the bands. Who has the best musical endorsement? Bob Graham has Jimmy Buffet. Howard Dean has Joan Jett, Melissa Etheridge, and Carly Simon. Gephardt has Barry Manilow, Michael Bolton, and Tony Bennett behind him. Edwards has Hootie and the Blowfish. Bush has Ricky Martin and Ted Nugent. Of all the musical endorsers, Moby prefers Willie Nelson, who is for Kucinich.

One week later Kerry and Moby took their show on the road and appeared together in New York City at the Intrepid Sea-Air-Space

Museum. This time the opening act was the disco staple Chic, singing their '70s hit "Freak Out." Kerry watched from the side of the stage as Moby did a cover of the Twisted Sister song "We're Not Going to Take It" and the Yuppie Kerry supporters were banging their heads.

Kerry took off his coat and Hermès tie, grabbed the rhythm guitar, and joined Moby in a duet of Johnny Cash's "Ring of Fire." The dynamic duo brought down the house of one thousand adoring fans. Then Kerry stepped aside and watched Moby play Lou Reed's "Walk on the Wild Side" while the drunken spectators got out of control.

On the way out, reporters were asking me if I heard "Moby call President Bush an evil fuck." I do remember hearing Moby say that his band was available to play bar mitzvahs, but I was standing right next to the amp and it was blaring so loud that my ears were ringing, so I don't know if Moby said that or not. Though no reporter on site could confirm it, the next day the papers said Moby said it.

Kerry closed down the month of September and skated his way into October (or "Rocktober") at a pick-up hockey game at the Fleet Center in Boston, along with the Boston Bruins and actors Michael J. Fox, Tim Robbins, and Dennis Leary. Before the game, Kerry had an interview on ice with MTV. Kerry skated over to pick up his interviewer and the first thing he said on camera was, "I'm gonna barf." Gideon Yago of MTV launched right into his interview: "Who were you in high school?" Kerry said, "I slacked off on studying . . . I was a daydreamer, the guy staring out the window."

After MTV and ESPN got their one-on-ones, he skated off to get warmed up. As we stood there, shooting video of Kerry bending over with his rear end right in my face, all I could think was: and you want to be my president?

It was time for the game to begin and you could just smell the testosterone in the air. When they introduced the players, each of them skated out to great cheers and "Boo-yas." Except for Tim Robbins, who got booed. When I ignorantly asked a guy with a beer helmet on why he was booing he said, "Because he is un-American, he was all against the war." (This explained why Tim Robbins refused to share his thoughts on the presidential election with me earlier in the day. He said he has already been "hurt enough by sharing his political views.")

After the game, the beer helmet guy said that he thinks Kerry is a "wicked cool guy," even though he "hasn't done squat but stand in Ted Kennedy's shadow." His buddy added, "I don't care if he can skate, I want to know if he can balance the budget and lead the troops to war." Another local hockey enthusiast remarked, "He is a good team player, but he never stood out." Maybe that's his problem: He is good on a team of one hundred senators, but people may have a hard time seeing him as the man to lead the whole party.

In 2000, Bush defied his ruling-class roots by making no secret of the fact that he'd rather be raking hay on his ranch than sitting in cabinet meetings talking about policy. And the common folk ate that up; they love the Average Joe. Kerry is now trying to market himself as a man of the people. By blatantly butching it up, his message to the world is: I'm not going to feel your pain, I'm going to fix your carburetor.

Kerry has eleven months to convince his party that he is the one who deserves to be back here at the Fleet Center for the Democratic National Convention as the nominee. It is now becoming clear that he is not going to be able to skate his way here.

Kerry getting warmed up.

Wes Clark or Puff Daddy: Who Would You Rather Party With?

New York City
OCTOBER 14, 2003

TONIGHT, WES CLARK and Al Sharpton both had parties within blocks of each other in downtown New York City. To get his Party for Young Professionals started, the general brought along his West Point buddies. To celebrate his forty-ninth birthday, the reverend had his hip-hop homies Puff Daddy and Jay-Z throw him a photo op. Guests at the Sharpton shindig were asked for a $500 donation to the campaign; the Clark crowd were invited to donate as much, or as little, as they wanted.

Debating which party to go to, I decided to check out the Clark event first, knowing that it would not be an all-nighter, and then I'd jump over to see Puff Daddy aka Puffy aka P. Diddy aka Sean Combs aka JLo's ex, known for being acquitted of all charges in the shooting at a Manhattan nightclub.

Standing in front of the nightclub waiting for the general to arrive, I decided to take an informal poll of New Yorkers about which party they would prefer to attend. Who would you rather party with: Puff Daddy or Wes Clark? I asked. "P. Diddy, 'cause I don't like Clark's rap," a guy in a Yankees jersey declared. When asked the same question, a pack of New Jersey women on their way to see Shania Twain at Madison Square Garden asked, "Who is Wes Clark?" An Upper West Side man in a suit and tie said in front of his date, "Puffy, cause I'd want to get some of that JLo action." (JLo hasn't been with Puffy for at least a year. Don't you read the tabloids?)

Wes Clark arrived, and as I followed him into the club, the doorman confessed who he'd rather see coming through the door: "Diddy, no doubt." The event was the standard political fund-raiser for the thirty-something crowd except that the candidate was whispering. "I am losing my voice," Clark told the crowd. "They told me the next thing to go is my grip, and I am afraid to ask what the third thing is." He then went on to make his supporters feel better about where their money was going. "I just want to tell you a couple of things because you are all insiders, you deserve to know . . . We are actually building this ship as we sail out from the harbor across the Atlantic, so don't pay too much attention to some of the things you may hear about the campaign and all that stuff."

Instead of watching this guy sink, I gathered my crew and sailed over to Sharpton's birthday bash. Upon arrival at rapper Jay-Z's club 40/40, we were ushered straight into a small back VIP room with a tinted glass door, a large-screen plasma TV, and comfortable couches. You could just tell that some kinky stuff goes on here on a regular night.

Tonight this is where the white media herd would be kept waiting for the photo op of two of America's most popular black men, Al Sharpton and Puff Daddy. Time passed as we talked among ourselves about the irony of how the only way Sharpton could get the cameras to show up at his event was by telling us that a celebrity would be with him.

The journos were getting restless. Across the room, the central casting *New York Post* reporter shouted at his editor through his cell phone, "I have to be with the mayor at 8 A.M. How much longer do you want me to wait here?" Next to me, a young black woman with an instamatic camera whispered into her phone, "I ain't shittin' you, sister, P. Diddy is in the house." P. Diddy was not in the house. In fact, he wasn't even in the neighborhood.

A press handler came in and announced, "In order for you to make your deadlines, we are going to start the photo op now." Al Sharpton rolled into the room with a superfly female sidekick, who was decked out in a faux Burberry jumpsuit with matching stilettos and a huge rhinestone belt.

Rap star Dr. Dre and record industry star Russell Simmons sang "Happy Birthday" to Al as he cut his birthday cake. "Thank you very much. Goodnight," a voice called out to the press. Quickly the crowd emptied the room and left the cake sitting alone in the corner. The pack followed the reverend out as he walked off into the dark, wet night.

It was time to go home, but not without permission from the assignment desk. All the disappointed young wannabe celebrity journalists stood hovering around the front of the club calling their bosses to fill them in on the Big Night, which turned out to be a little night. The doormen started barking at us. "Paparazzi are not allowed in front of the club." Paparazzi? We are not those blood-sucking scumbags. Or are we?

The more you think about it, there is hardly any distinction between paparazzi and political reporters. We chase the candidates just like they stalk celebrities. Only we never get to go to those exotic locales that paparazzi go to get their shots; we have to tread through hog lots in Iowa and house parties in New Hampshire. And when I say house party, I don't mean the off-the-hook, whacked-out, my-parents-are-out-of-town-so-let's-get-freaky kind of house party.

The advantage that the paparazzi have over us is that they follow real celebrities, so their time always pays off. I can spend a week with Wes Clark getting the scoop on how he plans to balance the budget, but most people don't even know who Wes Clark is and nobody really cares about his tax cut plan. Everybody wants to know what is new with JLo.

Because we cover men of substance, we feel superior, but it's all an

The lonely cake after the photo op.

illusion. The candidates fill our notebooks with promises that we all know will not last past election day. Don't kid yourself; the campaigns don't treat us any better than JLo would treat a pack of photo seekers sitting in her driveway.

"Paparazzi over to the side of the club," the bodybuilder–drill sergeant doorman screamed and we all instantly obeyed. This is not a man you want to mess with. He roped us off away from the door of the club and a big huge Hummer drove up.

Al Sharpton Photo Op Take 2

"I told you he'd be here," the relieved press handler bragged as she frantically called Al to get him back to the club. "Hold the press, we'll get the shot," the *Post* reporter howled into the phone with the excitement that should be reserved for a story of far grander proportions.

Like wet rats we all scurried back into the nightclub. Only this time a posse of street thugs dressed in Armani wouldn't let us get anywhere near the pop star. Puffy was positioned at the top of the staircase and huge black men with earpieces stood guard at the bottom of the stairs telling reporters they were not allowed to go near Mr. Diddy. There we all stood sheepishly at the bottom of the staircase with no chance of being able to shout questions at Mr. Diddy over the gangsta music.

Al arrived back on the scene and some of the more aggressive reporters climbed the adjacent staircase and attempted to get at Al and Puff Daddy from the side. But it didn't take long for Diddy's bodyguards to tell us all that it was time for us to go home. We were no longer wanted here. We were pushed out the door into the pouring rain.

It's 12:06. Do You Know Where Your General Is?

Manchester, New Hampshire
OCTOBER 26, 2003

His schedule frequently has been in chaos. On Wednesday, for example, he was scheduled to present his New Hampshire staff to the news media at 11:30 A.M. Not until 12:06, after reporters had assembled, did his campaign send out an e-mail advisory saying that he was instead appearing somewhere else at 11:30.

—NEW YORK TIMES

THIS IS NOT what you want the story of your campaign to be thirty-five days into the race. Reporters are already whispering that the general's best days are already behind him. He was fired up in the first week. After that, he got laryngitis and flamed out.

One month later, Clark is still green and it shows. On the stump, he has been leaving the crowd cold. He is a general, after all. Whenever someone asks him something, he answers with an old war story. From conversations with members in the crowd it appears that General Clark is not rocking people's world the way he thought he would. Although many women do point out how handsome he is and what beautiful hands he has. The first thing those who shook his hand reported was how firm his grip was. There was some talk about the huge gold and diamond ring he has on his wedding ring finger. Apparently it is his West Point class ring with a diamond from his father's pinkie ring set inside it. One woman found it endearing. "He's a strong man, strong men can get away with wearing that kind of jewelry." Another was not impressed. "The best thing he could do for his campaign is take off that creepy pimp ring."

Since Bob Graham dropped out and left an empty New Hampshire headquarters with some competent staffers, Clark already has an organization up and running. For a man who claims "I'm not a professional politician," Clark has accrued some of the best political professionals on the market, which is not necessarily a good thing.

The first thing journalists seem to notice at a Wes Clark event is how many staffers are in the room. His operation is bigger than the other candidates' (who have been at this for a year now). The staff is a constant topic of discussion among the reporters. We should be talking about the candidate and his positions, not how overcoddled we feel by his staff. On his first trip to New Hampshire, one photographer complained that he did not get one photograph of the supreme allied commander that did not have a handler's hand on his back. If the New York Yankees taught us anything, it is that you can have all the best players money can buy, but you have to know how to use them.

Originally the word on the street was that Clark was the invention of the old Clinton and Gore advisers getting together and trying to create the perfect candidate. Apparently the laboratory experiment is not going according to plan. In an attempt to rebound from a bad few weeks, today Clark emerged triumphant at the opening of his New Hampshire headquarters (or, as I wanted to call it, the Bob Graham HQ closing party).

As Clark entered the room to the tune of Van Halen's "Right Now" (the Bush campaign theme song), I had to wonder: Didn't his campaign hacks learn anything from their days with Al Gore? My colleagues and friends who covered the Gore campaign in 2000 have the same complaints about Wes Clark that they had about Al Gore. He is overmanaged by a stressy staff who try to control the media and keep their candidate as far away from them as possible.

The minute that Clark's communications director (who put Dukakis in the tank in '88 and directed trips for Gore in '00) instructed members of the press "We are going to do this like the White House. You stand there," I realized that Clark's staff is his own worst enemy. And he doesn't even know it. Doesn't this seasoned staffer know that we do not work for him? He does not own us, he should not tell us where we are "allowed to stand." So this is why the press hated Al Gore.

The difference here is: Wes Clark is not Al Gore, he was not the vice president, he does not have Secret Service, he is not the nominee, and he is not entitled to avoid all contact with the press. Even John Kerry has to grovel to all the local news geeks right now. Wes Clark is making a huge Al Gore–style mistake if he ignores the people who will be controlling his fate in print. After the month he's had, Clark needs all the good press he can get. Everyone thought that the man whose previous job was serving as a CNN commentator would have been more media savvy.

Clark is obviously still shell-shocked from his first round with the media firing squad. Within the first forty-eight hours of launching his campaign, he got shot down when a few of the political reporters who matter tried to pin him down on his position on the war (their verdict was that he could not declare definitively whether he was for or against it). This seemed like something he should have decided *before* getting into this race, since Iraq may very well be the defining issue of the 2004 election.

While the other top-tier candidates have been out on the trail for the past year busting their tails across the country, Clark was at home delib-

Clark meets the pack.

erating about the pros and cons of jumping into the race. We know now that he wasn't formulating his positions on the issues, or coming up with a good explanation for why he is running as a Democrat, considering that he voted for Nixon, Reagan, and Bush and he publicly praised George Bush within the past year. When he says he was taking time to decide whether or not to run, what on earth was he thinking about?

"What Are You Going to Do About the Chicken?"

Portsmouth, New Hampshire
OCTOBER 28, 2003

JOHN KERRY IS WORKING HARDER than he ever has in his entire life as a civilian. He really took a hit in the latest round of polls. With one hundred days before the official start of the primaries, the pollsters just predicted that Dean will reign supreme in New Hampshire. This must have put the fear of God into John Kerry. Now he's on the warpath.

This week he hit the house party circuit to recruit new supporters. And he didn't just show up, he gave each potential supporter his best shot. Tonight at the last party of the night he stayed to answer every single question in the room, including an animal rights activist who wanted to know "What are you going to do about the chicken?"

Sometimes you forget that the people at these house parties are a strange breed of political animal. They are following the horse race at a time when no one else in America can even name the candidates in the field. This revealed itself when Kerry made a reference to a joke he made at the last debate and the room laughed along knowingly. If you missed the debate (as most of America did), here is what happened: One of the panelists asked Kerry how he would dispel the impression that he's a "northeastern, liberal elitist." He answered, "Wait until you see my video, *Kerry Gone Wild.*" Tonight he joked that *Kerry Gone Wild* was now available in video stores. Kerry himself seemed surprised that the crowd knew what he was talking about. "How many of you didn't watch the debate?" No one raised a hand. "That sure tells you something about New Hampshire," he concluded.

This reminded me of another house party that took place on the last night of the World Series. Since New Hampshire is a part of Red Sox Nation it was assumed that the turnout would be low because everyone wanted to see the Yankees get their butts kicked. But it was a full house and the TV was off. The host explained that in New Hampshire, they don't need baseball; presidential politics is their sport. Kerry proclaimed, "Howard Dean has been a Red Sox fan as long as Wes Clark has been a Democrat." Then he moved on to say that Howard Dean is a carpetbagger and has absolutely no chance of defeating George Bush.

Whether it is the fear of humiliation, desperation, or the smell of a fight, the Massachusetts senator is fired up and he's going in for the kill. "This time of year, your juices get going politically." And the bad blood is flowing . . .

The senator made his best case yet against the one man he believes is the obstacle to his childhood dream of being president. "I am not attacking, I am just drawing distinctions. George Bush had no prior foreign policy experience. He told people, 'Don't worry, I'll hire a good staff.' Ladies and gentlemen, I believe very deeply that George Bush is the poster child/lesson to America that the presidency is not the place for on-the-job, post–September 11 foreign policy, national security training. There is an enormous difference between Howard Dean and myself. I think the Democrats will be enormously disadvantaged if we don't have the ability to stand up and keep America safe and secure."

A woman in the kitchen applauded loudly. This was the same woman who was at a Dean house party last week. When I questioned her allegiance, she told me she is recently committed to Kerry because "I had a lot of fun with Dean, but I knew he wouldn't last. He is the kind of guy you have a one-night stand with, but when you are ready to settle down, you come see John Kerry." She is one of the many New Englanders who has a bumper sticker on her car that says "Dated Dean, Married Kerry." Her Republican husband doesn't seem to mind. "She is voting with her head. Kerry is not her dream choice, but he is the only one who has a chance against Bush," he reasoned. "I'm voting for Bush, but if I were a Democrat, I would vote for Kerry because he has the best shot in the general election." Whom would you prefer to have over for dinner, Bush or Kerry? The couple agreed: If they were having a barbecue, they would invite Bush; if it were a sit-down dinner party with linens, it would be Kerry.

They are not alone in their belief that John Kerry is the most "electable" of the Democratic candidates. A self-declared McCain Independent told the senator that the reason he came tonight was because he thought Kerry was the best suited to take on Bush. That gave Kerry the opportunity to preview the material he will be using against the president. "We've entrusted him with the world and yet the world's waiting while the president is clearing brush."

The latest edition to Kerry's door-to-door sales pitch is: humility. He has decided to appeal to people's sympathies. "At these debates there is a doctor and a general. Do you have any idea how embarrassing it is to say, 'I'm just a senator'?" He's even using the "if" word. "If I am elected president . . ." Dean has been saying this for months as part of his underdog appeal. Everybody likes an underdog. Also, Kerry stole a line from Dean that has been getting a lot of mileage: "This is not about me, this is about us."

The senator is enduring a lot more than he used to from the crowds. This was evident from a series of questions he got at a house party last week in Merrimack. One man asked him, "Can you be fair about dealing with the situation in the Middle East because you are Jewish?" The candidate with the reputation for being the quintessential WASP talked about what should be done in the Middle East, and then had to explain that he is a practicing Catholic who has only a tad of Jewish blood in him.

Then an old Italian man accused Kerry of being "a racist just like Trent Lott." The Italian American demanded an apology for a joke

Kerry made on the Don Imus show. "The Iraqi army is in such bad shape, even the Italians could kick their butts," Kerry quipped. The old guy, who looked like his best days were behind him, scolded the senator: "You are anti–Italian American. You should be ashamed of yourself." He continued his attack, but the host had to step in to allow her other guests to get their questions answered.

Another man proclaimed, "Today, I found a cure for cancer." Then he demanded to know why places like MIT get all the research grants and smaller places, like where he works, never get federal money. Kerry talked about the unfairness in funding (but didn't congratulate the man on finding the cure for cancer). As Kerry kept talking, an older woman whispered to her friend, "I have never stood for an hour and a half to listen to anyone in my whole life."

John Kerry is running out of time. With only three months left until the New Hampshire primary, he has a lot more of these long nights ahead of him. You have to give the guy credit: The process of running for president really sucks the life out of you. It is monotonous, repetitious, and excruciating to watch. With his intelligence and wealth, John Kerry could be doing a lot better things on a Friday night than listening to some mad scientist claiming he found the cure for cancer and some vegetarian ranting about the living conditions of non-free-range chickens.

Who Will Ruin the Party?

November 2, 2003
WASHINGTON, D.C.

THE DEMOCRATS ARE ON THE VERGE of a civil war. It is Joe Lieberman and the Democratic Leadership Council versus Howard Dean and the grassroots activists. This will not be a velvet revolution;

heads will roll, and the only ones who will enjoy watching the blood-shed will be the Republicans because the winner of this battle is destined to lose the war with the GOP.

Every day in his stump speech Howard Dean says, "The only way to beat George Bush is by not acting like George Bush or being Bush Lite." Although it is meant to be an indictment of all his fellow Democratic candidates, it was custom-made for Joe Lieberman.

As the self-proclaimed "independent-minded Democrat," Joe Lieberman has spent his days in the U.S. Senate reaching across the aisle to compromise with members of the opposite party. This has earned him the nickname inside the Dean campaign of "the Republican footstool." As a centrist, Lieberman is making the same argument today that Bill Clinton made in 1992, that for a Democrat to win, he has to move to the center. (There is no proof that this argument is legitimate. Bill Clinton was a great candidate. Was it him or his swing to the center?)

Howard Dean believes that in order to win this election, the Democrats don't have to go to the right with Lieberman, they have to reach out to the base and then reach out to new voters. (Of course, words like left, right, and center are meaningless because they all mean different things to different people. But these are the words the campaigns are using.)

Dr. Dean's prescription for a new and improved Democratic Party is to isolate Democrats like Lieberman and cut off the centrists like the Democratic Leadership Council, the organization of moderate Democrats whose mission is to pull the party to the center. Dean calls the DLC "the Republican wing of the Democratic Party."

Lieberman is warning the world that Dean is pulling the party to the left, and the senator has declared this campaign "a battle for the heart and soul of the Democratic Party." Which, ironically, is the same line lefty Jerry Brown used against centrist Bill Clinton in 1992, when Clinton gave the Democratic Party a moderate makeover to bring in big donors and lobbyists. (The result of Clinton and the DLC's win is what Ralph Nader campaigned against in 2000: the two parties coming closer together and mirroring each other.)

In their manifesto, "The Real Soul of the Democratic Party," the

DLC proselytizes, "The great myth of the current cycle is the misguided notion that the hopes and dreams of activists represent the heart and soul of the Democratic Party. Real Democrats are real people, not activist elites . . . What activists like Dean call the Democratic wing of the Democratic Party is an aberration: the McGovern-Mondale wing, defined principally by weakness abroad and elitist, interest-group liberalism at home. That's the wing that lost 49 states in two elections, and transformed Democrats from a strong national party into a much weaker regional one." In other words, in order to win, the Democratic Party must excommunicate the liberals.

As Bush hatred grips the nation, there are many in the Democratic Party who believe that Howard Dean is the captain of the *Titanic,* cruising comfortably on his maiden voyage oblivious to the doomed future of his ship. They predict he will go down not because of what he is saying but because of how he is saying it. As one Blue Dog Democrat put it, "His angry tone will kill us. The image of the angry activists will not sell in the heartland."

In their editorial "Activists Are Out of Step," the DLCers give out more of their tough love: "Party activists are out of line not only with their party's historic tradition but with their fellow Democrats." Which means: Take a hike, all you stinking lefties, you do not fit the image of this party. (Even if what the DLC says is true, why would they go and pick a fight with the activists, the ones who do the legwork for the party?)

The bottom line is, the DLC doesn't think Dean can beat Bush, and the only thing that matters in politics is winning. So they are denouncing Dean as a liberal, which is ironic because his positions are more in line with the DLC than they would like to admit. Their objections to him have little to do with his ideology and everything to do with his electability, or lack thereof.

The DLC school of thought teaches that politics is all about the art of compromise. If you want to get elected, you have to learn to settle. If you are not willing to give in on certain issues, then go Green, and don't complain that your country is being run by the corporations and the Christian Coalition.

Are you going to vote with your heart or with your head? As Senator Evan Bayh, president of the DLC, put it, "It is our belief that the Democratic Party has an important choice to make: Do we want to vent or do we want to govern? The administration is being run by the far right. The Democratic Party is in danger of being taken over by the far left."

Howard Dean is not radically far left. He is just being characterized that way for political expediency. Which is why every time the DLC firing squad hits Dean, it only helps him raise more money. Trying to destroy your opponent as "far left" and "dangerously liberal" does seem gratuitous, especially when it is coming from inside your own party. If the Democrats lose this election, they may have only the DLC to blame. Which may not matter to the DLC; from what they are saying, it seems as if they would rather lose in 2004 than see Dean in Washington.

There is no proof that going right would improve a Democrat's viability in the general election. We don't really know how many liberals there are over there on the far left (there is no shortage of them on the Internet). But we do know that going left is a guaranteed formula for failure; just ask George McGovern and Walter Mondale. A move to the left will help the liberal Democrats feel good about themselves, but they better not expect to win any presidential elections for a very long time.

Will the conservative Democrats abandon Dean if he is the nominee? Will the DLC abandon the party? Does anyone really care what the DLC thinks? They say that their work to get Clinton elected makes them the only group of Democrats who has gotten anything done in the past decade. One wonders how much credit they deserve for Clinton's victories, but we'll give it to them, along with the blame for Al Gore's loss.

In the months to come, as the Democratic Party cuts itself open, we will see if their future depends on appealing to moderates. If the moderates lose, it will probably leave a huge open wound for the Democrats. But will it ensure Bush's reelection? Soon the Democratic primary voters will be forced to choose: Do you want someone who will tell you everything you want to hear? Or do you want to win? And is it possible to have both?

Meeting McGovern

New York City
NOVEMBER 4, 2003

> You guys never know what goes on. How could you, traveling
> with the candidate all the time? Of course, that's why we want you
> traveling.
>
> —ATTRIBUTED TO ONE OF "NIXON'S MOST ABLE
> MANAGERS," *HARPER'S,* 1971

WE COULD REALLY USE some perspective right about now. As
luck would have it, George McGovern, the antiwar hero who won the
Democratic nomination in 1972, is in town. It's time to go pay him a
visit.

Killing time at the offices of *Harper's* magazine (where McGovern
moonlights as a columnist), I flipped through a 1971 edition as I waited
to meet the elder statesman. There I found an article about life on the
campaign trail in the good old days. Here is what it said:

> There's a knowledgeable, if mild, contempt for the press among
> politicians—they feel the same way, incidentally, about clichés
> like "the public's right to know." That attitude was institutionalized
> in 1968 in a little manual carried by Richard Nixon's staff: The
> central point of scheduling is that campaigning is symbolic, i.e., it is
> not what the candidate actually does as much as what it appears he
> does.

The article, which was written around the time of my birth, went on
about how "television is the most important part of a modern campaign." Reading this today makes me doubt the theory of evolution.

Here we are, thirty-two years later, and the man who just walked in the door ran back then a lot like the Democratic front-runner is running today: against an incumbent president and with an antiwar message that many feel is too angry for the country. Does it look like history is repeating itself?

Who better to ask than the man who will be featured in the next issue of *Playboy* magazine, sandwiched in between the buxom bosoms of Playmates, talking about how the Dean campaign reminds him of his own. As I rose to meet the political icon, he reached into his back pocket Elvis-style and pulled out a pocket-size comb and began combing the hairs remaining on his eighty-two-year-old head. Then he picked up today's newspaper. "Sixteen GIs are killed," he read aloud. "This looks like Vietnam."

This led into a discussion about whether the Democrats should speak up against this war even if it means losing as badly as McGovern did. This is his position: "Is it better to speak the truth and lose? Absolutely. I lost big in 1972 to Richard Nixon. I don't envy him. He misled the American people. He kept us involved in a foolish war for another four years. Forty percent of all the young Americans who died in Vietnam died in Mr. Nixon's first four years as president of the United States, after he promised that he had a secret plan to end the war. I would not want those 40 percent of American casualties, some forty thousand American troops, on my conscience. He was impeached, he was threatened with conviction for that impeachment and had to resign the office. Do you think I would feel better about my position in history if I were in Mr. Nixon's shoes? Not on your life. I am proud of the campaign I waged. I sleep soundly every night knowing that I did my best to alert the American public to what was going on."

McGovern went on to praise history's great losers. "Some of the great figures in American history are the ones who lost. William Jennings Bryan lost three times; Adlai Stevenson lost two times; Wendell Willkie lost to Franklin Roosevelt. But every single one of those men contributed something of lasting worth to the United States. And I would wager, wherever they are, they are glad they tried even though they didn't make it. Certainly I am glad that I tried. I will be eternally grateful that I ran in 1972, that I won the nomination over sixteen other candidates, some of them very capable people. I think that campaign helped force an end to the Vietnam War. Because when we lost, almost 30 million Americans were on record as saying, '*We* don't support this war.' When 30 million people stood up and said, 'Let's get out of Vietnam,' I think the McGovern campaign in 1972 ended the war in Vietnam!"

There are many in the Democratic Party who do not share McGovern's romantic notions about the glory of losing. They want to win; that's why they founded the Democratic Leadership Council. McGovern does not have much respect for them. "These DLCers don't like anyone who isn't standing squarely in the middle of the road, and leaning a little bit to the right. They have never seen a war that they didn't like. I never would have won the nomination thirty years ago if I were doodling along in the middle of the road. That can sometimes be the most politically dangerous position in the end. When you are walking down the middle of the road you can get hit by traffic coming both ways. I think it is better to take a position, what is in the best interest of the public, not a theoretical position about where the middle of the road is."

George McGovern is advising all the candidates not to make the biggest mistake he made. He reminisces, "I wish I had listened to one piece of advice that LBJ gave me. He said, 'I would advise you to start by thanking the American people for giving you the opportunity to serve your country. And then, if you have some criticism, you can express it but not until you've thanked America.' Years later I was in the Senate cloakroom and I heard a senator say, 'I think the mistake George made was he sounded too angry at the country. It sounded like he was mad at America. I don't think you can win on that kind of platform.' When you show a great deal of anger on policy like I did in Vietnam or Iraq, you have to be very careful to emphasize that I don't have any animosity toward the troops and toward our commanding officers out there, they are not the policymakers and it is the policy I am against. I wish every candidate would remember that, especially when you talk about the issues of war and peace. I am for our troops; that is why I don't want to send them into a needless war and to get them killed needlessly in a struggle that has no real relevance to the security of America. It is very important to draw that distinction. I wish I did that."

As we were on the topic of regret, I asked George about the effect running for president had on his family. "I had four daughters and a son and I think every one of them paid a heavy price for my political career, and that is my overriding regret about politics. I would still do it over again if the opportunity arose. I have to admit it took a heavy toll on my family." But he considers himself one of the lucky ones. "You can be hurt in a presidential race. You can start as a person with great prestige and end up with nothing. The hazards involved in running range from divorce to death."

"I suppose that Robert Kennedy would say if he were here or his family would say that running for president cost us a good man, shot down like a stray dog in the street. That is an awful price to pay to run for president, to give your life. I think that if Robert Kennedy was here that he would say, 'I don't regret that. I had to speak out on those issues. It cost me my life, it cost my brother his life, but we did what we thought was in the public interest. Those are some of the prices you pay.' "

McGovern explained how the families of the candidates seem to be the ones who pay the biggest price for the candidates' oversize ambitions. Once a man decides to run, his wife and kids get sucked into the bubble. He told a story that seemed to capture what it is like to be inside a presidential campaign. "At the convention in Miami my family and I were assigned to the sixteenth floor of the hotel we were in. After three days my daughter Terry said, 'Dad, it seems to me we are in a different world. We are sixteen floors above the world. We don't really know any longer what's going on out there. We are isolated from America up here on the sixteenth floor looking out across the ocean.' That struck me as an astute observation." (Years later, his daughter Terry's alcoholism and depression left her frozen to death in a parking lot.)

McGovern remembered what it is like to live in a campaign bubble. "In a campaign you are in the hands of your staff, the schedulers, the advance people, they determine where you are going, how long you will stay, how many hands you will shake until you move on to the next, how many speeches you are going to give in a day. All of those things, you race from one event to the other, all this time protected from the [people]. You are always being ushered in and it does create a bubble effect. You are inside the bubble and the rest of the world is out there."

The best part about being inside the bubble is everyone kisses your ass. The worst part is you have to kiss up to the voters; even when they are rude to you, you can't tell them to kiss your ass. McGovern explained, "It was near the end of the campaign. I was exhausted. We were working our way along the fence. This one obnoxious character was yelling at me four-letter words and everything you can imagine . . . Finally I said, 'Come here,' and I said, 'You little miserable SOB, how would you like to kiss my ass?' " Of course, that ended up on CBS that night and his advisers told him, "You can't talk that way, particularly on television."

Every former candidate expresses frustration with the political game, but deep down they are still itching to get back on the field. When asked if he would do it all over again, McGovern admits, "I did in 1984 and I almost did in 1992, before Clinton came into the race. There is no thrill in this world that can top running for the presidency of the United States. Whether you win or lose you are out there campaigning night and day for the most powerful and influential office in the world, the same office that was held by George Washington, Thomas Jefferson, Abraham Lincoln, Franklin Roosevelt. They were out there campaigning the same as we are today. That in itself is a head-filling, heart-stirring experience.

"It reminds me of something Coach Marv Levy said when someone asked him what it felt like to make it to the Super Bowl and lose all four times: 'You want to know how to avoid that pain? Just don't be good enough to get into the Super Bowl.' You want to avoid the pain of losing an election, just don't be good enough to be nominated. Running for president is like making it to the Super Bowl. Once you've run for president and you lost, I think every four years you think, 'Gosh, maybe this could be my time. Maybe I ought to give it another try . . .'"

At the end of our talk, the distinguished senator from South Dakota rolled his red minisuitcase into the elevator. As he struggled to get out the front door, no one offered to help. I asked him if we'd be seeing him again at the Democratic Convention next summer. He said it was doubtful; his wife refuses to go to any more conventions because no one from the Democratic Party ever officially recognizes him from the stage.

The former nominee walked out into the street and tried in vain to get a taxi. As he stood there, with a distressed look on his face, in the middle of Broadway at rush hour desperately trying to catch a ride to the airport, I couldn't help but think how different this man's life would have been if this country had seen through Richard Nixon fourteen months sooner. The anonymous old man who couldn't hail a cab could have been . . . But as Richard Nixon said, "Second place is oblivion." Hail to the candidates.

George McGovern trying to catch a cab.

I See Dean People

Loveland, Iowa
NOVEMBER 15, 2003

HOWARD DEAN STARTED OUT by taking on the Democratic Party. Now he thinks he can go toe-to-toe with the president of the United States? Where does he get this kind of confidence? The secret to Dean's self-assurance is *money*. The reason the media are paying attention to him is because he has the most money and he knows how to raise more! He has earned respect by showing Washington that he is a cash cow.

When you have the dough, you can start turning political functions into pure theater. Like at the Jefferson Jackson Dinner in Des Moines, a night intended for the Iowa Democrats, when Dean showed the prowess of his grassroots organization by paying to bus in loads of screaming kids from all across the country who yelled their lungs out all night long. This is not your grandpa's C-SPAN. As all the other candidates walked in waving when they were introduced, Dean appeared on the balcony, in a sea of his supporters, who were expressing at ear-splitting decibels how much they worship their idol. You usually don't see this kind of lavish rock star staging until the general election.

Regardless of who the guests at the dinner came to support, everyone was polite enough to clap along with bits and pieces of all the candidates' speeches. Except for the Deanies. While the other candidates spoke, they sat on their hands and talked among themselves. (This is their MO. If you go to a convention hoping to hear all of the candidates, forget it. It is common to hear the Dean supporters chanting in the hallway when the other candidates are on stage speaking.) When Dean took to the stage, his adoring mob hooted and hollered. By the time he reached the crescendo of his speech, they were in a frenzy. The doctor pointed his finger in the air and hollered "You have the power" fourteen times, like he was casting a spell on his followers. Kool-Aid alert! "Are they all brainwashed?" the man standing in front of me asked his friends. "This is like Nuremberg."

Near the Dean cheering section a huge, hand-painted banner along the wall said I SEE DEAN PEOPLE a takeoff from the movie *The Sixth Sense,* in which the people were dead but did not know it. One of the Deanies who painted the sign explained its significance: "All the Democrats in this room are all Dean people, but they do not know it yet." A Kerry aide had his own interpretation of how ironic the sign was: "The Dean people think that we are all dead. What they don't realize is that they are the dead ones."

A Dean staffer walked up to a Kerry staffer and said, "Dean is going to kick your ass." Later that night, at the Kerry after-party, that same Deanie was walking around announcing, "I am recruiting. After tonight I'm sure I can find defectors." Another Deanie announced, "Soon all of these people will all be working for Dean." "I doubt it," a Kerry aide responded. "It is awfully early for that kind of patronizing and it is never a good time to treat your colleagues this poorly. Unless you have walked precincts, knocked on doors, and asked for votes, you don't deserve to be so arrogant."

For a campaign fueled by anger, the Deanies sure seem to be happy these days. Two weeks ago at the Howard Dean Halloween party in Manchester, New Hampshire, the Deaniacs were having the time of their lives. They all dressed up as something from the Dean stump speech (for example, one woman was dressed as a one-way ticket to Crawford, Texas; another was dressed as voodoo economics). A Dean impersonator gave his speech and they acted it out on stage, while the room full of his supporters mouthed along, *Rocky Horror Picture Show*–style. Dean himself seemed to be enjoying it, but by the time they got to the Dean sing-along he looked freaked out by the whole scene. The question is: Is he walking the dog, or is the dog walking him?

The Dean movement seems to have taken on a life of its own. He is more than just a candidate; he is a lifestyle choice. People put money in their budget for Howard Dean each month. They come from all over the country to worship him. Despite the hoopla, the candidate remains remarkably unaffected by the explosion created by his candidacy.

As the leader of a movement, Howard Dean is undisturbed by the sideshow that goes on around him. With Dean, what you see is what you get. He is selling a message, not some sappy sentimental son-of-a-millworker story. His success is turning presidential politics on its head by revealing that people don't want to be glad-handed and they don't want to hear about your dad the milk-truck driver. Unlike Bill Clinton, the son of a traveling salesman and stepson of an abusive car dealer, who won in 1992 with his feel-good, "I feel your pain" propaganda, Howard Dean is not emoting and sharing details of his personal life. He is on a crusade to overhaul the American government. He is not going to get on the couch and open himself up so that the entire world can psychologically evaluate him.

Dean refuses to get autobiographical. But in this tell-all Oprah Winfrey society we live in, people want to know something about who you are and where you come from. If you want to be president, people feel like they have the right to know everything about you. When *Esquire* magazine did a photo essay entitled "Democrats in Their Natural Habitats," Dick Gephardt and his family got in the kitchen and cooked "party chicken"; Bob Graham wore a plush toy monkey around his neck as he read to his granddaughters; Senator Lieberman did the old "pretend to pull his finger off" trick in front of his whole family; Senator Kerry sat in his home, surrounded by books and expensive art on the walls, with his wife, Teresa, in pearls and a power suit, drinking tea next to him; Howard Dean was photographed in his headquarters with his staff. That one image told you everything you need to know about Howard Dean. He is all substance, no B.S.

The governor refuses to coddle and seduce the press. When Howard Kurtz reported in the *Washington Post* that "reporters who have spent hours with Dean express surprise that he never asks a single question about them," columnists ridiculed those reporters for being egotistical and making it all about themselves. But that is missing the point. What those reporters were conveying is Howard Dean's lack of people skills. (If you went to the office every day and a guy you saw daily never said hello to you, you would think that he didn't have any personality.) Howard Dean is either oblivious to the people around him, or he is awkward socially. If you had to spend one month straight with him and he never acknowledged your existence, you would say he is an odd duck.

Since he was declared the front-runner, Dean has had all the cameras on him nonstop, and he obviously is not comfortable with it. When cameras turn on, he acts like a deer in the headlights and smiles an uncomfortably tense grin. When asked what it feels like to have all the cameras in his face, Dean replied, "I have to be very careful about what I say." Every time he is talking to a reporter, it turns into a press conference, so when reporters try to talk to him when he is not in the mood, he says, "This is not a press conference." He has established his own set of rules: You cannot take pictures of him when he's eating, sleeping, or wearing his glasses.

Watching John Kerry play with the press, you can tell that he has had years of experience at this game. Every campaign staffer you talk to spins fantastic tales about how their candidate is going to pull off winning the primaries. Even though the Deanies are new to this business and are kicking Kerry's butt, the senator's staffers don't seem nervous. You have to wonder, why isn't Bob Shrum breaking a sweat? What does he know that these Deanies don't?

Republicans have made no secret about their lust for Dean to be the nominee. Maybe it has nothing to do with the candidate and everything to do with the image of the Deanieboppers running his campaign. To them, Deanies look like Greenies and the whole thing looks like Kiddy Camp.

The Dean groupies at the JJ Dinner, November 2003.

We all remember them from the Sleepless Summer, August 2003.

Selling Out

New York City

DECEMBER 9, 2003

THE CHATTERING CLASS has been saying it for months: "The Democratic race is over. Dean has wrapped up the Democratic nomination for president of the United States." At least that is what the Capitol Hill newspaper *Roll Call* said in their story entitled "It Ain't Over 'til It's Over, but It's Probably Over." Everybody's saying it. The *Christian Science Monitor* declared, "Dean Gaining Aura of Inevitability," and the *Boston Herald* reported, "Howard Dean barrels toward the presidential nomination with increasing velocity."

If you need more proof, just ask anyone at *Newsweek* who is working on yet another Howard Dean cover story and they will tell you, Dean has all the things the race watchers look for in a front-runner: the most money, the best poll ratings, and all the best endorsements. "Today marked the unofficial close of the primaries with Al Gore coming out to endorse Howard Dean," one *Newsweek* reporter declared at the endorsement ceremony. "Getting Gore sealed the deal for Dean."

The *New York Times* front page is saying, "President Bush's political advisors are now all but certain that Howard Dean will be the Democratic presidential nominee." The *Washington Times* is declaring, "Mr. Gore's support was a signal to many in the Democratic Party that Mr. Dean has the nomination sewn up. 'I think that anybody who knows squat about Democratic politics knows this—Dean's the nominee, he's in. And I think Gore is just one great tremendous shot in the arm,' " said David "Mudcat" Saunders, a Democratic strategist.

Despite what all the people in the know are saying, what I want to know is, who in the world cares what Al Gore thinks? For the past three years he has been in hibernation. We saw Osama bin Laden on TV more than Al Gore this year. And now all of a sudden he shows up in Harlem to reemerge as the Comeback Kid? It's a good thing Bill Clinton was out of town.

When Al got onstage in Harlem in front of all the white people and declared, "We need to remake the Democratic Party," I realized it was officially time to stage an intervention. Reality check: The last person to serve as the head of the party was Al Gore. So if the party is broken, who broke it?

Mr. Gore, who do you think Howard Dean is talking about when he complains that the Democrats have ignored their base? You, your former running mate, and that group you founded, the DLC. Didn't you read the editorial praising Dean because "Democrats need an anti-Gore"? In 2000, the voters ignorantly said there was no difference between George Bush and Al Gore because you failed so miserably to represent the party. If you had won in 2000 the party would be just fine right now. But now that you have killed your own party and been the first to declare it DOA, we don't need your mea culpa right now, as the party is on the verge of spontaneous combustion.

Dean has already made it perfectly clear that he intends to win by solidifying the base, bringing in new voters (who never liked Washington insiders like Gore), and bringing back the Naderites who were turned off by Al Gore in 2000 (because he was a career politician who started off as Green-friendly but then re-created himself for a national election). Why didn't anyone tell Howard Dean about Al Gore's historic power to screw things up?

This whole endorsement was not such a surprise. Howard Dean is everything Al Gore wishes he were. After all, he was the original Internet candidate. Dean offered Gore the perfect opportunity to reinvent himself, and at this point, Al Gore would grab any microphone he can get his hands on. But I don't really see how the Gore endorsement does much for Dean, except give him some K Street cred, which is everything his campaign is against.

The last thing Howard needs is for the people to think he is becoming The Man. Up until now, Dean was like a great indie rock act; the minute Gore stood next to him, he became a sell-out. As the outsider becomes the insider, what will happen to the little people who power

Howard? Like the comedians who donated their jokes to Dean at a series of New York City fund-raisers on the night that news of the Gore endorsement broke, who ended up getting a tongue-lashing from Howard for the content of their jokes.

Some "edgy" downtown comics performed their "racy material" for Dean supporters. They were there because, as comedian Judy Gold poetically put it, "We have to get this piece of living, breathing shit out of the office" (referring to our commander in chief).

Throughout the night, there was a lot of heterosexual bashing, pro-lesbian punch lines, and jokes at Bush and Cheney's expense. In her performance, antiwar activist Janeane Garofalo critiqued the Medicare bill that Bush just signed into law as the "You can go fuck yourself, Grandma, bill."

Comic Kate Clinton commented on the new pedophile allegations against Michael Jackson and quipped, "Frankly, I'm far more frightened of Condoleezza Rice." Sandra Bernhardt made more Condi jokes with a "Yes, Massa" accent. Then she went on to do what she does best, curse like a sailor throughout her raunchy routine full of abortion and lesbian jokes, eventually calling Dick Cheney's daughter Mary "a big lezzie."

Comedian David Cross did a bit in which he pretended to be Republican Senator Trent Lott (who lost his post as majority leader for saying, "The country would have been better off if Strom Thurmond had been elected president in 1948." Since Thurmond was a segregationist candidate, Lott's statement was considered racist). Imitating Lott, the comedian used the word "nigger" and joked about how "the media distorts and misconstrues everything."

Ironically, the candidate who is known for telling it like it is (and hating the media) found the jokes "offensive." His political instincts must have told him that not all Democrats are so into nigger jokes. Dean took to the stage and reprimanded the entertainers, "I just don't have much tolerance for ethnic humor." Still, he didn't refuse any of the $2 million they raised for him.

It is doubtful that any of these comedians will be invited to perform at the convention. But whoever gets the nomination will have Al Gore right by his side. Howard Dean ought to be a little more selective about the friends he is choosing to share the stage with. Because as Al Gore's old friend Joe Lieberman was the first to point out, "Al Gore is endorsing somebody who has taken positions that are diametrically opposite to what Al himself has said he believed over the years."

Howard, beware of the fair-weather friends. And don't become one. The only thing more embarrassing than standing onstage with Al Gore is not inviting him to the party and being known as the guy who dumps the people who helped him get where he is today.

Everyone Says John Kerry Is Done

Defiance, Iowa
DECEMBER 26, 2003

ON AN ICY COLD, snowy Saturday night in Davenport, Iowa, in the middle of the holiday season, John Kerry took an hour and forty-five minutes' worth of questions from the audience. Desperado, why don't you come to your senses?

Even though the primary is still a month away, suddenly everybody we talk to, from the woman sitting next to us at a diner in New Hampshire to the old man driving the hotel van in Iowa, have all come to the conclusion that "John Kerry is done."

It reminds me of when we used to ask the nuns in Catholic school for proof that there is a God. The best defense they gave was that people from around the world, who spoke different languages and had no means of communicating with one another, all believed in him. Today, nobody believes in the candidacy of John Kerry.

It is hard to pinpoint the exact date and time when everyone started saying that it is over, but today, it is a given. The first time I heard it said as fact was when a *Washington Post* reporter asked Clark, "Now that

Kerry is dead, are you vying for the number-two slot in New Hampshire?"

For over a month now, ever since he threw out his campaign manager and other staffers walked out in protest, the emerging consensus among reporters is that Kerry's campaign has ruptured.

Rumors have been circulating about the fallen front-runner ever since the *New York Times* reported on November 11 that Kerry had a conference call to discuss his staff shake-up and "a participant said, Mr. Kerry—who could be heard eating his supper over the speakerphone as he conducted the meeting—blamed the news media coverage for his problems."

These days all you hear or read in the paper is that Kerry is "not connecting." In the past month alone, the *Washington Post* wrote, "Kerry's performance has been one of the year's great political disappointments." Another write-up read, "Of all of the candidates, Kerry is considered the biggest disappointment by many Democrats, who say he has failed to clearly articulate a vision for the country." Another one said, "For Kerry the moment has come to accept the fact that the game is over. That moment has arrived this week with the release of a poll that finds him trailing the Rev. Al Sharpton." They also wrote, "The last time John Kerry was engaged in this hopeless a mission, he was dressed in fatigues and running around Southeast Asia."

The *Boston Globe* wrote, "A funny thing happened on the way to the nomination. Kerry collapsed . . . His epic downfall, which has taken him from the cover of news magazines early this year to an afterthought these days, has an almost Shakespearean quality to it." Another *Globe* column called him a "jackass" who "morphs into Ed Muskie," and WGBH reported that Kerry's "gone over like the metric system." The *Boston Herald* talked about the "ugly scene for a troubled campaign . . . sinking Kerry's faltering presidential bid into even deeper disarray." In a story entitled, "Kerry Tries to Rejuvenate His Faltering Campaign," *USA Today* reported that "Kerry could be in line for a different distinction: the first major candidate to be pushed from the race."

In an attempt to stop the hemorrhaging, Kerry showed up at Concord High School and gave a speech to the students about what he plans to do in the first one hundred days of his presidency. A senior who was yawning during the speech complained, "He speaks like the teachers talking in the *Peanuts* cartoons: All you can hear is noise." He also said he had a hard time watching Kerry because he looks like Count Chocula, the cereal box character (with a yen for chocolaty goodness).

A history teacher said, "He should be talking about what he is going to do in the first one hundred days when he gets back to the Senate. He has missed so many votes campaigning that he can't talk about his work in the Senate . . . He talks more about the few months he spent in Vietnam than he talks about his twenty years in the Senate. He talks about Vietnam so much, he might as well go campaign in the Mekong Delta."

After all the work Kerry has done on behalf of the POW-MIAs, they found the remains of Howard Dean's baby brother, Charlie, just in time for Thanksgiving. The way Joe Trippi explains it, "John Kerry set the table and Howard Dean is sitting down for dinner."

Kerry appeared on Jay Leno's show after a two-part segment with Comic, the insult dog, who was making his pooping jokes at Kerry's expense. Kerry stayed for only one segment.

Standing in the empty parking lot of Shaw's Supermarket without gloves in the dead of winter, trying to get shoppers to shake his hand, Kerry pleaded, "I need your help. I am asking for your help." A young guy refused him, "I've got to get home to feed my dog . . . I have a life."

After going door-to-door with the senator in Portsmouth, New Hampshire, to meet voters, I asked a bereavement counselor who met him, "Does he give good retail?" She replied, "Maybe too good."

The bellboy at the hotel who carried Kerry's bags told me, "He is burnt out; the road is getting the best of him. There is not much fresh left."

A Dean spy who crashed a Kerry event offhandedly remarked, "I can't believe this is the man we were afraid of."

One of the reporters covering Kerry said, "He is acting like the guy who knows he is about to be dumped but keeps telling you, 'We can make this work.' "

On the day that America was glued to their televisions to watch Saddam Hussein get the lice picked out of his hair, John Kerry was having a live town hall meeting with undecided voters, which he paid to have aired all across Iowa.

To revive his ailing campaign, he has come up with a new gimmick to lure crowds: a home-cooked meal. His entire schedule now is full of "chili fests," at which the voters line up, soup-kitchen style, and wait to be served a bowl of chili from the senator and his billionaire ketchup-heiress wife. Kerry claims the chili fests are working. "There are a lot of hungry people who want to be fed." He has proved that there are a lot of people looking for a free meal, but we still don't know if giving out a hot bowl of beans will translate into votes.

The new and improved John Kerry has more than just chili, he has a new motto; now he's "The Real Deal." To which my producer responded, "The real deal? It's more like the real Dean" (based on the amount of material Kerry has co-opted from Dean). It seemed his old motto, "The courage to do what is right for America," wasn't working; as one of the *Newsweek* reporters said, "Kerry is as phony as a three dollar bill."

In defense of John Kerry, what they say about him is not all true. When he is talking to voters he is not arrogant or aloof; he is sincere and warm. He has been working so hard and he deserves credit for the amount of energy he has put into talking with people about the issues. But reporters don't care about issues. All they want to talk about is the horse race. When an Associated Press reporter tried to ask him about the latest round of polls, the senator had to defend his desire to talk about something real. "Forgive me if I want to talk about substance for a minute. I know that all you care about is the polls but I really think we should be talking about this tax cut."

The falling out with his staff apparently was about whether Kerry should have been tougher on Howard Dean earlier on. Initially, Kerry didn't want to go on the attack early, he took the high road. Of course, that could not last, but it's good to know that Kerry is not the aggressor who wants to take the fight head-on.

It is said of some candidates that they were doomed because they got in too late (Graham and Clark always use this excuse for their poor performances). If John Kerry loses it will be because he got in too early; people had time to get tired of him, as they seem to have now. As his outgoing communications director said, "It's hard to get two bites from the apple."

The signs of Kerry's demise have been hard to ignore, but it is hard to feel sorry for a guy whose house burnt down before anyone smelled the smoke. As his own employee let the whole world know, when John Kerry's campaign was going down in flames, he was at home eating dinner. Which is where the *Boston Globe* predicts he will be in six months, when the Democratic Convention comes to his hometown, just one mile from his townhouse (which he just mortgaged to pay for his dying campaign).

Even though the professional political class has given up on him and the headlines are now saying "Pressure Grows on Kerry to Drop Out of Race," he is not giving up. Because even though the media have declared this race over, not one voter has been to the polls and anything can happen. He said it himself when he was asked, "Are you disheartened that the media have declared 'Kerry Is Dead'?" "Nobody should celebrate prematurely. This race is really wide open. Anything is possible."

ACT II

Confessions of a sinner:

"I, a former card-carrying member of the National Press Corps, have sinned. I have engaged in 'horse race' and 'fuselage' journalism. I have written stories that focused more on campaign tactics than issues. I have interviewed political aides and consultants as if they, and not voters, should decide the content, if not the very outcome, of an election campaign. I have pretended to know what the country wanted, when in fact I had little or no idea because I had not really done the hard-precinct-level reporting from which such knowledge might stem. I am truly sorry and I humbly repent. So should anyone who is similarly sinning today, for it is clear to me that we who are privileged to call ourselves political journalists have a great deal to be repentant about. The bad habits of what I call 'know it all' reporting have become so ingrained that many of us have actually begun thinking of them as principles."

—STAN CLOUD, FORMER NEWSPAPER EDITOR AND
TIME MAGAZINE'S WASHINGTON BUREAU CHIEF

The Invasion

WE'RE HERE! And to the locals, you know what that means: overcrowded restaurants, lines in stores, traffic jams, and no parking spaces. The local businesses have jacked up their prices and the hotels have doubled their rates to welcome the hordes of visiting media. At this time, every four years, those who live here know not to eat out, not to drive through the center of town, and not to go anywhere near the big hotels, no matter what, because they are journalist-infected infernos! In other words, lock your doors and keep your kids inside; the media mafia has arrived.

Every four years a new wave of young recruits comes to New Hampshire with dreams of being political reporters. Four years ago, that was me, fresh off the plane with that first-day-of-school glow. What you learn on your second time around is that journalism is a job, not an adventure; nothing is new; campaigns have been covered in the exact same way since the dawn of democracy; and there is no institutional memory. Every election season the new breed experiences for the first time what the old-timers come back for every election.

The first-timers always think that they are the first on Earth to see it. Inevitably, some freshman newsy writes a story about how being on a presidential campaign is like *Groundhog Day* and that the campaigns herd us around like sheep. Within the first week, you hear an old-timer preaching their motto, "What goes on the road, stays on the road" (meaning you can sleep with everyone on the bus and no one will tell your wife).

To accommodate the onslaught of new journalists interested in covering the candidates, this is the point in the race when the campaigns officially organize traveling press corps. In theory, each news organization

97

assigns one person to cover each candidate. From now on, the candidates will not be seen without a pack of reporters in their shadow. From a distance, the pack moves flawlessly as an organized group that relies on the candidate's cues. The problem that this flocking dynamic presents is that the more there are of us, the less you get to see of the candidate. It is not an issue about the quality of the reporters, but the quantity.

So here we are at the end of yet another long mind-numbing day on the road and I'm sitting on the big yellow school bus with a pack of reporters heading back to The Hotel Ottumwa (whose motto is "Where hospitality begins") and we are placing bets on what the hotel is going to smell like (the best guess is "ass"). My mom just called to check in, and while we were chatting the boys on the bus burst out into a Neil Diamond medley. As I try to yell over them she asks, "Haven't you grown out of being on the bus? That is no place for a lady." I tried to redeem myself in her eyes by telling her that Eleanor Clift was onboard.

Getting back on the campaign bus is a lot like exercise. The first day it hurts a lot and you don't see the benefits of being there, but the longer you stick with it, the more it starts to pay off. The danger of staying too long is that you are forced to take orders from staffers and you become susceptible to the group psychology. That's when you know it is time to drop off and go join a new ship of fools.

This time around, my former employers at NBC (who wouldn't air any of my camcorder footage in 2000) have armed all of their producers with cameras and sent them to get wacky "on the road" footage. Soon the other networks followed suit. Now every time a candidate gets on his own bus, he is stepping into his own reality TV show. Like a pack of Japanese tourists, not many of them seem to be taking pictures; they are just randomly shooting reams of video. Howard Dean was the first to ask, "Who on earth is going to watch all this?" It is no secret that politics is really boring. Just because you have a camera rolling behind the scenes does not mean that it will be interesting or that anyone is going to want to watch it.

The candidates are not the only ones who are not thrilled with the embeds, or, as the real reporters call them, "inbreds." The serious scribes (who were never too keen on my camera in 2000) complain that the cameras prevent the possibility of ever getting a candidate to have a candid moment. And many of the old-school professional photojournalists who have lost work to "the amateurs" have expressed their anger at me. Their argument is that the networks' photojournalism experiment proves that you have a lot of cameras, but most of them are pointed in the wrong direction.

The best display of this is when a crotchety old man was trying to eat his breakfast in his local diner and an overzealous embed turned her camera on him for his close-up. The man barked out, "Don't point that thing at me. It doesn't go very deep with you newsgirls, does it? The label that they put on you, there is a core of truth to it, isn't there? What do you know about presidential elections? You are living in oblivion of your own history."

Nobody likes it when the press swarms. As soon as a local in Nashua, New Hampshire (voted "best place to live" in 1997 by *Money* magazine), saw a presidential candidate walk into his bowling alley he announced, "Send in the clowns." A woman trying to do her grocery shopping in Sully's Supermarket in Goffstown, New Hampshire, observed, "You guys are like a plague of locusts." Clark was at Sully's (home of the "Best Meats in Town") for a bagging groceries photo op, but a shopper named Robby never did get to see the general actually put groceries in a bag because "there were so many reporters around." This is not unusual; locals rarely get to see the candidates these days due to the large number of media circling around them.

Here is how Robby saw the Clark event: "As soon as [Clark] stopped to talk to real folk, the press just swarmed, like 'Get out of my way.' It was amazing. It was like watching flies buzzing on a pile of manure, tripping over each other. Sad for them that they have to feel so cut-throat. Time is important, but not at the cost of manners." She concluded, "It is a wonderful and terrible thing to have you in town. The wonderful part is, of course, you bring a lot of excitement and promotion to a store like Sully's, you put our name in the national news and that is great for us. But boy, oh boy, you push and shove. I would not

The Wes Clark reality-TV show.

want to be a presidential candidate. You would be swarmed by reporters and people pushing and shoving and cameras in your face. Some courtly manners are in order for press, I would say."

As soon as the Clark entourage left, the Sully's cashier ripped off the Clark '04 sticker that a Clark staffer asked her to wear and the staff stood around making jokes, like "How many cameras does it take to screw in a lightbulb? Fifty and a general." A customer who missed the commotion listened to the cashier retell the story of how the general bagged groceries. The old man replied, "At least he is good for something, unlike those press people!"

After seeing how the sausage (or in this case, the press) is made, the clerks in Sully's admitted to feeling used and concluded that they will never be able to look at a newspaper or magazine the same way again. When I asked one of the clerks if I could interview her about that on camera she said, "No, I don't like TV. I don't have a TV because it hurt my self-confidence. It started to make me feel ugly. I think TV is unhealthy. You TV people are toxic."

Across town Joe Lieberman swung open the doors of a diner with a cluster of press people talking on their cell phones, playing with their BlackBerrys, looking for outlets to plug in their laptops, and screaming things like "What is the name of this place?" and "I need sound, I need sound!" One regular customer who was scared off by the mob stood outside and gawked at the ratio of camera crews to customers. He expressed his disbelief: "It's a surreal scene. It is as if you are at a party and a camera goes on and everybody acts different. The event changes by the mere fact that the media are there." He determined that we were "infecting the town."

A customer who was man enough to brave the mob scene complained to his waitress, "How am I supposed to eat my lunch with all these cameras in my face?" On his way out he was annoyed that all of the reporters who were interrupting his lunch hour were asking so many questions. "Why do you care so much about what I think? I am just a guy trying to have lunch," he remarked. "The only opinion I have is that you guys ought to let us eat our lunch in peace."

The guy next to him growled at the reporters, "Get a real job!" This reminded me of something one of my old colleagues used to say to his interns on their first day on the job: "Don't get along well with people? Can't stand the sight of blood? Too dumb for law school? Welcome to TV news!"

A videographer from the local station who hit me in the head with his camera in one of those scrums in New Hampshire wrote me an e-mail apology. "Is it just me, or is the media getting nastier and more out of control than last time around? The still photographers in particular seem to be really out of control. One large smelly photog from the *New York Times* almost knocked three people off the stage. I'm really afraid that this political coverage is becoming a media Death Sport!"

One of the waitresses at Richard's, the most expensive restaurant in Manchester, told us that this was the first week since they opened that they were booked solid. I explained that since we are here on someone else's dime, we eat at only the most expensive restaurants. She told us that she figured that out when a CNN anchor sent his seafood back because it had a "piece of glass" in it (the cook was forced to come out and explain that it was not glass, but sea salt).

This was just one of the many examples our friendly waitress gave us to prove that it is not just the quantity but the quality of customers that has changed this week. She complained, "Hon [they call everyone Hon], you guys talk about nothing all night long. It reminds me of how we used to talk about boys in junior high, when I had a crush on a guy and he didn't even know I existed, but I would talk to my friends about it endlessly." She told us that all she hears customers doing is psychoanalyzing everything about these presidential candidates, but "it is obvious that no one really knows what is going to happen. But you can't say that on TV, so people get on talk shows and talk out of their asses." My dinner guest, who makes appearances on TV, tried to defend himself. "We don't know, you can't know, nobody knows, but we are here trying to figure it out."

The one thing the waitress wanted to know is why the only people who don't seem to talk about politics are the candidates. She gossiped, "Wes Clark was in here and the waiter who served him said he overheard his conversation and all he was talking about was sports or something."

At Picollo Italia, the best Italian restaurant in town, the staff is forbidden to talk about politics with the customers. Our favorite waiter there told us that if you worked in a restaurant in New Hampshire the first thing you learn is to "shut your mouth and serve the food." When I tried to get him to break the rules he swore, "There are two things I never talk about: politics and religion."

My general conclusion from talking to the locals in Iowa and New Hampshire is that they all hate politics. Every waiter and hotel clerk and cashier I talked to said they were not going to vote.

The front desk clerk at the Center of New Hampshire Holiday Inn confided that this month the staff renamed their hotel the Center of the Universe Hotel in honor of their media guests, who have "the biggest egos in the universe." The manager on duty (who estimated that his venue has made at least $1 million already this year from all of the media staying here) said, "I still haven't figured out why you are here. Why should a small all-white state like New Hampshire have so much influence?" He makes a good point. New Hampshire is 95 percent white (like Iowa, which is 93 percent white). A guest at the front desk defended his state, "You can't complain that New Hampshire is all white because you (the media) are all white, too."

Even though FEC records show that our presence is a boon to their states' economies, it is hard to find anyone who has anything nice to say about the reporters they have dealt with. They disdain the media because, as one cabbie put it, "They are big city slickers disrupting our small town." One of the bus drivers who was tired of cleaning up after the press corps complained, "You people are the trashiest. When I get home I have to deodorize my bus all night." The manager of catering services at our hotel said, "I think you are all just a bunch of pampered little brats."

When a bartender in the hotel bar griped about how busy the place was these days, a reporter told him he should be happy because we are bringing more money into their establishment. He complained, "You bring more money, but you also bring a lot more work" (implying that there were many things he would rather be doing than working). The bartender admitted that "journalists are great tippers, but the campaign staffers never tip."

A barfly (who has cable at home but came to watch the football game at the hotel bar because he "had to get away from the missus") complained about the clientele. "What I can't stand about reporters is . . . they have no interest in substance, all they talk about is 'who's on top today.' " Throughout the game, he cursed at the TV screen because every commercial was for a presidential candidate. He pointed to the screen and shouted, "You want to know why everyone in this town hates politics? The only thing I hate more than my wife and you reporters is these politicians on TV."

Everywhere you go you overhear people talking about the candidates. If you were sitting at the hotel bar last night, you would have overheard the makeup artist giving her opinions of the candidates she made up for the last debate: "Kerry has a lot of anger inside of him . . . Lieberman has the best personality." You know you are sitting next to a journalist when you hear things like, "Thank god I am not covering the Martha Stewart trial" and "I don't like this bar. I hope that I'm going to be rotated to Colorado for Kobe Bryant."

There was a guy standing outside a convention center who loves the political process so much that he traveled to Iowa and New Hampshire just to check it out. He told me that the one thing he has seen as a political tourist is how shallow the media are. "I have been a little too close to some of the press and, my god, it is as vacuous as Hollywood, it is just really, really bad. I wish we had a more respectful media. Most of these guys off camera, I wish everyone could see them."

If you ask me, the worst part about the primaries is not the people who are paid to be on camera, it is the people trying to get on TV, the screaming supporters, people who travel from all across the country to stand outside in below-zero weather waving signs and screaming for the candidate they love. One time a frustrated local who was sick of hearing the kids scream asked a group of Edwards supporters what in the hell they were doing. The head cheerleader told him, "We are doing visibility." (Visibility? You mean to tell me that there is actually a term for standing on the side of the road and shouting at cars that drive by?) The man asked, "Don't you have anything better to do?" She explained to him that she was a poli sci student getting immersed in the process. The man told her to "study it, don't be it." It is a good thing that he walked away before she led her crew in a dance-off with a rival campaign to see who had better dance moves for their campaign chants.

As the campaign buses crisscross each other on their way to the local high school gym or the VFW hall for yet another rally, the locals will be sitting home, watching their calendars, waiting for the day when we get lost so that they can have their town back. But even there they are not safe, for at any given moment, one of the candidates could show up with that swarm of locusts at their front door.

Hi, honey, I'm home.

Not Ready for Prime Time

Sandwich, New Hampshire
JANUARY 14, 2004

WES CLARK'S NEW YEAR'S RESOLUTION is that he is not going to settle for the number two job: "I'm not going to be Howard Dean's Dick Cheney." According to Clark, Dean offered him the job, but Clark shut him down. (Dean flatly denies having made this offer. One of these men is lying, but we don't know who.) But that is not the only sign of Clark's arrogance.

He says things like "If I'd been president, I would have had Osama bin Laden by this time." And he likes to spread rumors. Like when Donald Rumsfeld's "long, hard slog" Iraq memo came out, Clark said, "Rumsfeld had to leak his own memo." A reporter challenged him on how he knew Rumsfeld leaked the memo and he said, "Well, that's what the rumor is."

But wait, there's more. According to Clark, there are only two men left in this race. He declared, "What I think is you're seeing this emerge as a sort of two-person race in the Democratic Party, and that's what's really shaping up." Clark is not alone in this assessment. The Republican Party tracker, who shows up at all of the Clark events to videotape the opposition, agrees. He said that the only two candidates the GOP is tracking now are Dean and Clark (they stopped tracking Kerry after his campaign manager quit). And the anointed newsmen at *Newsweek* have already named Clark the "Un-Dean." (All of this is just further evidence that nobody in this business has a clue what they are talking about.)

Since we last saw Clark, he has fine-tuned his stump speech, he has an explanation for why he voted for Republicans, and he's got a pretty good Web site (which displays his motto, "You've Gotta Believe," which he stole from Dean!). Some nights he is on fire, like when one man told him, "You are the closest I'll get to God." Other nights he's a mere mortal who is nervous and out of rhythm like a fish out of water. He is book smart, but not K Street smart.

By now, the general has been through Campaigning 101 and has figured out that if you want to run for president, you have to talk about "family values" (which he now does early and often). And he is on a baby-kissing crusade. When a woman stood up with her baby in her arms at a pancake breakfast to ask a question, the general beat her to the punch. "Can I kiss that baby?" The protective mother asked, "Do you have a cold?"

Clark is selling himself as everything Howard Dean isn't: a religious southern general. After Dean confessed "I don't go to church," Clark added a minister to his stump speech: "Before I decided to run, I went to see my minister . . ." Clark's new closing line is "I want to put the joy back in America!" Joy back in America? When did we lose the joy? Clark is suggesting that Howard Dean has no joy to offer; he thinks that if he can corner the market on joy, voters will choose him over that angry Dean.

Clark has all the joy because he has all the patriotism, a word he used twenty-three times in one sermon (which is what we will call his speech because when he was speaking he got an "Amen" and an "All right," as if he were a preacher who came to save the Democrats).

So now that Wes Clark has his stump speech down, and there is no doubt about where he stood on the war (he's against it), it's time for the Q and A. Today he was asked, "How do you feel about sending George Bush to Mars?" and "Who will you pick to be your running mate?" On a day like this it is clear to see that as long as Clark is still introducing himself to voters, he is still immune from the attacks and criticisms that come with being a serious contender. While Wes Clark fielded mostly softball questions, Howard Dean was across town taking a beating.

One woman lectured Dean, "You're getting a tremendous amount of tutoring about foreign affairs, and frequently you've come up with a lot of misstatements to show your lack of knowledge." Dean defended himself, but she followed up with a question about Dean's sealed records as governor: "To me, there's something you want to hide."

Then a seventeen-year-old high school student challenged him on his opposition to the war, charging him with hypocrisy for originally supporting the president's intervention in Iraq.

As the front-runner, Dean is being critically challenged and held to a much higher standard than his competitors right now. Everyone in New Hampshire already knows who he is. The voters are just getting to know Wes Clark; they are still in the foreplay phase. Copies of his home movie *American Son,* brought to you by the producer of Clinton's propaganda film *The Man from Hope,* are now arriving in their homes (which includes a testimonial from Wes's only son about how great his dad is and one of Wes's childhood buddies: "Wes included me when all the other kids wouldn't"). Right now New Hampshirites just want to come and check him out. So they are packing the pews to hear him pontificate about patriotism.

Politics attracts freaks, but of all the candidates, Clark brings out all the weirdos with their conspiracy theories. After all, what do conspiracy theorists talk about? The military and the government; Wes Clark is now associated with both. One man who shows up at many Clark events demands answers about what Dr. Strangelove (Clark) did in Serbia. Another Clark stalker is convinced that the general comes from the "dark side" and wants to know what "America's military-industrial complex had to do with 9/11." While most campaigns just ignore the crazies who come around, you can just imagine how freaked out Clark's staff gets.

His flack factor is still high, but there was only one incident today. A Clark advance girl was fighting with the photographers, insisting that they stand where she told them to stand because "that is what Little Rock wants." One photographer reminded her that he is not working for Little Rock and he intended to stay standing where he was standing because it was public space and he did not want to ruin his camera by standing out in the rain (where Little Rock wanted him to stand).

Clark still relies entirely on the counsel of his campaign staff, which is why Joe Trippi calls Wes Clark the *Weekend at Bernie's* candidate (based on the movie in which Bernie dies but they keep carrying him around because they need him as a prop).

A media studies class would have a field day watching Wes Clark with his press corps. Traveling inside Clark's cocoon, I experienced the strangest case of déjà vu. It seemed like every move the general made was mimicking W. in 2000. He popped caramel corn into his mouth, W. style, while standing in the aisle of the airplane, acted goofy and chatted with his embeds about what his favorite foods are, and flirted with his press corps à la George Bush. Being there, I feel like I was stuck on the George Bush 2000 reality TV show. When asked, "Are you living *The Truman Show?*" Clark said he did not mind having the cameras in his face all of the time. "Who wouldn't want three pretty young women following them?" referring to the three network producers assigned to cover him (whom he has asked for hugs, taken out to dinner at Chili's, offered sips of his milkshake and handwritten letters about how much fun he is having in New Hampshire). And what did he do with his press corps of three pretty young women? He took them shopping, of course, at the L.L. Bean factory store, where they waited outside of his dressing room to see him model his new sweater.

There have been a few times on the Clark campaign when the whole thing felt like a media creation; the storyline of Clark surging seemed contrived by the news media to play up the horse race. Like the event that was open to the public at the Manchester Public Library, for which only two real voters showed up. They said they heard about the event on the radio and they wanted to meet Clark, but when they arrived they realized that this event was for media only. They apologized for crashing a press conference and got up to leave. A librarian assured them that this event was for the public, so they ended up staying.

The same thing happened the day before. There was a rally at the airport and although it was advertised, only media showed up. A campaign staffer explained that no one came because it was 14 degrees below zero. Still, this was the first time I got an answer to the question. What happens if you have a campaign event and no one shows up? There are always enough media to fill the room.

Just like George Bush four years ago, Clark's idea of delivering a major policy address means reading a piece of paper. (It's hard to believe that this man wants to be the leader of the free world and he has never used a teleprompter before!) If you watch Clark campaign you can tell that he doesn't know how this whole presidential election game is played. To win this sport, two important skills that you need (which Clark seems to be lacking) are being able to project from the stage and managing to defuse reporters. The general is used to giving orders, not taking them from voters and groveling to reporters.

The one area in which Clark has shown his prowess is fund-raising. He has raised a phenomenal amount of money quickly, but he picked all the low-hanging fruit. His two biggest supporters are Madonna, "I am endorsing Clark not just as a celebrity but as a mother," and Michael Moore, "I would like to see the general debate the deserter" (while this may be true, this comment is not politically correct for a presidential campaign and makes Clark an easy target). Interesting side note about the Michael Moore endorsement: When planning the event, Moore's people asked the Clark campaign how big the venue was. Afraid the place would be too small, Moore's staff instructed the Clark campaign to get a bigger facility because "Michael gets five thousand to ten thousand people every time he speaks." News reports estimated that one thousand people showed up.

In the next few weeks, people will decide if they are going to stick with Dean, who has already made many mistakes but has been thoroughly tested, or if they will go looking for someone else. Clark is waiting in the wings for people to lose faith in the front-runner so that he can rise to the occasion. There is only one problem with the general's logic: If electability is the issue, why on earth would voters choose another Washington outsider with no national experience who has not been in this war long enough to be subjected to the harsh artillery of a presidential primary and isn't ready for prime time?

Handling Howard

Battle Creek, Iowa
JANUARY 16, 2004

HOWARD CAN'T BE HANDLED. Every time his staff tell him to use "maximum self-discipline," he completely ignores them. Coming to terms with the fact that he is totally unmanageable, the staff have given up. Their motto is "Let Howard be Howard," but that is a coping mechanism, not an intentional campaign strategy. Someone ought to do something before this guy self-destructs.

"Why can't Howard keep his mouth shut?" a flustered flack flaps. "I wish he would just shut his quote hole." Dean is so off message that he even makes news in interviews with local papers. No one ever makes news when they are talking to the locals because the locals usually ask softball questions, like "Why is [insert town name here] important to you?" or "Are you going to win [whichever state you are in]?" or "Senator Edwards, is America ready for another good-looking senator to be president?"

This is why, in 2000, Bush denied the networks interviews but would talk to any and all the affiliates. My favorite local reporter was a blonde-haired blue-eyed Barbie who launched into her interview with a ferocity that would break Edward R. Murrow's heart: "Are you happy to be here?" And then followed up with "Will you do a plug for my show?" She instructed him to say something to the effect of "This is George Bush and you are watching Action News with Valerie." Then she asked for his autograph and posed for a photo, squealing, "My parents are going to be so stoked that I got to meet the governor of Texas." At the end of the "interview" Bush put his hand on her back and said, "Good job." Good job? She got five minutes alone with the future leader of the free world and the only question she asked was "Are you happy to be here?" I couldn't help wondering whose job Valerie was doing well, hers or his?

The former governor of Vermont would never put up with that kind of horseplay. He is not here to make friends with the local yokels. So they are forced to ask him real questions and he is happy to share his views on a range of topics that his handlers don't want him to talk about. The boys on the bus say Dean's lack of discipline reveals that he is not acting professional or presidential.

The bigger problem seems to be that in the sound bite society that we are living in, Howard Dean is speaking in paragraphs and many of the things he says are taken out of context. For example, there is a line in his stump speech that has gotten standing ovations from many crowds of party activists. He says, "I'm going to go down south, and I'm going to say to white folks who have been voting Republican, 'All right, the Confederate flag may be an issue for you, but what about your children's health care? There are sixty thousand kids in South Carolina that don't have health insurance—and most of them are white. If you keep voting for the Republicans, they're never going to get health insurance for your kids, they're never going to help your schools, you're never going to get a better job, you're never going to get a raise. Come back to the Democratic Party—the party of Franklin Roosevelt where everybody was included. There's no reason why white guys who have a Confederate flag in the back of their pickup truck shouldn't be walking side-by-side with blacks, because they don't have health insurance, either.' "

Dean is simply saying that the Democratic Party has to convince poor southern whites that the Republican Party does not represent them. Why shouldn't he be able to say this? It is true. Dean has said this many times, but the press never reported it.

The "Confederate flag controversy" did not become a story until the shorthand version of Dean's statement was printed in the *Des Moines Register.* Dean said, "I still want to be the candidate for guys with Confederate flags in their pickup trucks." John Edwards and Al Sharpton jumped all over Dean, calling him an elitist and a racist. Now we've got a fight: That's front-page news! The *New York Times* explained, "Dr. Dean stepped headlong into a reality of presidential politics: It is not about what you say but when you say it. Context is everything, particularly when eight rivals are trying to do you in."

As all the candidates take potshots at the front-runner, the only stories you will read in the paper now are about their catfights because the press get paid to report the naughty, not the nice. No one wants to read something nice; naughty is what sells papers. Think about it, when was the last time that you read something nice in the newspaper? A bad news day for the candidate is good for his press corps. Newsmen pray for a storm so that everyone will tune in to hear about it!

All the relentless scrutiny has made the Dean campaign believe that the press is lobotomizing Dean. The reporters' response is, "Don't blame the messenger." You can blame Dick Gephardt or John Kerry for keeping the attacks coming; it is not the reporters' fault, they are simply asking for a response. It is their job to ask the questions. And besides, Dean would be complaining if he didn't get a chance to respond to the attacks.

Every day now Howard Dean is getting the crap beaten out of him. Until now he dissed his fellow Democrats with impunity; their counterattacks never stuck to him (earning him the nickname Teflon Dean). But it appears that all the fighting is bruising him. He tried to cry foul, urging the DNC chair to "make them stop." (If he thinks this is bad, he has no idea what Karl Rove has waiting for the nominee.)

Dean likes to criticize "Washington politicians" and the "Washington-politics-as-usual club," but he doesn't like it when they gang up on him to fight back. If you throw a punch, you have to expect an even harder punch in return. Dean aired an ad in Iowa with a photo of Gephardt in the Rose Garden with Bush; the announcer said, "Dick Gephardt agrees to coauthor the Iraq resolution, giving George Bush the authority to go to war." And then mysteriously a new ad appeared featuring Osama bin Laden on the cover of *Time* magazine with a deep apocalyptic voice declaring, "It's time for Democrats to start thinking about Dean's inexperience." The words "Dangerous World," "Destroy Us," "Dangers Ahead," and "No Experience" flash on the screen. The voice continues, "Americans want a president who can face the dangers ahead, but Howard Dean has no military or foreign policy experience and Howard Dean just cannot compete with George Bush on foreign policy. It's time for Democrats to think about that—and think about it now."

Where did this come from? A 527 (named for the Internal Revenue Service code that allows a tax-exempt group to organize and raise money for political activities) called Americans for Jobs, Health Care and Progressive Values, which sounds like one of those crazy right-wing organizations, but their spokesman is Kerry's former spokesman and their executive director is a former fund-raiser for Gephardt.

The Dean movement is officially at war against the Stop Dean movement. Everywhere John Kerry goes there is a group of loud, young, screaming Deansters nipping at his heels. They show up with Dean signs and shout their cheers just to mess with the senator's head. This is their revenge. They are angry about what they call the "conspiracy to stop Dean." They are convinced that every time Dean makes a mistake, Kerry and Gephardt practice the dark art of calling in a hit (they call their friends in Congress and ask them to speak out against Dean). Of course, they're right.

Everyone knows that the Gephardt campaign and the Kerry campaign are in cahoots; surely they are sharing information that will hurt Dean. As Trippi complained, "They have a mutual interest right now in trying to tear us down." Of course they do! They want to win. This is presidential politics. No one said that it was going to be fair. What made you think these guys were going to play nice?

Since Dean has made his name by attacking Washington, he doesn't have many friends on Capitol Hill to call; he has few congressmen in his Rolodex who will rush to his defense. Making all of his true believers believe that all of Washington, D.C., is against him only helps raise funds for the movement. Joe Trippi writes letters to Dean supporters that say things like "They'll do anything to stop you!" and "You have heard about the efforts to stop Dean. But they're not trying to stop

Howard Dean—they're trying to stop you" and "Our opponents will do whatever it takes to stop us." By using the us-versus-them propaganda, Trippi encourages people to send in money now, not for Dean, but for their own good.

But no matter how much money they raise, they cannot find a way to make Dean stop giving his opponents more ammunition. After Saddam Hussein was captured, Dean came out and said that we aren't any safer now that Saddam was captured. Yes, it was impolitic, but if you think about it, how are we any safer? What Dean said is true, but people don't want to know the truth. If they did, they would watch shows like *Nightline* (which is about to be canceled because, as one Disney executive said, "People don't want to go to bed mad or sad"). Americans want to feel good about their president and their country, and the more Dean tells people that their government is lying to them, the less they are going to want to hear.

John Edwards Is Hottt! *But Boring*

West Ossipee, New Hampshire
JANUARY 16, 2004

JOHN EDWARDS DOESN'T FLIP the pancakes. He doesn't ride a Harley or play ice hockey either; you will not see him performing any of those cute little tricks for the cameras. The only thing John Edwards wants you to know about John Edwards is that he is "the son of a millworker" who believes "there are Two Americas."

This son of a millworker goes from town to town preaching about the Two Americas (one for the rich and one for the poor) with the discipline of a religious disciple spreading the word of salvation. As the political currents change, John Edwards is unflappable; he is consistent and on message, never deviating from his script. All of the candidates have their stump speeches, but they mix it up now and then. Not John Edwards. He delivers his lines on cue without interruption. Using the stage like a courtroom, the former trial lawyer has every move and hand gesture perfected as he paces back and forth, whipping the crowd into a frenzy.

This is the dream of every campaign adviser, and the nightmare of every working journalist. "We are in the news business, there is none of that here. Everything John Edwards said today is already in my notebook from yesterday," a disgruntled member of his press corps complained. "Why see it again? It's in the can. I can go home and put it on a loop and replay the same tape over and over again to simulate being here. All he will say this week is what he said last week." By now, I am guesstimating that I have heard the term "Two Americas" at least two thousand times. I got it. Edwards is so on message that there is nothing interesting about his campaign.

One of the old-school scribblers concluded, "I have never known anyone as strict on the message as he is. I have developed this amazing ability to write so much about so little." Another reporter covering the Edwards campaign philosophized, "This is the existential campaign, it's like *Waiting for Godot.* We are waiting for a story, knowing there will be none."

Though it is common for the print people to get shut out, campaigns usually grant photographers backstage access so that they can put out flattering images of their faux-private moments. Not here. The shooters complain that there is "nothing to shoot" but the same thing they shot yesterday and the day before that. "We have to educate them about our needs," a magazine photographer complained. "We need pictures and there aren't any here." He said that the one time he was granted permission to snap some shots in the front cabin of the plane, the senator "did not act natural, he was just waiting for us to go away." The last time John Kerry posed in the exact same setup, he pretended to read the paper and then spontaneously looked out the window.

Whenever I am backstage with another candidate and Senator Edwards sees us, he says something like, "What are you doing here?" As if he does not approve of or understand why people with cameras are allowed anywhere other than in the roped-off press section. Perhaps he is afraid that I will overhear something, like the time another candidate asked him for his position on an issue and he replied, "I'll have to do a focus group on that."

On the Bush campaign we always used to joke that we could train monkeys to do our jobs. I am confident that I could get a monkey to cover the John Edwards campaign without missing a beat. When comparing the candidates with some of my former colleagues over cocktails, I came to the conclusion that of all the candidates, John Edwards is the toughest nut to crack. To which someone suggested, "Maybe that's because there is nothing inside."

Despite the message management, when you talk to people at an Edwards rally the one thing they all say about him is "John Edwards is *hottt!*" At least that is what one young man's sign said at a rally. Turns out that he did not actually make the sign, his Republican girlfriend did; they have "a couple's crush on John." (The campaign would not allow the Edwards is *hottt!* sign on stage because this was "not the image they want of the candidate.")

"John Edwards is Brad Pitt with a poli sci degree," one college coed observed. There is never any shortage of ladies who cut class to come out and see him. "He's so boyish," an admiring female whispered to her girlfriend. "I'm from the South and that's how we like our men, *hot.*" At a union convention a woman concluded, "If it were on looks alone," she would choose Edwards. "He's like cream cheese, smooth on the eyes." At one event, a mom actually abandoned her kid, hiding him in his stroller behind the press riser so that she could go get a closer look at the young senator.

There are two kinds of John Edwards lovers: the stale old grandmas who say they like Edwards because "he reminds me of JFK," and the college-age girls who like him because "he's like a young JFK" (repeating something they must have heard somewhere). Despite what all these women see in him, I just don't get it. But maybe there's nothing to get.

The day I decided to stop covering John Edwards was the day I followed him going door-to-door in Nashua, New Hampshire, to invite people to come hear him speak at the Nashua City Hall (where John F. Kennedy launched his campaign in 1960). The baby-faced Breck boy pulled up in an SUV, climbed out in his duck boots, and marched down the block with all the camera crews in tow. He rang the first doorbell, stood there long enough for the cameras to get the shot, then marched on to house number two, where the whole family was ready and waiting in their doorway. He went through the motions and then moved on. After he finished up at house number three, he climbed into his SUV and drove off. That's it? You call that working for a living?

Immediately after Edwards walked away from each door, I rang the bell of the house he had just visited. While he was still within earshot, the first guy said he was for Joe Lieberman, the second was a Republican household, and the third did not plan to vote. Of course, his staffers advanced the trip and had preselected the three houses for the senator to visit (to make sure that the people were not caught off-guard or seen opening the door in their pajamas). So if these were not real undecided voters, what was the point of this whole exercise? Was it only for the news crews? John Edwards doesn't do things just for the cameras! Maybe someone told him he had to. After all, that's what all the other candidates do. But at least the others stand there long enough to make us believe that they are enjoying this whole dog-and-pony show.

Down at the Nashua City Hall about a hundred people (many press, a lot of staff or volunteers, and some real supporters) huddled in the rain waiting for Senator Edwards. When he arrived a half-hour late, he stood across from the bronze bust of John Kennedy and talked about the Two Americas, but this time he added JFK into his usual political slogans. "John Kennedy understood cynics didn't build America, optimists built America. It is time for you and me to inspire America again, and lift this country again. Isn't it time for the people of the United States to have a president who believes in them?"

After the speech, a local who saw John Kennedy here over forty years ago said of Edwards, "He arouses nothing in me. I don't love him, I don't hate him. I have no opinion whatsoever. At least Dean makes me angry. To get my vote, you have to make me feel something."

Where is Lloyd Bentsen when you need him? Sorry, John Edwards, but you are no Jack Kennedy. (And by the way, America will never elect a president who doesn't flip flapjacks.)

Gephardtpalooza

Burlington, Iowa
JANUARY 17, 2004

IN THE FINAL PUSH to draw attention to his campaign, Dick Gephardt is busting out with Gephardtpalooza. Named after the rock-and-roll jam festival, this traveling road show will be bringing congressmen on the road to sing the praises of Dick Gephardt. But behind the music, things are not looking good for this guy. At the rallies, they have started playing Bon Jovi's "Living on a Prayer." And on the charter, the flight attendant has started serving us our meals before they serve Dick. Can't this man get any respect?

Even though Gephardt and Dean are tied in the polls and battling it out for first place in Iowa, Dean is getting 1,000 percent more coverage daily than Gephardt. Obviously, the editors who sit at their desks inside the Beltway or in Midtown are not interested in the Dick Gephardt story because it has no hoopla. He will never say anything shocking or irreverent. In other words, he is not going to sell newspapers. He will talk about trade policy and health care for every American. Who wants to read about that?

The most commonly heard expression on all the other press buses is

"Dick Gephardt is yesterday's news." Says who? Says all those Washington political reporters who have had to cover Dick Gephardt at some point in the past twenty years. Where are they all now? They are hot on the trail of that vociferous Dean.

Looking around the Gephardt charter at the seven journalists covering Dick in the days leading up to the caucus, it strikes me that the media have already determined that he will not make it to the next round. Where is *Newsweek*? *Time*? The Associated Press? Reuters? CNN? The *Washington Post*? They are all on the Howard Dean bus tour. Dean is the shoot-from-the-hip renegade; the reporters love that stuff! And he has Martin Sheen, Rob Reiner, Al Gore! All Dick's got is '80s crooner Michael Bolton (who will be singing for him at the UAW Hall in Burlington, Iowa). Now that's rock and roll!

There is a fundamental unfairness in the way the media cover the candidates. Why should one candidate have so many in his press corps while others have so few? How do the editors decide who to cover and who to ignore? Those decisions promote certain candidates over others. It is no secret who the media have preselected as fittest to survive to the next round. But there is no reason why Dick Gephardt should not get coverage, at least until the voters have their say.

Why aren't more reporters fighting to join Gephardtpalooza? Probably because there are only two kinds of Gephardt events: Either he is in an overlit machinist hall with big fat macho Teamsters wearing bomber jackets chanting their union cheers, or he is in a room full of people who want to tell him about the day they met Harry Truman. These folks are either knitting, fussing with their dentures, or breathing from an oxygen tank (yes, I saw all three at one event). After delivering his speech, Gephardt stands in the doorway like a greeter at Wal-Mart and asks each person to come out and caucus for him.

Unaware of the huge crowds and excitement on the other campaigns, those working for Dick Gephardt do not seem to realize that this campaign is heading for a train wreck. Based on the small size of his crowds, the one recurring question that the reporters ask is: "Will Gephardt get blindsided in Iowa?" That prompts his campaign spokesman to dismiss the talk about crowds: "Size does not matter," not just because crowd size is like penis size (all campaigns exaggerate), but because they only need to pick up a handful of new voters in these small little pockets of Iowa for Dick to win. When I shared that possibility with a pack of blue-collar Iowans drinking Pabst Blue Ribbon in the bar at the VFW Hall in Ottumwa, one lady dismissed my theory. "You're thirty-three years old and you don't have a husband. You're here in Ottumwa, Iowa, on a Saturday night. What do you know?"

Of all the campaign caravans parading around those ninety-nine counties, Dick Gephardt's has the nicest vibe. His small circle of staff is easy to work with and they never bark out orders or give any attitude. The journalists are some of the sharpest people I've met on the trail. They respect their candidate and are not cynical about or suspicious of him (as many press corps seem to be of their candidates). Of course, they have healthy skepticism about his prospects, but they challenge him on the prowess of his organization instead of insulting him for not being a sexier candidate.

In the small but serious platoon of journalists who are assigned to cover Gephardt, they try to make sense of the limited coverage their candidate is getting. As the *LA Times* reporter put it, "This should be Dick Gephardt's moment. The issue in this election is security—national security, job security, social security. When you are looking for security you should pick someone with experience. Dick at least deserves to be heard on a national stage."

Just like the tree falling in the woods, if there is not a busload of press there to talk about it on the talk shows, who cares that it fell at all? And so the fall of Dick Gephardt will be nothing more than a sideshow to the big noisy election madness on the main stage.

Everyone Says Kerry Is Surging

Oskaloosa, Iowa
JANUARY 17, 2004

SITTING AT THE BAR at the 801 Steakhouse in Des Moines with some campaign reporters and a couple of bottles of wine, we played a game: What is the one story you wrote that you did not believe but you had to write because your editor told you to? The group agreed that was an easy one; it was "Kerry is surging."

Ever since the *Wall Street Journal* printed a story calling Kerry "the Comeback Kid," every paper in America has copied it just in case (to cover their ass). As a result, people are now giving John Kerry a second look. And they seem to like what they are seeing. Things have been running a lot better ever since Kerry hired Ted Kennedy's gang to run his operation.

Ironically, at the very time the reporters were writing Kerry off, he was in the process of turning it all around. He gave up on New Hampshire entirely and put all of his chips on Iowa. He shipped 120 paid staffers out to the state and he climbed aboard the Real Deal Express and rode around the Hawkeye State. This is Kerry Incorporated, a slick, professional operation. It's nothing like Gephardt's mom-and-pop campaign.

Along the way, friends have popped in for cameos. Ted Kennedy stood by JFK's side, in a passing-of-the-torch-style series of campaign stops. Seventies folk hero Peter Yarrow, from Peter, Paul and Mary, rode along and sang an antiwar anthem he wrote in honor of Kerry (who voted for the war). Max Cleland, the former senator who lost three of his limbs in Vietnam, came out and campaigned for Kerry. The locals seemed to love him even though some had no idea who he was—one man said "the highlight of the night was meeting Larry Flynt."

But the celebrities are not the ones who resuscitated Senator Kerry.

If there is one man who deserves the credit for saving Kerry's campaign, it's Jim Rassman, the Republican whose life John Kerry saved thirty-five years ago in Vietnam who came to Iowa for a surprise reunion to let the world know that he will switch his registration to vote for John Kerry for president because "John Kerry served his country with distinction."

In the past week, John Kerry has been letting us see him sweat. It is not uncommon for him to be the last man left standing, shaking hands in the room. He is not taking anyone for granted; he is showing the kind of patience that it takes to earn one caucus-goer's vote at a time.

As Kerry's crowds begin to grow and he rises in the polls, I can't help but wonder: Is the whole "John Kerry is surging" story line a myth created by news editors to add some drama into this otherwise dull race (readers love survivors)? Do the polls mirror reality, or are those being polled just responding to what they read in the paper? What came first, the good press or the good poll numbers? And does John Kerry really care? After all, he can beat the polls, but he can't win without good press.

The Deanies Versus the New York Times

New York City
JANUARY 18, 2004

EVERY MAJOR MEDIA OUTLET has given Howard Dean so much attention that it makes me wonder: Is every editor in America drinking and peeing Dean's Kool-Aid?

As all the candidates complain that they are not getting enough media coverage because the Dean media phenomenon is sucking up all of the oxygen, Dean supporters have declared war against the *New York Times* because they are not satisfied with the coverage their man is getting.

Dean loyalists have started a campaign against the reporters whose stories they do not approve of. They have been inundating the *Times* editors' inboxes with complaints. One fellow even started his own blog, Wilgoren Watch, "dedicated to deconstructing the *New York Times* coverage of Howard Dean's campaign for the White House." Another blogger accuses the *Times* reporter of "smearing the candidate" to the point that "this reporter has engaged in the moral equivalent of a terrorist attack."

Amid threats from Deanies canceling their subscriptions to the paper because of what one former reader called an "effort to topple Howard Dean," *New York Times* public editor Daniel Okrent took it upon himself to reread all of the *Times*' Democratic campaign coverage in the past seven weeks to examine any gross violations of the rules of good journalism. He said that he did not find "enough that could signify a pattern of behavior or betray a partisan agenda . . . the tilt they identify is invariably a part of the story under examination. An article detailing what Dean's opponents perceive to be his weaknesses is legitimate news. All the 'on the one hands' and 'on the other hands' you could stuff into such a piece wouldn't dissipate the negative aura it necessarily emits. Individual articles may be rough on the candidate, but individual articles do not constitute coverage. What the paper does over time, through the long slog of a campaign, is what matters."

Okrent offers this suggestion to bitter readers: "Think of a politician you dislike—maybe one of the Democrats Dean is battling—and substitute his name for Dean's in any piece about your man. If it still sounds unfair, there's the possibility it is. But without passing such a test, you're left not with 'an insult to our democracy,' as one of my correspondents calls the paper's campaign coverage, but with journalism."

He also points out that in his research, "The *Times* published 59 major stories or editorials about Dean. Wesley Clark has been up for view 30 times. No other candidate has enjoyed (or suffered) more than

20 appearances in the paper. Carol Moseley Braun got only three shots—and two of those were about her decision to leave the race."

Dean has not taken a public position on the fairness of his own coverage. He denies that he reads his own press clips (even though his aides provide commentary to the reporters on what the candidate thought about what they wrote). From what his staffers tell us, it is clear that Howard Dean shares his supporters' disdain for the media. And most of the reporters would agree with what the *New York Times* reporter told a Deanie who confronted her and told her to "report reality"; she said, "I do report reality, just not the reality in your head."

Most reporters resent the fact that readers have the right to interfere with their work because there are a lot of crackpots out there and the ones who have the time to write usually have a host of issues (and are never going to be satisfied). Reporters feel that they should not have to deal with every person out there with a laptop and a sense of entitlement that their opinion belongs in print.

Giving everyone a microphone isn't always a good thing. The *New Republic*, dubbed the *New Republican* after they endorsed Joe Lieberman, have their own anti-Dean blog. And the *Washington Post* has written so many editorials ranting against Dean that if all you read is the *Post's* editorial page, you would think that Howard Dean is Public Enemy Number One.

No matter what any other media outlets say, the only one that matters is the *New York Times* because they are the leader of the pack; every major media outlet follows their lead. On every presidential campaign, the *Times* always has way too much power: It is the paper all the big media honchos read, so what they write influences what everyone else does. Some of the candidates seem to have a strange obsession with what the *Times* writes. One day, in front of all the other reporters, Senator Kerry complimented the *Times* reporter four times on a story he had written. The reporters on all the campaigns complain that the *Times* reporters monopolize the candidates' time and influence their moods, setting the tone for the day. It is not uncommon for the *Times* reporter to have an interpretation that no one else had, but that everyone was forced to follow.

In 2000, the *New York Times* reporter who covered Bush talked about his struggle with his role in the whole process. "Who am I to have any sort of influence on who the next president of the United States might be? I do try to be fair and I hope that because I ask the question 'Who am I to have any influence on this progress?' it keeps me humble enough to make sure that whatever smidgen of influence I have isn't exerted in a petty or malicious or uneven way. But that said, one of the problems with covering an election is reporters are individuals with individual voices, individual perspectives. And when you have different reporters covering different candidates, it is hard for there to be any assurance that the person covering each of the candidates will do it in a similar enough way so there isn't in the end some imbalance. That is a real challenge for the editors. The pace of this is so furious that there is a danger that things don't come out quite even because the different pieces of the puzzles are in different hands."

In an effort to force the reporters to be more vigilant, the bloggers have started the Adopt-a-Journalist program, through which anyone with a computer can volunteer to monitor and deconstruct any working journalist.

As one disgruntled blogger wrote:

We must do it every day, for every story, by every reporter, in any medium and hold them accountable on a daily if not hourly basis for the contradictions, hypocrisies and sins of omission and commission which our deconstruction efforts reveal.

Just as fish are not aware of water, reporters such as this one are probably not aware of the "water" of their environment as participants in a socially and culturally elitist capitalist institution—The watchdog that once spoke truth to power became the lapdog and now is the attack dog for power. The news media has shifted from afflicting the comfortable and comforting the afflicted to the opposite: comforting the comfortable and afflicting the afflicted. The corporate/capitalist news media are hired hands—agents—of the powerful and agents of the institutions of wealth, power and social regression. The news media have become little more than scoops, scribblers, propagandists, press agents, hacks, liars and misleaders for raw capital, power and Dark Age mentality against Truth, Justice and the American Way.

This election cycle is the first time that no act of journalism will go undeconstructed and no journalist will go unpunished. It is good to see that the Internet is not just for porn anymore, and I salute all those little guys with enough time on their hands to take on the media dinosaurs from the comfort of their couches. But it is scary to think about what will happen when the online lynch mob, with its electronic nooses, starts calling for all the journalists' heads, and none of the media moguls have the balls to stand up to them.

The voice of the people is a good thing until only the squeakiest wheels get the grease, when only the loudest voices start getting the same kind of power that they seek to destroy. With every small victory that the bloggers have (like forcing the *New York Times* to review their journalism), any anonymous drive-by blogger is being given the same, if not more, power than those with credentials to get into the front door of the *New York Times*. Let's hope the revenge of the nerds doesn't go too far.

Besides, the individual boys and girls on the bus are only a small piece of the puzzle. Their power is limited; they cannot make or break a candidate. Everything that a writer or producer does in the field gets sent back to the home office, and that is where it gets edited. The editors who actually edit the stories decide what makes it into the paper and control which candidates merit coverage. These are the people with all of the control. Who will monitor them?

This whole movement to patrol journalists may actually just be hurting the readers. It is clear that all of this new pressure is making the reporters so self-conscious that it is merely forcing them to water down their stories and limit the amount of information they actually share with their audience. One *Times* reporter explained, "Working under pressure in fear of offending anyone and obsessed with fairness, the more inclined I am to play it safe, which means excluding all the interesting stuff. I have to water everything down because I don't want my boss to get any bad letters."

Dean Versus the Media

Des Moines, Iowa
JANUARY 19, 2004

"THE MORE YOU HANDLE US, the worse it is for you. We are getting pissed off," a disgruntled journalist tried to explain to the Dean staffer who announced that yet another event on the People Powered Howard Bus Tour was "pool only."

Everyone covering the Dean campaign knows all too well what the word "pool" means. A pool is when they allow only a small pool of re-porters and all of the photographers into an event (who are supposed to share what they get with all the other news organizations). At the White House, everything is pooled. But this is the primaries, and journalists have a hard time being told what they can and can't do this early on. Campaigns are not really entitled to control the media like this until they win a primary or two. The whole pool situation on the Dean bus tour is out of control.

The campaign had three busloads of media caravaning around the state, and even though the news organizations paid good money to fol-low the candidate, the journalists are not allowed to get off the bus. So they have buses full of working journalists held hostage. Every so often you can hear one of them calling the home office to complain, "What am I doing here? Everything is pool."

At the next stop on this thirteen-hour trip, the bus arrived at the Dairy Queen and reporters were told, "Only the photographers are get-ting off." The bus erupted. "This campaign is all about the stills [as in still photographers]!" Eventually the reporters revolted and crammed into the Dairy Queen with Dean. After all, it is public space. A fight broke out between a photographer and a reporter. One called the other "a jerk" and he replied, "Do you want to step outside?" The two took their shoving match to the parking lot.

Dean Versus the Media ~ 127

You never want to keep a bus full of reporters on deadline waiting because all they are going to do is write about it. This is how the *Des Moines Register* reported the whole episode:

> Hours later when told that yet another campaign stop would be open to only a handful of reporters Australian journalist Olivia Rousset spoke up. "So there's nothing left for us to do today?" "Sleep," a staff answered. It was only 3 P.M.—still eight hours to go.
>
> "The way I understand this," a national reporter quipped, "the latest development in the campaign that will decide the fate of the free world is that the governor will stop somewhere in the middle of Iowa, buy ice cream and distribute it?"

"Wasn't this campaign supposed to be about power?" someone else asked. "No," Rousset said. "This campaign is about ice cream."

There are a few basic rules in message management. Here is one: Australian television should *never* be complaining in the newspaper about your campaign. But this is what the campaign gets for hosting everyone from Japanese television to a French Internet magazine.

Disgruntled American reporters were not pleased with the campaign for allowing the foreign press to come along. "It's megalomania. The world does not need to get to know Howard Dean right now," the bureau chief of a leading American magazine complained. Dean's press staff in Iowa obviously have no idea what they are doing; they defended their decision to let everyone on board by calling it "being inclusive." But they never should have agreed to take German TV along; the small precincts of Iowa are not big enough for this many journalists.

There are more media here than Bush ever had in 2000. With little historical perspective, it is hard to know for a fact, but I am guessing that there has never been this much interest in a presidential primary in the history of presidential politics. Or maybe there are just more media organizations than ever. And they all have needs that are not being met. The wheels are coming off the bus.

Howard Dean, the antimedia candidate who became a media darling, is being punished for not playing by the media's rules of providing access. Clearly not comprehending the needs of his press corps, Dean has wondered aloud, "Why do they need to be coddled?"

What Howard Dean does not seem to grasp is the symbiotic relationship between press and politicians. Every candidate has to find his own way to feed the ravenous media monster. The reporters have to write stories and the candidate has to get his message out. How they use each other is the sacred dance that has been danced since the dawn of the first news day.

In the beginning, the unknown governor needed the media to get his name out there. He gave them access and they wrote the stories that he wanted written. They put him on the cover of their magazines and helped Dean become a household name. Now that he is on top, he doesn't want to have anything to do with these people. He thinks he doesn't need them anymore. He is dead wrong. Someone should have warned him that if you cross them, they will turn on you. And they can't lose because they own the ink.

The last thing you want is for your press corps to hate you (see Al Gore in 2000). If George W. Bush taught us anything in the last election, it is that if you make nice with your press corps, they will be sedated into submission. The minute you started asking questions that W. didn't like, he would put you in your place by threatening to cut off your access.

Dean advisers tried this old Karl Rove measure of threatening to kick a network producer off the campaign plane if the network reported a story that the campaign did not approve of. The story ran without any

Soprano-style retaliation, but the incident highlighted that the media's honeymoon with Howard is over.

Sitting in the back of the bus with the Dean staffer who now only half-jokes that his job is to "try to get the press not to be evil" because "you are bad for democracy" and "a force against progress," we reminisced about the good old days back when Dean was a hot new hit. Now his routine is getting old. The Deanie blames the media for turning the world against his candidate. "That is how the media works— what goes up must come down." There may be some truth to that, but Dean has to share the blame.

His deep-down disdain for the media comes out in odd moments. He has been caught on tape reprimanding a camera crew and pushing microphones and tape recorders out of his face. Once he was talking to an old man about veterans' issues and he pushed a tape recorder out of the way, saying, "This is a private conversation." There is no such thing as a private conversation at a public event when you are running for president.

On January 9, the *New York Times* published a story entitled "Tide of Second Thoughts Rises among Democrats" with quotes from locals saying, "Dean has turned a lot of people off by acting cocky" and "He was too good to be true." In the copycat culture of the media, all the reporters wrote their own version of the same story. By January 14, when CBS News ran a story called "Buyer's Remorse," suggesting that people may want to trade Dean in for a new nominee, it was clear that Dean needed some backup.

This was just around the time the first wave of the Perfect Storm hit. That is what Joe Trippi was calling the 3,500 volunteers (the zealots from the blog) who descended on Iowa from all across the world, "some from as far away as Tokyo, Japan," to go door-to-door, like Jehovah's Witnesses for Howard Dean. (I never did understand that whole Perfect Storm concept. Didn't they all drown in that movie?) Trippi declared that their motto was "Fear the orange hats" and it definitely worked. Locals were afraid, very afraid.

All of a sudden, everywhere you looked there were Dean Storm Troopers wearing fluorescent orange hats, driving cars with out-of-town license plates, and you could overhear people saying things like "That is so going on the blog." They were sent door-to-door (covering 200,000 doors and making over 50,000 phone calls) to talk to people about why they love Howard Dean. Apparently they did more harm than good.

One waitress in Des Moines asked, "Have you noticed that there are a lot more gays in town?" A cab driver said, "I drove around a group who called themselves the 'Dumb Floridians Headed North for Dean' and they were dumb, young, and annoying." An old lady reminisced, "In the good old days, campaigns sent experienced people who were well-versed on the issues, this time all these kids showed up wanting to chat."

But what about all those letters they wrote at the meet-ups? When I went to some homes of the people who were sent letters from Dean meet-ups in New York City, few seemed to have read or been moved by what they got in the mail. The man who answered the door at a house that was sent a letter by the Hudson River lover said, "Listen lady, I can't tell you about every piece of junk mail I've gotten in the past year." At a farmhouse, I asked a young farmer about the letter addressed to him from New York City, and he said, "Yeah, I read it, but why do you think I would listen to anyone living in Freak Nation?"

As we head into the caucus, it appears that Howard Dean is going to have a much worse night than he ever expected. Is it because Iowans are turned off by the Deaniacs, or is it because of all of the bad press? This morning, the whole Dean-versus-the-media struggle came to a boiling point when Dean tried to stop by a Martin Luther King Jr. event with his entire press corps in tow. What was intended to be a solemn ceremony turned into a media mob scene when the all-white media descended upon the all-black audience and stormed their way to the front row to get near the candidate. The journalists are supposed to document the event; instead, they ended up totally disrupting it.

The whole episode obviously pissed off the participants. One woman on the planning committee of the ceremony said, "I think it was very disrespectful. The intent of today was not to look at Howard Dean."

Dean's spokesman blamed the media for making Dean look bad.

Is nothing sacred? All the white reporters in the black church.

"The crush of the press was distracting and not showing the respect that Dr. King deserves." Can't we all just get along?

After leaving the event, when asked how he feels about his chances tonight, Dean told off the press: "I'm feeling great, we're going to win, but you guys got to behave yourselves out of respect for Dr. King . . . You know why I wasn't able to attend this event? Because you guys are behaving so badly. You've got to get a new life."

Whatever happens next, one thing is clear: When it comes to the media, Howard Dean can't win.

Dean with the media monster.

Heroes or Zeros

THE PAPERS ARE SAYING that the new polls are showing a four-way tie: Dick Gephardt has monster trailer trucks circling Des Moines (with James Hoffa, the head of the Teamsters, telling folks "Dick Gephardt's gonna kick their ass"); Howard Dean has thousands of funny-looking young volunteers living at a Girl Scout camp and running around town in their orange hats trying to convert people; John Kerry has all of his old war buddies by his side, reminiscing about their good old days at war; and John Edwards, aka the nice one, has what the *New York Times* called "the best hair in the business."

The candidates have been saying privately that whoever wins Iowa is gonna win the whole thing. As we wait for the results to come in, there is little left to do but pace around in the lobby of the Fort Des Moines Hotel. That is where I found Joe Trippi. I reminded him that when Iowa delivers their verdict, we will know whether Trippi is a genius or a moron. If Dean pulls this off, Trippi will be credited as the political mastermind behind the throne (à la Karl Rove); if he loses, Trippi will be a dead man walking. "If we lose, I bet I will never see that camera again," Trippi predicted. So, Joe, which are you, a kingmaker or a moron? "Neither. You guys fabricate this stuff because you need a story." But you know that none of these reporters will ever want to speak to you again if you lose? "I am perfectly aware of that. It's the story of my life."

Each of the campaigns claims that they have the secret formula to deliver a victory on the ground here based on focusing on the precincts they need to win. As the organizers scramble to get their supporters to the caucus, the only thing we know for sure is that the man with the best ground organization is going to win.

So this is what it all comes down to: 100,000 Iowa Democrats. Heck, I (as one of the 1,200 journalists covering this story) have spent more than $100,000 on hotel, restaurant, bar, and transportation costs in this state in the past year. After all the time and money the candidates have spent in the Hawkeye State (it is estimated that the campaigns will have spent $100 per caucus-goer), it seems that the people of Iowa are still undecided. Half of the people polled said they were ready to change their mind about who they were going to support at the caucus. It is clear who the real winner is in all of this: The governor of Iowa estimated that the visiting journalists have spent $60 million in his state during the caucus season.

"Tonight, live from Des Moines, it's Tom Brokaw's election coverage!" (Don't you love how the networks give their anchors more attention than they give the candidates?) Brokaw is in position, the satellite trucks all have their parking spaces, the streets are full of nothing but out-of-town license plates, and as soon as the results are in, we are going to hightail it out of town. New Hampshire awaits . . .

Dick's Last Day

St. Louis, Missouri
JANUARY 20, 2004

JUST BEFORE THE IOWA CAUCUS, a ten-year-old from the *Scholastic Kids* press corps asked Congressman Gephardt, "Will you be sad if you lose?" Without blinking Dick replied, "The problem with that question is you used the word *if*." Minutes later on the bus, the Knight-Ridder reporter asked Dick, "Do you ever have moments when you are not so relentlessly optimistic?" He answered, "No." Again he tried, "Ever?" And Gephardt said, *"No.* It doesn't do you any good to sit around in a funk and be pessimistic. My mother used to put on my desk when I was a kid Norman Vincent Peale's magazine called *The Power of Positive Thinking* and my mother was very positive. She would always preach the glass is half-full, it's not half-empty. And that's the way to be. Cynicism comes from a lack of hope, and I believe we can make this country better. I've given up on giving up."

Dick Gephardt is a great example of someone who worked to change the country from the inside. He worked his way up in American government and reached the summit of congressional power. The system rewarded him; he had many good years, and he got to go places you and I can only dream about. But tonight, after twenty-seven years of dutifully serving his country, Dick Gephardt is being sent out to pasture.

In the room where Dick's victory party was supposed to take place, the few remaining loyalists stand around watching voters give testimonials on the local news. One lady said of Gephardt, "He's a nice man, but nice people don't make good leaders." Another confessed that he voted for Edwards, even though "I don't know anything about him, but those other guys are all the old guard. I wanted to go with a new face." It seems the less the voters know about a candidate, the more they like him.

Just last night the room was packed with Gephardt lovers. Where did they all go? It seems everyone wants to be around you when they think you might be a winner. The minute the results came out, they all disappeared. We did not fly on to New Hampshire as planned; instead, the charter headed to Dick Gephardt's home in Missouri. When we landed, Monty the Republican/Fox News enthusiast/flight attendant (who said he respected Dick Gephardt for voting with the president on the war) announced over the P.A., "Welcome to St. Louis, the last stop of Dick Gephardt's political career." The final indignity.

So the guy with the better hair won. The fact that Dick Gephardt is sitting at home and John Edwards gets to go on to the next round proves that the system is dysfunctional. This country is not based on meritocracy. Those who actually do the work never get the glory. In fact, Dick's experience was a liability; he suffered from what the *New York Times* called the "inevitable result of a career spent in Congressional leadership, trying to find common ground in the ideologically sprawling Democratic caucus. History suggests that legislative leaders become, in a way, their party's sin eaters, too loaded up with baggage and compromise for the message-driven simplicity of a modern presidential campaign."

We don't want the good guy; we like bad boys who lack principles. We reward those who look good and spin the best myths about themselves. This is a flashy, fickle, unfair business. No one—except the winner—is going to tell you that it works.

After all he has been through, in his concession speech Dick had no bitterness. With tears rolling down his face he said, "I love this country and I love my family." I could not help but think that most people go to great lengths to avoid having to be with their families and they are embarrassed by what George Bush is doing to this country. Still, Dick can see only the bright side.

The worst part about Dick Gephardt's loss is that today all the political pundits are talking about how Howard Dean came in third place in Iowa. The big story is not "The end of the former Democratic leader's political career"; it is "Can Dean recover after losing Iowa?" Even on CNN, when Judy Woodruff introduced a story about Gephardt's loss, there was a technical error and they rolled a different story by mistake. Poor Dick couldn't even win the losing game.

The Scream

New Hampshire
JANUARY 24, 2004

HOWARD DEAN DIDN'T HAVE a concession speech written on caucus night. When the results came in, he was not ready to accept the fact that he came in third. Shell-shocked and bleeding, Dean was forced to face three thousand of his diehard supporters to admit that he got his ass kicked.

It has been called many things: the "I have a scream" speech, "Dean unglued," "Dean gone wild." Whatever you want to call it, the last five seconds of Dean's Iowa concession speech changed the entire world's perception of Howard Dean, and ultimately doomed his campaign.

Everyone had their own interpretation of "the scream." If you were in the room and you saw Tom Harkin on steroids pumping up the crowd, and you saw the hyper young Dean worshippers in the orange hats screaming so loud that you could barely hear what their fearless leader was saying, you never would have known that you were watching the last few seconds of his political career.

Those who were in the room agreed that it was not nearly as over the top as it looked on TV. They were underestimating the power of television. The Dean movement worked well on the Internet with real people, but it would not play well on television with a nation of cynical spectators.

My Dutch boyfriend knew that the whole scene didn't look right, but since this was his first presidential concession speech, he thought that this was how Americans lose (and we never have been good losers). He kept asking the old-school journalists around him, "What is wrong with Americans, how come they can't accept defeat?"

They made fun of the little foreigner. "This is why we rule the world, Dutchie," the *New Yorker* correspondent told him. Others explained that Dean's performance was perfectly normal; he was "saving face" and "performing for his supporters." But this was not the night to play to the room. The sole purpose of primary night victory celebrations and concessions is for the cameras. It doesn't matter how anyone in the room sees it; the only thing that matters is how the world sees it on television. And on TV it did not look good.

For many Americans, this was the first time they were meeting Howard Dean. To those who already knew him, this moment confirmed their worst suspicions. All along, the Washington establishment has been saying he is a loudmouth, a hothead; now they could say, "We told you so."

According to the newspapers, no one at home liked the Howard Dean they saw that night. They thought the Monster Truck Madness/World Wrestling Federation–style howl was evidence of what *USA Today* called "Dean's emotional instability." Was it the media or the American people who decided that Dean wigged out?

Overnight, "funky and danceable shriek remixes" hit the Internet and the late-night comedians had their way with it. "Did you see Dean's speech last night?" Jay Leno joked. "Oh my God! Now I hear the cows in Iowa are afraid of getting mad Dean disease. I'm not an expert in politics, but I think it's a bad sign when your speech ends with your aides shooting you with a tranquilizer gun."

Craig Kilborn quipped, "I don't want to scare anybody here, but we just received word from police that Howard Dean is loose and may be armed with a microphone."

David Letterman kept reairing the clip with Dean's head exploding for the finale. "Did you folks see President Bush's State of the Union address?" Dave joked. "How about that surprise announcement? Howard Dean has been captured and he's in the hands of interrogators."

Even after the president delivered the last State of the Union (of his first term), promising a trip to Mars, a constitutional amendment against gay marriage, a war against steroids, and a defense of his war with Iraq (despite intelligence report failures that prove that there are no weapons of mass destruction in Iraq after all), all the anchormen asked their guests was, "What did you think of the scream?"

Because the cable channels have twenty-four hours to fill (in which they essentially have twenty-one hours of entertainment and three hours of news), they just kept playing it. By the time media trackers reported that the scream had aired at least seven hundred times, Joe Trippi complained that the way the networks were using it was "unfair . . . it was entertainment masquerading as news." Of course the networks were going to unfairly, gratuitously exploit the moment. How could they resist? What is more satisfying than watching a televised political suicide?

While some reporters on the trail kept asking Dean if he was "apologizing" or "sorry for" the scream, Dean defended his right to be a human being. "What I'm saying is, I'm not perfect. I have warts, sometimes I get very passionate . . . All I can do is be who I am."

Those who work in TV know that the camera does strange things, like add ten pounds or dark circles under your eyes, or make you look like a raving lunatic even though all you were doing is trying to cheer up your supporters. The camera will suck your soul right out of you if you let it. You are not allowed to be honest in front of it. Reality does not work on television because TV is not reality.

It is easy to say that the media blow things up; everyone knows that they do, but they need a specific moment they can break down and the scream was an easy piece of video to make use of. Dean gave them exactly what they needed. Still, it is absurd that the networks felt the need to keep re-airing the same stale bit.

Dean is free to be who he wants to be, but the network executives will never be anything more than ratings whores. They will always find a way to defend their practice of exploiting others to entertain their viewers.

Some felt they had the right to constantly reair the clip because, as Paul Slavin, senior vice president of ABC News, said, "It took on such a life . . . the amount of attention it was receiving necessitated more attention." Others, like Princell Hair, the general manager of CNN, said, "We've been wrestling with this. If we had to do it over again, we'd probably pull ourselves back." Andrew Heyward, the president of CBS News, admitted, "The cumulative effect was the event was covered more than [was] editorially justified . . . It's just inherent in the structure of the news media today, especially with the role that twenty-four-hour cable plays . . . Cable thrives on repetition and, let's be kind, exhaustive analysis, which has to constantly be freshened. If there's a powerful piece of video to fuel it, it's going to be repeated even more."

Trippi argued that the clip itself was not a fair representation of the event because the television cameras did not pan the room to capture the whole scene and therefore what you saw on TV was not a complete picture. (Why would a lifelong political operative expect anything different?) Everyone in this business knows no clip is a "fair representation"; the minute you edit a piece of video, it changes.

There was a debate about how it sounded on TV compared to how it sounded if you were in the room. ABC ran a story about how those watching at home were listening to a live feed from Dean's microphone and did not hear the roar of the crowd. The more he tried to scream over the crowd, the better it sounded to those in the room, but the worse it looked on TV. They aired the videotape shot by their producer who was in the room and all you could hear was supporters yelling at the top of their lungs. This gave the moment some context. Still, if you had five different microphones, you would have heard five different things, and those who saw the ABC segment heard only two. So the discussion of how you heard Dean's scream is fair, but not exculpatory.

The reason the "Howard Dean in the room versus Howard Dean through the directional microphone" debate is moot is because the television cameramen shot the Dean speech the same way they have shot every candidate's concession speech since the dawn of television. Why should Dean be covered any differently? It was shown on television the way every other candidate running for president has been shown. Dean's performance is being compared to every other man who ever ran in a presidential primary, lost, and had to give a concession speech. How you deal with losing is just as important as how you deal with winning. People are remembered only for their worst days.

This was not how candidates are supposed to accept defeat. They are supposed to be humble and gracious. Dean was manic and melodramatic. But this is how we are interpreting the behavior of a loser. He did not lose because he screamed; he screamed because he lost. You have to wonder: If Dean had won that night, would the scream have been seen as anything more than a reaction to a joyous and happy occasion?

The fact that this has become the central moment of the campaign and perhaps the only memorable moment so far in this election is a disturbing reflection of how cheap the news business is. This man spent two years trying to get his message out on a broad range of issues, and now that Americans are finally tuning in, all MSNBC is airing is the extended dance remix version of the Dean scream.

Dean's spokesman Jay Carson finely summed it all up: "The real question is, why are we talking for the fourth day in a row about less than thirty seconds of a speech in Iowa when there are 9 million Americans unemployed, 43 million Americans without health insurance, and people are dying in Iraq?"

The Center for Media and Public Affairs reported that in the week following the scream, only 39 percent of Dean's coverage on the evening news was positive, compared to the 71 percent of positive coverage of John Kerry's campaign and 86 percent of positive coverage that John Edwards got.

Since the infamous event, everyone I have talked to who was there admits that they still don't know what they saw that night (if they saw anything at all; most of the journalists were roped off in the back of the room, near the food spread, with no view of the stage). For most of us, it took a few days for the media to tell us what we had seen. The reruns forced us to reevaluate what we saw; the image on the screen became our new version of reality; what we experienced live was changed by what we saw on TV.

Some of the pundits who were in the room that night telling my boyfriend that there wasn't anything unusual about Dean's speech were on TV in the days following the event talking about how "bad it looked" when Dean "flipped out." This is either an example of how ignorant the pundits are (they don't know what they are seeing when they see it) or it is a clear example of the power of images. They were not speaking about their version of reality, they were talking about the reality created by television.

For years to come, the scream speech will be used in journalism schools as a case study of what is wrong with the media. The worst part about the scream is that it confirms what media consultants have been saying all along: If you are running for president, you must stick to the script; you are not allowed to express how you really feel. The more a candidate gets ridiculed for and hurt by living in the moment, the less chance there is that we will ever see an honest moment in American politics. If the candidates are not allowed to ever be themselves or to say anything that is not in the script, then all of American politics will be as boring and monotone as John Edwards.

Top Ten Things You Are Not Allowed to Say in a Presidential Campaign

1. "If I win, members of Congress are going to be scurrying for shelter, just like a giant flashlight on a bunch of cockroaches." (Howard Dean, October 14, 2003, in Iowa)

2. "If you look at the caucuses system, they are dominated by the special interests in both parties . . . the special interests don't represent the centrist tendencies of the American people. They represent the extremes. And then you get a president who is beholden to either one extreme or the other, and where the average person is in the middle." (Howard Dean on the Canadian TV show *The Editors* in 2000, but not reported until January 8, 2004)

3. "Eleven companies in this country control 90 percent of what ordinary people are able to read and watch on their television. That's wrong. We need to have a wide variety of opinions in every community . . . We're going to break up giant media enterprises." (Howard Dean, December 1, 2003, on MSNBC)

4. When asked why President Bush is suppressing evidence in the 9/11 investigation: "The most interesting theory that I've heard so far—which is nothing more than a theory, it can't be proved—is that he was warned ahead of time by the Saudis." (Howard Dean, December 1, 2003, on National Public Radio)

5. "The capture of Saddam has not made America safer." (Howard Dean, December 15, 2003, in Los Angeles)

6. When asked who he will pick for VP: "I'm going to pick somebody with defense and foreign policy experience . . . The fact is, it's a résumé problem. I need to plug that hole in my résumé. And I am going to do that with my running mate." (Howard Dean, December 21, 2003, in Litchfield, New Hampshire)

7. "I still have this old-fashioned notion that even with people like Osama, who is very likely guilty, we should do our best not to prejudge jury trials." (Howard Dean, December 26, 2003, to the *Concord Monitor,* New Hampshire)

8. "I still want to be the candidate for guys with Confederate flags in their pickup trucks." (Howard Dean, October 1, 2003, to the *Des Moines Register*)

9. When asked by an old retired man to "Please tone down the garbage, the mean-mouthing, the tearing-down of your neighbor [Bush]: "George Bush is not my neighbor . . . You sit down. You've had your say and now I'm going to have my say." (Howard Dean, January 11, 2003, in Oelwein, Iowa)

10. "Not only are we going to New Hampshire . . . we're going to South Carolina and Oklahoma and Arizona and North Dakota and New Mexico, and we're going to California and Texas and New York. And we're going to South Dakota and Oregon and Washington and Michigan. And then we're going to Washington, D.C., to take back the White House. Yeeeeeeeearrrrrrhhhhh!" (Howard Dean, January 19, 2004, Des Moines, Iowa, concession speech)

Look Who's Back!

Nashua, New Hampshire
JANUARY 25, 2004

ABOUT A MONTH AGO, when my boyfriend's parents were visiting from Europe and we were desperate for new ways to entertain them, we ventured over to the Barnes & Noble to see historian Douglas Brinkley read from his new book *Tour of Duty: John Kerry and the Vietnam War.* Also there were Kerry's sister Peggy and the usual cast of wackos who hang around those book readings because they have nowhere else to go. We were among the few actual book buyers with any interest in the book.

In 2002 Brinkley had approached the senator and made an exclusive deal to get full access to his Vietnam diaries, with one "string attached"—that Brinkley's book would be written "within two years," meaning that it would come out before the election so that it could be used as a campaign tool.

But something happened on the way to the bookshelf. Kerry's campaign collapsed and now this guy is stuck with a book that no one but Kerry's sister wants to read. The author explained that his subject "exerted no editorial control on the manuscript" and that this book is his, not Kerry's, and that there is no relationship between himself and the candidate or the campaign.

Perhaps it was the language barrier, or the pro-Kerry nature of the presentation from the author, who was introduced as a historian and a professor, but my boyfriend's parents (who are both professors) kept asking us questions like "Does he work for John Kerry?" and "Did John Kerry pay him to write this book?" and "How can he be a historian if he is writing about a candidate with an election deadline?" They were not the only ones in the room confused about the relationship between the writer and his subject.

Brinkley defended his work by saying that "Kerry's purpose was to spread the word about the history of Swift Boats in Vietnam." The author went on to praise his subject, but the audience wasn't buying it. One man asked why Kerry's presidential campaign "isn't catching on," and the author was forced to use words (that were not approved by the senator's campaign spokesman) like "glory seeking," "privileged," "pretty boy," "remote," "too ambitious," and "Yalie." Perhaps I wasn't giving this guy enough credit—maybe he really does know John Kerry!

Now here we are, one month later, and our hero John Kerry has come back from the dead. And look who's by his side. It's Douglas Brinkley at his service! Kerry's ploy to publish his heroic war stories seems to have paid off! And just in time.

Of course, there are a lot of reasons why Kerry won the caucuses: the guiding light of Teddy Kennedy, the sophisticated organization his campaign ran on the ground in Iowa, the fact that after serving eight thousand bowls of chili in New Hampshire he realized that he wasn't going to win so he gave up and went for the Hail Mary in Iowa. But when all was said and done, it was the Vietnam vets coming to his rescue. What really put the senator over the top were the testimonials from his old war buddies; you can't do any better than having the man whose life you saved cry on TV for you. (And it didn't hurt that they had copies of *Tour of Duty* on sale at Kerry's events and that Brinkley was having book signings all around Iowa.)

Voters work in mysterious ways, but on caucus night the one thing that seems to have resonated with them was all that stuff they heard about Kerry being a war hero. Who would have known that Americans respect military service? By selling himself as the Vietnam War hero, with a popular book extolling his military service as proof, Kerry successfully sold himself to the voters and Brinkley sold enough copies of *Tour of Duty* to make it to the best-seller list. But there is trouble on the horizon . . .

The same story that he used to become the front-runner is going to be used against him in the general election. The veterans who are not happy with Brinkley's book are energizing the Swift Boat Vets Against Kerry. The same "inspirational story" that is driving Democrats to the polls in the primaries is galvanizing the Kerry haters to show up and protest him.

Tonight at the big chili fest at the Nashua Firehouse, one of the angry swift boat vets was trying to get the press to listen to his side of the story about Kerry in Vietnam, but no one was listening. Only one guy from Japanese TV gave him the microphone and let him rant: "Brinkley and Kerry belong together—they are both opportunists who are exploiting the vets to make themselves famous."

The fliers for tonight's event said "Come meet Ted Kennedy" at a "Chili-fest for John Kerry." But there was no chili and no Ted Kennedy. Sitting around waiting for the candidate to arrive, one of the Kerry faithful complained, "Last time he was early and this time he is making us wait all night. That is the biggest problem with this guy—he is the most inconsistent candidate I've ever seen."

With nothing else to do while we waited under the fluorescent lights with the bad music blaring, I talked to some recovering Deaniacs about their first impressions of John Kerry and how they managed to overcome them. A new mother holding her three-week-old baby said, "A few months ago I couldn't say John Kerry's name without rolling my eyes, but now we are in that 'anyone but Dean moment' and Kerry doesn't look so bad. Actually he looks like a prize, a savior." Her husband, a divorce attorney, said, "I used to have a problem with Kerry, but I got over it."

A carpet cleaner who drove from Vermont to see Kerry explained, "Dean was a revolution. Kerry is a politically correct stump speech, but we have no other choice." The fur dealer standing next to him added, "Howard Dean is the best thing that ever happened to John Kerry. He made him a fighter. Kerry didn't start fighting until he was staring defeat in the face. Now I think Kerry can win this thing, so I'm voting for him." So there really is a whole psychology of momentum. People want to go with a winner and the minute they see who that is, they jump on board.

The softball coach from the local high school gave me his explanation of what is going on right now: "There is this myth that I keep reading in the newspaper that all of a sudden 'Kerry is connecting,' people are now starting to get turned on by John Kerry. After that scream, Dean looked like a loser and losers turn people off, so everyone is looking for someone new. That is why Kerry is rising. He did not grow a personality overnight." An encyclopedia salesman added, "Howard Dean helped Kerry grow a spine, he served his purpose, now it's Kerry's turn to carry the torch."

Remember back when Joe Trippi used to say "Kerry set the table and Dean sat down for dinner"? It now appears that Kerry was just letting Dean keep the seat warm until he came to claim it. The hip-talking journalists have an expression that they keep using to explain Kerry's return: "After the Internet crash, everyone went back to the blue chip stocks."

My favorite teen idol, Gideon Yago from MTV, put the whole "dated Dean, married Kerry" phenomenon in terms that we can all relate to—by comparing them to David Bowie and Iggy Pop. Iggy was the original; Bowie stole his act but made it slicker, more distinguished and commercial. "It's not who does it first, it's who does it second." Howard Dean was the original and he had the stage to himself for a while, but once Kerry stole Dean's material and refined it, we did not need Dean anymore.

When Kerry finally showed up (two hours late), he said, "While you were sitting around here eating chili, I was meeting with . . ." To which a cranky old lady who was tired of waiting around without chili screamed back at him, "Don't tell me about where you have been. All you are telling us is that you were with someone more important than me."

Now that he's back on top, he doesn't have to show up on time, or scoop the chili, or deliver a Kennedy. It looks like the cocky old senator is back! While he was speaking, the young lady in front of me whispered to her date, "He looks tired." He whispered back, "He looks much better on TV."

On the way out an old man who was not impressed with the show said to his wife, "You promised me a new Kerry . . . That's the same old Kerry we saw last month." So it's true: John Kerry really is back!

Death by Nuance

Waterloo, New Hampshire
JANUARY 26, 2004

EVEN THOUGH we still have a long way to go before all the other candidates drop out and John Kerry actually gets the nomination, the White House is mounting their offense.

There are two distinctly different tactics in this campaign: the tactic of clarity and the tactic of distortion. The Bush campaign is going with the distortion approach; that really seems to be working for them. Kerry is going with clarity, which means he is killing us with long-winded explanations that don't explain much. Professor of linguistics George Lakoff says it best: "How many times have you heard the Republicans give a sound bite and the Democrats give a paragraph?"

Doesn't anyone in the Kerry campaign watch Fox News? They make everything simple. Gay marriage? We do not like gays. We are against them having any rights. As George Bush says, "You are either with us or against us." The Democrats know that gay marriage is an issue that will hurt them, so they are coming up with these lengthy defenses of their positions that sound like apologies (making defending the rights of gays sound like a crime). So are you with us or against us? Senator Kerry: "I am against gay marriage *but* for civil unions because . . ." But? Every time you use the word *but* you start to lose people.

The biggest threat to the Democrats is nuance because television news is not about nuance; it is about giving the audience bite-size little mind snacks with no informational value. Because we have a two-party system, our political culture is two-sided. On TV everything is reduced to two flavors: chocolate or vanilla. Every debate is framed as Democrat versus Republican, red versus blue. That's it; these are your only choices, even though in reality, there are usually at least twelve different sides to an issue. The conservatives have mastered the politics of language; they use the right words to frame the debates to their advantage.

Fox News talks about very complicated issues in a language that we can all understand. My friend Rich Lowry (aka the leader of the Young Conservative Movement) has a theory: People like Tim Russert and Chris Matthews know all the people they have on their shows and they have already discussed the issues with them at length. So by the time they get on the air, they sound like they are in the middle of a conversation that they were having at a dinner party last night. People don't want to watch know-it-alls chew the fat on television—they are looking for a conversation they can participate in. That is why Fox News is so successful.

George Bush used to say in 2000, "You have to define yourself before they define you." If you turn on Fox News right now, the question the Republicans are asking is, "How can you nominate a liberal guy from the Northeast and think he is going to win?" That is everything they want you to know about John Kerry: He's a liberal. They are setting John Kerry in concrete before he gets the chance to define himself.

Television is like a bad odor wafting through the air; very little of it stays with you. Just one line, one catch phrase is all that people will remember. The Republicans are going to spend seven days a week on TV over the next year calling Senator Kerry the one thing that they want to stick: liberal flip-flopper. What is Kerry going to call Bush? How about incompetent liar? That ought to stick. Most of the millions of words that will come out of the senator's mouth over the next year will be completely forgotten; only a few of his phrases will be picked up and repeated because the news is only going to report the planes that crash, not the planes that land safely.

To demonstrate Kerry's lack of economy of words, just take a look at this excerpt from Fox News on Sunday, January 25, 2004. You can see everything that you need to know about the challenge Senator Kerry will face in this election:

CHRIS WALLACE: Senator, are you more liberal than Ted Kennedy?

JOHN KERRY: That is so funny. I almost—first of all, it's flattery. I'm complimented that they're attacking me that way. Secondly, it proves what I'm saying, that I'm the strongest person to go against George Bush, or they wouldn't be attacking me this early. Thirdly, as they say in the South, that dog won't hunt. I'm the guy who led the fight to put 100,000 cops on the streets of America. I've been a prosecutor. I've sent people to jail for the rest of their lives. I led the fight in 1985, with Fritz Hollings and others, to reduce the deficit and be fiscally responsible with Gramm-Rudman-Hollings. I have fought again and again against special interests that divert the taxpayers' money and put it into favored, powerful crony deals. I fought to protect the middle class in the course of this campaign so we don't raise taxes. I voted for lower taxes. I voted to create jobs. I don't think that's going to work. I voted for welfare reform. I mean, I . . .

Senator Kerry, he asked you a simple question: Are you a liberal, yes or no? All you have to do is come up with a funny one-liner to defuse this question. And by the way, why do you sound so offended by the word "liberal"? You are running away from it like it is a dirty, perverted word. Okay. Let's move on to the big issues that Fox News is going to use to pound on you all year:

WALLACE: Let's look at some of the other issues, though. Over the years, you have voted against banning partial-birth abortions six times. You voted against the Defense of Marriage Act, which defined marriage as a union of a man and woman, and you have voted against the death penalty, even for terrorists who kill Americans overseas—let me finish—although I know that you later changed your mind on that. Any second thoughts about those other votes?

KERRY: No, absolutely not, Chris. They were votes of principle, and let me explain them, and I'll be able to explain them to Americans. I don't support marriage among gays. I've said that many times. That was not my position. But I also don't support the United States Senate being used for gay bashing, for, sort of, discriminatory efforts to try to drive wedges between the American people . . . I don't support gay marriage. But I also support equal protection under the law. I support not having a president who wants to drive wedges between people and try to divide Americans . . .

Senator Kerry, how come you always have a big *but*? All we are looking for here is a simple yes or no sound bite, not a whole explanation of the issue. You know that you can't win on issues like gay marriage and partial-birth abortions—these are losing issues for you no matter what. Can't you see what Chris Wallace is doing to you here? He is giving you the rope. Don't hang yourself with it. Change the subject. Ignore the questions and talk about your own agenda.

WALLACE: You voted against banning partial-birth abortions six times.

KERRY: Yes. *But* I'm against partial-birth abortion, as are many people. But under the law of our land, I believe it is a constitutional right for a woman to be able to make a choice with respect to her health. If a doctor—all we wanted to do was allow a doctor, two doctors, to be able to write a letter saying that if there were grievous bodily injury to the woman—grievous bodily injury, not just health, but grievous bodily injury—that they ought to have the right to be able to make a medical decision. The Republicans didn't want that because they wanted, again, to drive a wedge issue. That doesn't mean—you see, these things, they're always more complicated than people think. And what we need to do in America is have an honest conversation about the future of our country. People aren't frankly—that's not what divides America. What divides America, whether it's in the South or Southwest, North, Northwest, people want jobs, Chris. People want health care. People want schools that work. People want clean air to breathe and clean water to drink. And we're going backwards on every single one of those major issues before the country. Now, what the Republicans want to do is divert it . . .

Senator Kerry, enough already. It was a simple question: are you for or against it? Why are you rambling on? You are killing us here with your epic answers. This is why people are calling you Senator Nuance and why Fred Barnes from the *Weekly Standard* said, "His emergence as the Great Explainer is a problem for Kerry."

Last question, and this is an easy one here. The Republicans are slandering you all over the place. They are calling you a liberal flip-flopper and they are attacking your record. In the next year they will try to crush you like a little bug. Your party believes that the president went to war under false pretenses. Here is your chance to take a hit.

WALLACE: Do you trust George W. Bush?

KERRY: I believe that Dick Cheney exaggerated, clearly. When they talked about weapons of mass destruction that could be deployed in forty-five minutes, there were none. When they talked about aerial devices that could deliver, there were none. When they talked about the linkage to al Qaida that they've now exaggerated, but they themselves said then there was no smoking gun. They said it. Now they say there was a linkage. I think there's been an enormous amount of exaggeration, stretching, deception. And the question is still unanswered as to what Dick Cheney was doing over at the CIA personally in those weeks leading up to the war.

WALLACE: And when you see what David Kay said, do you believe that the president was part of a willful effort to mislead the American people?

KERRY: I would never suggest that about a president of the United States without adequate evidence. I don't know the answer to it. But I do know this . . .

WALLACE: But you're suggesting it about the vice president?

KERRY: I know the vice president either misspoke or misled the American people, but he did so in a way that gave Congressmen and

-women, who have since said—I mean, very good people, good Americans who voted in good conscience, have stood up and said, "I was misled." This administration has to be accountable for that. And they haven't yet accounted for it.

So you don't trust Cheney, but you give George a free pass, and if you aren't giving me a reason not to trust George, then I might as well vote for him. Bill Clinton, the man who bounced the other Bush out of office, says that the trick to getting elected is you have to give the American people "a reason to fire the other guy."

It is time for Senator Kerry to come to terms with the media environment he is living in. Cable news does not have the appetite for his long, drawn-out answers. He thinks too much, and in this instant-gratification cable culture, anytime you give more than a simple sound bite, everyone (including the media) is absolved from having to think about what is actually being said.

Dean's Demise

Manchester, New Hampshire
JANUARY 27, 2004

AS THE PRIMARIES BEGIN, Howard Dean is not wearing well. All that Internet passion is not the grassroots network that the Deanies thought it would be. It just isn't happening on the ground, and there is no shortage of people taking great pleasure in discovering that Dean's grassroots were Astroturf. The signs around town sum up this whole race: "Doubting Dean? Vote Kerry!" As Dean falls off the screen, Kerry is there to fill the void.

The Dean campaign is starting to pay for their hubris. Why did they believe what they read on the blog? They should not have listened only to the true believers. What made them think the bloggers were the key to victory? Ignoring the "too many cooks in the kitchen" principle, the campaign let the people speak. Perhaps the lesson here is that not everyone should have a voice.

After getting knocked around for showing too much passion, Dean put on a sweater, switched to decaf, and lost his edge. He has become *Howard Dean Unplugged,* and without the fire, he sounds like all the other politicians. A college kid who was bused in from Chicago to see her superhero said that after his mellow performance she asked backstage, "What happened to my Howard Dean?" And the excuse the campaign used was, "He is losing his voice and we don't want that to happen."

At that same event, Dean showed his lack of political skills in dealing with bumps in the road. A supporter of Lyndon LaRouche screamed profanities at Dean, calling him a liar, and he was unable to cope with it gracefully. LaRouche is the illegitimate fascist presidential candidate on his eighth campaign whom no one takes seriously. His followers disrupt all the candidates, and they have found clever ways to cope with the expected interruptions. One group of LaRouchies likes to serenade John Kerry: "John Kerry, what a Hamlet, grow some balls." But when a LaRouchie went after Howard Dean, he instantly instructed security to "throw him out." As the heckler heckled on, Al Franken had to tackle the guy to the ground. The whole scene was not pretty.

Just as things were spiraling downward, Dean did what he promised he was never going to do: He dragged out his wife. Judy was the big "get"; all the talk shows were trying to book her for months. Finally she agreed to do Diane Sawyer. If they had only done this interview the week before, when ABC wanted her, they could have gotten the nice Diane Sawyer; instead, they waited until they needed Diane, and when you need Diane, you get the nasty Diane.

Now that Judy was obviously standing by her man (which she said she never wanted to do), Diane had to ask, "Do you feel like a prop?" Judy politely said, "No." This was their big chance. The Deans could look like real ready-made-for-prime-time human beings. But under the soft TV magazine lights, Howard Dean's wife told Diane, "We never argue." Are they freaks of nature? Every couple argues now and then. Have you ever met a couple that has *never* argued? Besides, no one in America is going to believe that when this man told his wife he was running for president and she refused to be involved that there was not some form of an argument. Now it is looking like the biggest loser in this whole campaign is Dr. Steinberg, now known as Dr. Dean, who got brought on board just as the ship was sinking. The cruelest comment one TV commentator used was, "The fact that she looked like Yoko Ono didn't help much either."

A common theme at Dean events these days is "Annoy the media, vote for Dean." People have been writing this on their signs and chanting it in front of cameras. Annoy the media? They created Howard Dean. *Newsweek* and *Time* and all the others put Dean on their covers and they gave him more ink than any other presidential candidate ever. Without the media, Howard Dean would be Dennis Kucinich. Now that Dean is not doing as well as the Deanies hoped, they are blaming the media? If you want to blame someone, blame the candidate for not knowing how to use the media and doing a terrible job of managing his own campaign.

When the results came in, Dean placed second to Kerry in New Hampshire. He took to the stage and said he was "pleased." For the past two years he has been driving through the back roads of every county in this state and you expect us to believe that he is actually pleased with second place? If he can't win here, he can't win anywhere.

There was a dark sadness in the room, despite all the signs with the new buzzword: HOPE NOT FEAR, HOWARD = HOPE, and GIVE 'EM HOPE, HOWARD, which replaced GIVE 'EM HELL, HOWARD. They were trying to send the signal that this campaign has gone from attack mode to hope mode. In the back of the room, Tucker Carlson was live on CNN asking, "Where do the Dean supporters go from here?"

During his speech, Dean had yet another odd onstage moment. As he was speaking, he spotted a supporter in the crowd from San Francisco. Midsentence he asked, "Did you come all the way from San Francisco?" Didn't he learn in Iowa not to play to the room? You want the millions of people at home watching TV to think that all of those people in the room are your local supporters, not the Dean Heads that stalk you across the country. And besides, I am from S.F. and I love that city, but I know that when you say San Francisco the first thing people think is (the stereotype Dean is trying to overcome) "liberal." Or perhaps they think "Internet bubble," which is what Howard Dean is turning out to be.

There was no sign of Al Gore or Bill Bradley or Tom Harkin tonight. Everyone wants to be on the winning team; on nights like tonight, they are nowhere to be found. But I am not really sure those guys would be welcome here. Everyone openly acknowledges that ever since Al Gore and the old party warhorses endorsed Dean, the campaign has gone downhill. Or, as a veteran of the 2000 campaign so plainly put it, "Everything Al Gore touches turns to shit."

Joe Trippi (who explained the Iowa loss as a "murder-suicide" between Gephardt and Dean) was replaced by Roy Neel, a Washington lobbyist who personifies everything the Deansters are against. Neel's résumé reads, "He lobbies on issues relating to telecommunications policy on behalf of the Baby Bells." The man running this Internet movement is a lobbyist for the old-fashioned phone companies?

Now that times are getting tough, it is hard to tell who Howard Dean really is. But what do you expect from a man who says he got into politics so that he could build a bike path and ended up running for president of the United States?

Feel That Joementum!

Hartford, Connecticut
FEBRUARY 4, 2004

ON THE SUNDAY MORNING before the New Hampshire primary, a collection of fifty—camera crews, print reporters, and the "Let's Go Joe cheering section"—assembled in downtown Manchester for another episode of "Operation Liebermania." Today we were following Joey Lieberman and the Liebermaniacs as they go door-to-door to spread their election fever.

This is not just any neighborhood, this is Joey's new home turf. A few weeks ago we were all at his house-warming party for the generic people-storage-unit-style apartment he is renting right down the road. So today Joey is not just meeting New Hampshire voters; he is meeting his neighbors!

As he sprung off his bus, Integrity One, in bitter, bone-chilling, below-zero temperatures, he asked, "Can you feel it? That's the Joementum!" (So that's what we're calling it these days! It feels an awful lot like frostbite.) Then he explained what we were doing. "This is how I started thirty-three years ago when I ran for state senate. I probably visited 2,500 to 3,000 households door-to-door. If you want to run for any office, you need three skills: You have got to learn to sleep on planes, you have to learn to eat in moving vehicles, and you have to know how to go door-to-door." So, as an old pro, Joey showed us how it was done.

The photographers were head-butting each other for the best view of Joey ringing doorbells. They had him covered on all sides: beside him on the porch, behind him from the front lawn, and the most ambitious photographer was shoving his camera against people's windows. A campaign staffer tried in vain to organize the horde: "Guys, guys please, people live here, this is their home!" Lights, camera, action. Joey rings the doorbell. Pause. Rings it again. No answer.

As all the big burly men with boom microphones traipsed through people's yards and climbed through the bushes to position themselves on the decks of people's homes, it was hard to find a neighbor bold enough to answer the door. So Joey left notes: "As my hands get colder my message will be limited to the single word 'Help!' " Eventually he found a brave soul to actually open the door, and although we do not know what exactly the neighbor said to him, after he left the house, Joey jumped into his Suburban and got the hell out of the neighborhood.

Maybe he will have more luck at his next stop, the TGI Friday's in the mall. As we walked into the red-and-white-striped theme-park-style sports bar known as a happy hour meeting place for single adults, the hostess greeted us with the chain's motto: "In here it's always Friday." Joey rejoiced, "Hallelujah!"

At one table, a woman in an "I love Jesus" sweatshirt could not contain her enthusiasm about what was going on in the restaurant. But as we got closer, it turned out that she was not getting excited about meeting Joe Lieberman, she was making noise about TGI Friday's new Atkins-approved low-carb diet menu.

Joey made his way around the joint trying to meet customers while they talked among themselves. One woman who completely ignored him told me, "I look at him and all I think is: rabbi." Asked about the senator's chances in this race, she said, "He is going to get run over because he is standing in the middle of the road. The liberals don't like him because he votes like a Republican, the Republicans don't like him because they don't like Democrats."

Over a plate of buffalo wings, Joey was telling a young woman (wearing an I AM DRUNK TAKE ME HOME T-shirt) about his efforts to go after Hollywood's violent films with his buddy Bill Bennett. It did not look like this position was going over well with the young ladies.

The funny thing about these impromptu drop-ins at local eating establishments is that over the course of the day, lots of people walked up to Joey and told him that he was a great American. But these are not the exchanges that anyone is going to write about. Reporters are only going to write about the funny or irreverent things that people say. In fairness, Joey made plenty of new friends.

The biggest problem this campaign has been having is finding people for Joey to talk to. In the past few weeks, the candidate has been seen in an uninhabited home for the elderly, roaming through the aisles of an empty drugstore, and at a series of diners with more reporters than locals (and all he has for a press corps is a "six pack"). When I asked the cashier at Kmart (who loves Lieberman) why she did not intend to vote for him she said, "I don't think he has any chance." The bag boy chimed in, "No, he doesn't have a prayer." Why not? "The media doesn't take him seriously."

When all the votes were counted, at the end of his one-year-and-nineteen-day mission of pitching himself to the American people, all Joe Lieberman got for his time on the campaign trail was 81,007 votes. In the beginning of 2003, he was a front-runner in all the national polls; one year later he is an also-ran.

On the day after he dropped out, his hometown paper, the *Hartford Courant,* concluded, "Something about the Lieberman campaign never clicked with voters. Nothing worked . . . perhaps the fact that he was Jewish . . . Or it was because of Lieberman's lack of charisma." This was surprising to me because every time I rode along with Joey he was Mr. Congeniality; he was witty and clever and a great singer. He was great one-on-one, but once he starting talking about the issues on the stump, the sound of his voice put people to sleep. "I am the only candidate taking a fresh look at tax reform," he declared often. This is not sexy, even for C-SPAN.

Joey feels the reason he did not resonate with voters was because in the polarizing world of politics, people were not interested in the guy looking for a compromise. He told me, "In the Democratic primaries people were really looking for somebody who they felt hated George Bush as much as they did and that's not my nature. I never believed the president was an evil person, I just believed he was wrong. I wasn't the right candidate." Why? Because you ran like a Republican in a Democratic primary? "No, I think that the voters who turned out in the Democratic primaries wanted a more partisan liberal candidate."

On the trail, Joey liked to paraphrase Winston Churchill by saying that politics is the only business where you can die and live another day. "Politics is almost as exciting as war, and quite as dangerous. In war you can only be killed once, but in politics many times." He got out just in time. If he dragged it out any longer he would have turned his perfectly solid reputation into fodder for the late-night talk shows. The last thing you want to do is stay in until the bitter end and be known as a big loser (see Howard Dean). Nobody, besides politicos, the journalists who have to cover this stuff, and voters in a few small states, has been paying attention to all the campaign noise in the past year.

As the old black man sitting next to me on the Peter Pan bus on my way to Joey's concession speech said, "Joe Lieberman did not lose, he got out before anyone in the country even noticed he was running. He got out with his reputation intact." In this case, you see how some candidates in these races have more to lose than others. As Dick Gephardt disappears into oblivion, Joey Lieberman will return to his life as a U.S. senator.

When I went to say goodbye to him he said, "Some senators run for president because they are tired of being senator. I haven't reached that point." Just then a supporter interrupted, "Joe, you would make the best president. I honestly believe that. You've made your mark on history." Joey responded, "We've got some good days ahead of us."

The General Dies Off

Little Rock, Arkansas
FEBRUARY 11, 2004

THE MAN WHO BEAT MILOSEVICH had a much harder time in the battle of the Democratic primaries. Poor Wesley Clark. Someone actually convinced him to drag his reputation through this presidential race.

The moment I knew Wes Clark's presidential campaign was coming to an end was when a woman who just shook his hand in a hotel lobby said, "My mother would disown me if she saw that." When asked why, she said her mother was "Clark's biggest fan, until she saw him in person."

What we learned from the Clark candidacy is that a man with no political history is not eligible to be president. If you are untested in a political environment, you will never really stand a chance against the professional politicians. You need to know something about the political process before you can run, and you must have a set of skills for presidential politics; novices need not apply.

Clark himself admitted early on, "Nobody has ever done anything like this before. The honest truth is, I didn't make up my mind to accept the call until Monday morning, the fourteenth of September at eight-thirty. And I called the office and I said, 'Okay, we are going to go ahead.' " But you can't merely accept the call; you have to plot and scheme for decades to get here. A pursuit as large as this requires a lifetime of preparation, image building, media training, public speaking experience, and relationships. To be able to sell yourself as a political product, you need all of these ingredients. Wes Clark was a war hero, but he didn't know how to talk politics. It is a whole different language.

And he got really bad advice. Someone should have warned him not to invite Michael Moore to stand onstage with him. Amateur mistake.

And whose idea was it to let Wes Clark say of Kerry, he is "a lieutenant and I'm a general"? Even if it's true, you can't say things like that in this business.

There was all this talk about how Wes Clark was in this race for the Clintons and this was a proxy war between Clinton and Gore (who is standing with Dean). If that is the case, we are learning how irrelevant both Clinton and Gore have made themselves. The Clinton mafia only hurt Clark. All those old staffers of Bill who were juicing to get back into the game and thought Wes Clark was their ticket did not have a clue how irrelevant they were. They had an unprecedented arrogance about themselves.

The best part about the Clark candidacy was Wes Clark Jr. He wasn't afraid to tell it like it is. Near the end of the campaign, he told reporters, "It's been a really disillusioning experience . . . You go out and see how politics actually works. It's a dirty business, filled with a lot of people who are pretending to be a lot of things they are not." The thirty-four-year-old son of the general didn't shy away from telling reporters that they were failing to do their jobs. "You've got to talk about what the man stands for and what he's done. Nobody does that. His stance on the issues or his qualifications for the job haven't been talked about at all. It's all horse-race questions," he said. "I told reporters, you're not honest with the American people about what's really going on. And this is just the way it works. It's about ratings. It's not about the truth. They just create conflict so that they can sell papers . . . It's this kind of childish gotchaism that comes out where you're not really reporting anything of substance."

In our postmortem conversation, this was Wes Clark Jr.'s assessment of the political press:

> They do a huge disservice to the American people. They are a threat to democracy. They don't care about reporting the facts. They don't care about getting your story out. It's about getting people excited enough to watch the news and the political coverage. What can you learn by following the circus around other than that it's a circus?

You don't get a deep insight into any of the candidates by looking at the campaign stuff because it's not designed to tell you who they are. It's designed to keep a story each day that comes into the press. What you've done in your life doesn't matter. What matters is what you say when you sit down with these people.

Wes Jr. suggested that in order to understand the media, you have to look at who they are. "What they are is a bunch of people separated from their families—if they're married, which most of them are—most of them in their late twenties, early thirties, and they ride around on a bus all day, and they get drunk at night, and they're pissed off because they're not getting ahead in their career and having a flash-bang story. What can you do? That's why you have campaigns the way they're structured, to keep them occupied. It's like, idle hands for the devil's workshop. So every campaign comes up with ideas to keep this roving band of semidrunk nerds occupied so that they don't burn down your house."

Wes Jr. came away from this experience with the conclusion that the media anoint the nominee and his challenger and there is nothing the other candidates can do to overcome that. "If you have the media relentlessly pushing two candidates, you can't get past that; it's just not possible." But the most frustrating part about watching his dad run was seeing how he was portrayed in the paper. "You read so much that's not true. Just even articles written about me, and there weren't many, but the few that were written, my age would be wrong or where I went to college was wrong, or they'd take a quote that I know I didn't say. And it was just like, okay, if they're doing that to me, think about what they're doing in every other story that you read." He guesses that half of the stories written about his father had mistakes in them, but what killed him was the little things that the reporters picked up on. "It's the subtle things, it's the stuff that you don't notice unless you're related to the candidate . . . My favorite was Dad wearing a sweater in New Hampshire one day. Maybe he was wearing a sweater because he was cold!" (This was a comment about all the stories that were written about the fashion faux pas his father committed by wearing an argyle sweater.)

Although the candidate never had the appeal that many hoped for, that used argyle sweater did. Someone actually paid $5,404 for it on eBay.

Interpreting Howard Dean

Wausau, Wisconsin
FEBRUARY 13, 2004

ON THE DAY Howard lost another round of primaries, he told supporters, "We're going to keep going and going and going and going and going, just like the Energizer Bunny." Later that night, a small incident in a Seattle hotel clearly exposed Dean's image problem. Here are two different reports of the same incident:

The *New York Times*

As Dr. Dean headed into the Westin hotel in downtown Seattle on Tuesday night a few supporters were waiting and asked him to autograph copies of his campaign book. He declined and walked by.

ABC NEWS.com

Walking into the lobby of the Seattle Westin Hotel, Gov. Howard Dean waved off two early 20-something autograph seekers. The brush-off was uncharacteristic of the candidate, who boasts that one-fourth of his supporters are under the age of 30. Perhaps it was losing to Al Sharpton in South Carolina or something that happened on the van ride from Tacoma to Seattle. Or maybe it was driving by the Sheraton Hotel and seeing the massive swarm of Kerry supporters.

Aide Mike O'Mary dismisses these theories and offers up this one. Of late the Governor has been approached by the same group of people asking for photos and autographs, which they are selling on e-Bay. A quick click on the electronic auction house comes up with some interesting Dean tchotchkes: A Perfect Storm hat, Howard Dean scream buttons, a 12-inch Howard Dean action doll and, yes, signed photos.

These two versions of the same episode reveal more about the media than they do about Howard Dean. Two different journalists reported the same incident in their own way, one more charitably than the other. That is what journalism is: the act of witnessing things. Everyone perceives things in their own way, and if you were standing in the lobby that night, you would have had your own interpretation of the moment. And most likely you would not have the campaign contact to call and clarify what happened. (And even if you did, would you believe him? Isn't it his job to apologize for and make his boss look good?)

We do not know if the two young people were genuine fans or capitalist vultures. There is no proof that they are the sellers of the eBay autographs, but if you knew that they were, would it change your interpretation of that moment? And if you had seen Howard Dean curtly blow off autograph seekers before, like the time in New York City outside his mother's apartment (to which an old man who witnessed the snub said, "Don't feel that badly, kids, Mickey Mantle did that to me when I was eight years old"), would that affect your impression of him?

Howard Dean is running for president of the United States of America, and whether he likes it or not, part of his job description is making nice with people, even if he is not in the mood. He can play by his own rules, but he can't expect immunity from the press for doing so. Politics is all about perception. You may be the greatest guy on earth, but if you can't show it on TV, you have a problem. This is a part of the business, just like medicine and law; if you want to practice it, you need to have a certain skill set. There is no way to avoid it; you have got to kiss the babies. Dean never even pretended to play the adorable role of emperor of ice cream. For many, he came off as brittle and unlovable, like a four-foot-tall Chinese dry cleaner told me, "Dean rubs me the wrong way. He is too short to be president."

There is speculation that he really will keep going and going like the Energizer Bunny, with holes in the soles of his black penny loafers, all the way to the convention. He would lose his staff and press corps and just go it alone on commercial flights, Dennis Kucinich–style. His staff concedes that they really have no idea how long their boss is going to drag this out. How far can he get on fantasy fumes?

"The entire race has come down to this: We must win Wisconsin," Dean wrote in an e-mail to his followers. He went on to beg for $50 contributions. "Anything less will put us out of this race." He told reporters, "The people of Wisconsin should have some say in who the Democratic nominee should be." You are leaving the fate of your entire campaign in the hands of the cheeseheads? But when he arrived in Wisconsin, he changed his mind about the whole "If I don't win Wisconsin, the campaign is over" thing. He says he never read the e-mail that went out to his supporters claiming that he would drop out if he lost Wisconsin and now he is saying that he will stay in the race regardless, even though the unions are taking back their endorsements and jumping in bed with John Kerry.

So now, every day the only questions the reporters are asking him are "Are you going to drop out?" "When are you going to drop out?" "Why haven't you dropped out yet?" Still, Howard Dean has more press on his deathwatch than Gephardt and Lieberman combined ever had covering their entire campaigns.

These days the former front-runner can be found doing things like dropping in on an eighth-grade science class to teach them about dog pee. "Which has more bacteria: dog pee or river water?" he asked the class. Then he went on to tell them, "I do not recommend drinking urine, but if you drink water straight from the river you have a better chance of getting an infection than if you drink urine." How the mighty have fallen.

In every race you need a Howard Dean, the sacrificial lamb who takes all of the risks. He got out there and said everything that the Democrats should have been saying all along, and they all stole his script. If he wants to stay relevant, he'll get out soon and take credit for rewriting the nominee's stump speech. But those who have been with him for some time now have no idea what he will do. People who work for him are saying that they hope he drops out soon so that their résumés will still be worth something. The longer he drags it out, the more embarrassed they will be to say they worked for him. All along he has said that this movement was not about him, now some staffers worry he may be "so selfish that he will turn this movement into a joke. If he stays in, he will become a punch line." Another staffer worried, "The more isolated he gets, the more he will believe he's right and the whole world is wrong."

His own press corps really seems to have no idea what he will do. So in the closing week, those who spent the past six months with the man don't know what he is all about. This is a problem. If the people paid to study you don't understand you, contradictions are bound to come out in their coverage. As the media obsess over trying to figure Howard out, a *Newsweek* reporter suggests, "Someone should write a story: The Many Personalities of Howard Dean."

A newspaper reporter who has been covering Dean all along admitted, "I still don't have any idea who this guy is. I am sure he is a great guy, but the view I saw of him I never could like." A network producer disagreed: "He's funny, you just never saw it." She pointed to the time on the airplane when he taught them to use the Dean playing cards (on sale now at reduced prices in all the primary states) to play the card game "Oh Hell" and swore out loud, grabbed the video camera and recorded one of the reporters sleeping, sang a Kenny Rogers song, and wore a Wisconsin cheesehead.

Ironically, George Bush did all of those things on his plane in 2000. As a television producer, I was entertained by George in those instances. They made good television, but I am not so sure the *New York*

Times reporter found W. all that amusing. This is the conflict between kids with camcorders and "the paper of record." More important, we all had our own experience with the same man. Many times things were printed in the *New York Times* that I did not see: The reporter had his own conversations in the front of the plane that I was not privy to. I had my own experience with George Bush; other reporters had theirs.

George Bush acted differently when he was sitting next to me than he did when he was sitting next to the *Times* reporters. When you are sitting in a long narrow tube like an airplane, you can't hear what is being said in the front of the plane and you have no idea what's going on in the back of the plane. All you know is what you see in your row; your row is your reality.

When my Bush movie came out, other journalists and the president's spin men were asked for their opinions about it. But what they thought was irrelevant because they were not there. The only opinions that mattered to me were those of the president and the members of the press corps who were sitting right next to me all year (who were featured in the film). My point is that on the presidential campaign, everyone has a different experience, and there is one journalist per million media consumers, what each press person sees and how they see it matters because in the morning, the reader or viewer will shape his or her opinion of the candidate from the way the person on the plane presents what they saw of that candidate.

Deanies who blame the media for his demise will be satisfied to hear that some of the journalists covering the Dean campaign blamed the *New York Times* for setting an adversarial tone with the candidate. They accused the *Times* reporter of making Dean defensive and brittle; they blamed her for ruining the dynamic of the press bus: "He closed up like an oyster whenever she opened her mouth" and "She drilled him without foreplay; she never let him do small talk." But isn't that what she is paid to do?

Some of the television producers on board admitted that they even tried to help their guy out. A network producer admitted, "When TV people told the campaign that they should make Dean more accessible, show the lighter side, the campaign ignored the advice." So all you saw on TV were those awkward moments, like the time he was standing close to a group of really cute kids and his press person had to instruct him to go play with the toddlers.

Or the time a school kid asked the governor, "Why are you at our school?" and he told the little kid he was there because someone put it on his schedule and he doesn't really have control over his own schedule. The superintendent had to step in and say something to make the kid think Dean cared about where he was.

Or that time on the eve of the Iowa caucus when he went all the way to Georgia to see President Jimmy Carter and he walked out of the meeting and said nothing to acknowledge the fact that President Carter was standing right next to him. All that came out of his mouth was, "Hey guys, new Zogby poll out tonight."

These are just a few little anecdotes that reveal that running for president requires a set of people skills that Howard Dean does not have. He became a caricature of himself and all we ever saw was that caricature. Which is why in the last week of the campaign, the Deanies were still passing out videocassette tapes of the Diane Sawyer interview; that was the only time he looked human on national television.

The reporter I admire most, Candy Crowley from CNN, has this take: "Here's a guy that is not an angry person, but he is different in person than he appears on TV. The little box blows things up, very, very big. I think all these candidates are different when they get up on stage. Any connection between who these people are and what you see on the TV is accidental because the camera changes things."

Last night I sat next to a reporter from Vermont who told me that he knows Howard Dean well, he has covered him for many years. He admitted that he was totally shocked by the angry, anti-Bush persona Dean adopted for the campaign because privately that is not who he is. He told me stories that proved that the governor is really a decent man. Really? Now you tell me.

This demonstrates an important lesson about presidential politics. If you want to run for president, you have to play a character. If you are not comfortable with that and you want to be principled and honest to yourself, don't run for president. More important, if we want to change the system, first we have to change TV!

Everyone Loves Kerry

Las Vegas, Nevada
FEBRUARY 14, 2004

"CAN YOU THINK of anything better than spending Valentine's Day in Las Vegas with me and my entire press corps?" Senator Kerry joked. "This is the life." (The closest I came to romance was getting a rose from the TSA agent after the full-frontal security pat-down.) We are here in Sin City for the Nevada caucus and everyone loves John Kerry.

Ever since he won the New Hampshire primary, people just want to touch him. Two months ago, he was struggling to get shoppers to shake his hand in the supermarket parking lot; today, in a different parking lot, people of all ages are throwing themselves at him. And they are bringing him gifts! On the rope line, strangers have been handing him everything from tennis balls to chicken burritos.

People are now placing all of their faith in John Kerry. They are projecting superpowers onto him. Everyone needs a Superman. This is what happens when you win: Overnight, people start to see you as an action figure.

This morning there was full-blown hysteria when the senator dropped by a caucus location to shake hands with supporters outside. It was a mosh pit of young screaming girls, big burly union guys, and wrinkly old women all trying to get a piece of him. There was a lot of pushing and shouting as a pack of seemingly sweet housewives bum-rushed the senator and nearly knocked him over. One woman in leopard pants and stiletto heels screaming "Mr. President!" almost trampled an elderly man and his grandson just to put her hand on John Kerry's back.

In an attempt to control the mob scene, the mean and macho union guys took it upon themselves to do security. A tough-looking guy chewing on a toothpick stood guard near Kerry, shoving people. "Someone is going to get the shit kicked out of them if they don't back it up." Not knowing anything about crowd control, he was obviously just making matters worse.

A fight broke out when one of the supersized wannabe security agents started pushing a female photographer, threatening her, "I can take care of you." Another macho man was bullying the other photojournalists, telling them their traveling press corps credentials were "no good here." The campaign staffers were being told that they were not allowed through the human chain of volunteer union firefighters surrounding the senator. "I am in charge here and you ain't going anywhere near him."

In fear of getting run over like you would if you went running with the bulls, I removed myself from the epicenter of the Kerry swarm and talked to a young lady wearing a T-shirt that she had made in honor of Valentine's Day: MY HEART BELONGS TO JOHN EDWARDS. She said she came to support John Edwards because "he is so dreamy." (When the results came in we found out that looks alone were not enough. Edwards got only 10 percent of the caucus-goers' support.)

Walking by a small group of Dean supporters, a converted Kerryite turned to her friend and asked, "What did you ever see in him?" Her friend reminded her, "He was against the war." Oh yeah, the war. Remember the war and how angry people were about it? Today it seems the war is to voters what Valentine's Day is to single people. It only mattered until they settled down; once they got a man, they didn't seem to care about it anymore.

A middle-aged man with a camcorder looking for some action asked me for an interview. When I suspiciously asked him if he was shooting for the GOP, he explained that he shoots porn. Why would a porn producer be shooting video of John Kerry? He explained, "Because under Clinton, the porn industry had no problems, but with Bush in office, the porn industry is under attack." He gave his endorsement on behalf of his industry. "Porn producers love John Kerry."

As Kerry tried to escape, a woman tossed her newborn baby through the open window of his moving vehicle. Kerry stopped the car and got out to return the child to its owner, admitting that he was really scared for the child. It is time to bring in the Secret Service.

John Kerry will not have a private moment between now and November. Everywhere he goes he will have a procession of camera crews. It is unclear whether he has gotten used to that fact. Just this morning he walked out of the hotel and stood next to a tree by himself and tried to do a chin-up on the branch. Instantly all the photographers sitting on the bus nearby started snapping shots. He strolled off alone to get some fresh air, and when he turned around, his press corps was there. Now that he is almost the nominee, if he takes one step, the cameras follow. So there we were, all standing on the lawn taking pictures and video of a man alone taking a stroll in the outdoors. Knowing how to capitalize on the moment, Kerry shouted to his aide, "Wade, I need a football," and made the motions of tossing a football. But the football never appeared, so Kerry was stuck taking questions.

The photographers like John Kerry and John Kerry likes having his photo taken. He understands the power of the images and he exploits the photographers shamelessly. He even calls out to them, "Hey guys, the photo is over here." He is good at creating moments for the camera and he knows what a videoworthy moment looks like: having an impromptu snowball fight (he had dozens in New Hampshire), doing a chin-up on a tree, or tossing a football. My really smart and principled friend Thaddeus said the moment he decided to vote for Kerry was when he saw him tossing a football on TV. At that moment he thought to himself, "Kerry couldn't be all that bad." How could you not see through that? How can you look at that image without imagining the absurdity of a pack of accomplished journalists standing on the tarmac analyzing how an adult man throws a football?

A cynic would say that everything Kerry does is just for the cameras, like taking a walk alone (knowing that the photographers will follow) so the image that gets out there is Kerry all alone, not being overhandled. His handlers are more than accommodating to the cameramen. They promise things like "I am going to set that up for you," strangely blurring the line between helping and staging.

Like this afternoon, when a staffer came back on the airplane and announced, "We have a photo for you. The senator is going to be looking out the window." The photographers grabbed their cameras and ran up to the front of the plane. They snapped their photographs and came back smiling. Meanwhile, the reporters complained that it is unfair that they are not welcome to participate in the photo opportunity. But what do you need them for? Let's face it, not everyone reads the paper, but everybody looks at the pictures.

Whose idea was it to call the cameras in for a shot of the senator looking out the window? Maybe it was Kerry's, or maybe it was Bob Shrum's. Come to think of it, it looked awfully like one of those JFK-style portraits, the senator staring out into the sunset. When I watch these pictures being made, it makes me wonder if any of the pictures that we have ever seen of a politician are real, not just a setup. Probably not.

Sitting on the Kerry plane watching the photographers shoot photos of him rolling oranges down the aisle, I am reminded of 2000, when George W. did the exact same thing. Been here and done this. Four years have gone by and they can't come up with a new trick? Campaigns are so unoriginal; there is no institutional memory.

It is strange how everything looks so different when you are inside the bubble. For example, in the outside world, or at least in the outside political universe, everyone is gossiping about the latest rumor that threatens to destroy this campaign. But you would never know it in here.

Yesterday, Friday the thirteenth, the entire day was consumed with talk of the Drudge Report and a British tabloid story about a mysterious woman who allegedly had something to do with John Kerry. Don Imus asked Kerry about the rumor on the radio and he said, "There is nothing to it." Then the photo op of Kerry's departure was canceled. On the plane, everyone circled around to eavesdrop as the senator spoke with two of his embeds about how he really needs to get back on his exercise routine. But there was no mention of the scandal. He got off the plane in below-zero degrees in Wisconsin and the pack was there to watch (just in case), but no one asked him anything. The million-dollar question all day was, "Who is going to be the first to bring it up?"

You can make the case for and against asking Kerry about the rumor. On the one hand, it is a sleazy unsubstantiated rumor. The man is running for president of the United States, he should not have to answer to every piece of gossip that comes off some wacky Web site.

On the other hand, this did not come off just any Web site. This is the *Drudge Report;* it has credibility because it broke the Monica Lewinsky story. If you don't ask about it, Drudge can say that the mainstream media are afraid to touch the story because they don't want to jeopardize their access. What good is access if you don't use it? Just ask the question, let him deny it, and move on. For God's sake, when you are running for president, it goes with the territory.

While reporters played with their PDAs to check in on the latest gossip and checked the *Drudge Report* on their laptops at the filing center and whispered among themselves, there was no actual drama inside the bubble because no one was going to bring it up with Kerry. Eventually, a reporter did ask him in a pool-only situation that had no cameras and the whole thing went away.

He denied it; the woman denied it. Who cares? We live in a media society that believes that you are innocent until the press can come up with enough proof to convict you. "If it ever comes up again," a reporter joked, "all he should say is, 'Hey look, I am campaigning with Ted Kennedy, at least I didn't kill my girlfriend.'" Though in poor taste, this is a clear example of how reporters really feel about politicians.

Howard's End

IN THE FINAL DAYS on the Dean bus, as his press corps saw their White House dreams going down the drain, some of them seemed to be stuck in the denial stage. All I seemed to hear was Kerry-bashing, including "How can Kerry be the nominee, he has not been vetted?" (not true: The *Boston Globe* has probed every Kerry cavity) and "I heard he hasn't had a media avail all week; his press corps is giving him a free pass" and "What a bunch of pansies" and "Hey look, it's Botox One" (pointing at Kerry's much bigger plane). They said things to newcomers like "You are only here for the funeral" and "You haven't been out in two weeks. What do you know?"

Riding on their press bus that said "Lamers" on the side, they had their own inside jokes and riffs that people who have been covering a candidate too long always have. Like their candidate, some of them were paranoid about the media. One young network producer was so paranoid that I would shoot him wearing his cheesehead that he announced, "Cheeseheads on, cameras off. I am talking to you." I was amused that he thought I would waste my film on his little antics, as if America really wants to watch him in his cheesehead.

Now all Dean sees are empty tarmacs. The screaming kids are all gone. When I asked the reporter who has been covering this campaign the longest, Carl Cameron of Fox News, where all the young loud Dean lovers went, he said, "They've grown up into the serious establishment voters."

At a town hall meeting in Wisconsin, a supporter said to the governor, "What I am having trouble with is, what happened to the tone? You have almost overmoderated. You don't wear that ugly gray suit anymore. You've got a movement going on here. Have you figured out where it's going?"

Dean told the man, "We are going to change this country one way or the other . . . We were the front-runner, the insider Washington folks were very uncomfortable with that and did a lot of things that weren't helpful. Reform and change is not easy—there are going to be enormous institutional powers against change, powers of Congress, powers of establishment media, it's not in their interest to have change. I already publicly said we ought to re-regulate the media—break up the enormous conglomerations."

On the Sunday before the Wisconsin primary all there was left to do was pray. Dean went to a black church in Milwaukee (again with the all-white press) and sang along, "Help me, Jesus." That night, as Dean was getting into the elevator, Steve Elmendorf (who was Gephardt's right-hand man and now works for Kerry) got in and introduced himself. It seemed funny that Dean did not know who he was. This is one of those Washington insiders who helped engineer Dean's demise. Riding along with the man who plotted to destroy him, Dean mused aloud, "This is such an incestuous business."

On his last day, Dean went to visit a root-beer plant and bought boxes of his new favorite drink to take home with him. His press corps, who are now used to getting booed at the events, wore the T-shirts they had made (most traveling press corps do this at the end). One of the funnier network producers suggested the shirt should read, HOWARD DEAN SPENT $50 MILLION AND ALL I GOT WAS THIS CRAPPY T-SHIRT, but the group thought that would have been in poor taste. Instead they went with ESTABLISHMENT MEDIA on the front and WE HAVE THE POWER, DEAN PRESS CORPS 2004 on the back. When they presented a T-shirt to the governor, the woman who ordered them said she did so on the Internet; Dean mused, "The establishment media trumped the Internet, but not for long." He seemed to appreciate the T-shirts because he knew that the twenty- and thirty-year-old press people sitting on the bus do not have that much influence in the media hierarchy. Perhaps in the studios and the bureaus there was a sinister plot to take the candidate down, but these guys and gals could not be blamed. He even said, "You have to remember, a lot of what goes wrong in the press is not the reporters' fault. They have editors that are forcing them to write things that may be different than what actually went on."

When we arrived in Burlington at two in the morning the Deanies all came and cheered for Howard as he carried his own bags (and lots of cases of root beer) off the plane. He gave out some hugs and high-fives, loaded the root beer into a small car, and pulled out. It was painful to watch those diehards who believed that they could change the system standing on the tarmac in tears.

With the fall of the antiestablishment hero, a great sigh of relief can be heard over the Beltway. As everyone tries to come up with an original explanation for what really happened to Howard Dean, we all know deep down how it went. Just like the hula hoop or the latest fad diet, we had our fun with him and then spit him out. Just like all those who came before him: John McCain, Ed Muskie, Jerry Brown, Gary Hart, and all the other renegades who never made it to the nomination.

There are so many factors that contributed to this story line: Howard was not media savvy, he did not have enough foreign policy experience, he put too much faith in young voters, he did not come off as likable, everyone knew what he was against but no one ever really knew what he was for. And the list goes on. At heart, he was not a good politician and he wasn't ready for the world stage.

But his supporters blame only the media. A Deanie at his concession speech explained, "It was a media lynching. Dean said things that the media didn't like, and this was the media's revenge. They built him up so they felt like they could tear him down." The lesson that many Deanies are taking from this experience is: Don't believe most of what you read in the newspapers or magazines or what you see on TV, because this time around most of them got it all wrong.

Dean explains his own loss by saying that it was a direct result of his criticism of the media monopolies. I'm sure that didn't help, but if he truly believes that, he is shirking his own responsibilities. He did not run a good campaign. Howard Dean failed because he was a real person and real people make crappy candidates. He was not averse to speaking his mind or changing his opinion on an issue. He was willing to say things that nobody else was, and in the end, voters were convinced that was a detriment.

Whether you see this as a media conspiracy or a Greek tragedy of a flawed candidate who brought on his own demise, his is a classic tale of a Washington outsider who inspired the status quo to conspire against him. Every four years, a candidate becomes a hit by selling himself as the outsider. But Washington does not like outsiders and outsiders don't like Washington. We saw this in the 2000 Republican primaries. Both John McCain, the chairman of the Senate Foreign Relations Committee, and George Bush, the son of a president, marketed themselves as outsiders. Like Dean, McCain did a remarkable job of soliciting contributions on the Internet, but in the end, they both got their unjust desserts handed to them on a plate by the Washington establishment.

If you deconstruct the Dean campaign you will probably learn everything there is to know about how the media work, how Washington works, and how the game of presidential elections is played. If you could break that code, you might just understand American politics.

Here is what we know for sure: In 2004 we learned that you are not allowed to leave your wife at home. You are not allowed to show any real emotion, and you are not allowed to say how you really feel about a sensitive issue (race, war, corporations that run Washington, the corporate media), because telling the truth is a liability in American politics.

Looking back at how Dean had everything going for him: He was ahead in the polls, he had the most money, he got all the right endorsements, he attracted all of the media's attention. But all of that meant nothing when it came down to how you win elections: You need votes. Believe it or not, the voters still matter (at least in a few small states).

Dean took the Internet to the next level, but before we decide if it is a tool that will transform democracy, someone has to use it to actually win. Maybe some day. But with the new spine that Howard Dean gave John Kerry, the Democrats have a better shot at the White House.

As Howard Dean prepares to keep working to change the system, the one lesson he seems to have learned is: The only way to fix the system is to work within it, not against it—you can effect more change on the inside than you can on the outside.

What Howard Dean Taught Me

After dropping out, here is what Dean had to say about the media:

> "The press has enormous problems in this country. There's enormous pressure in the newsroom to, as they said in Britain about the Iraq stuff, sex up the news. And that's what they do. Editors put pressure on reporters, reporters don't often get to write the stories they want. If editors don't like the slant of the story, they change it."

> "I think journalism is an institution that's in deep, deep trouble because it's lost its moorings. The work product is deeply flawed, and that's got to be fixed, and unfortunately that's one thing I can't fix. But it's a deeply flawed institution. I think that American democracy is suffering because the press has lost its way."

> "The *New York Times* did do some really bad things by putting stuff in the paper that they knew wasn't accurate and they sort of backed down when we pushed them a little bit, but it got in there anyway. And there were other papers, of course, that did the same thing. And that is very disappointing. Most people under thirty-five don't think the *New York Times* has any more credibility than whatever they want to read on the Internet. And in the long run, that's a much bigger problem for the *New York Times* than it is for people like me."

> "I grew up revering the *New York Times* and I don't anymore."

Seven Women Discover the Meaning of the Word "Propaganda"

Hempstead, New York
FEBRUARY 21, 2004

IN 1937, ED FILENE, the man who became famous for selling discount clothes out of his Basement, formed the Institute for Propaganda Analysis to educate Americans about propaganda. This organization is famous for identifying the seven key devices used in propaganda: name-calling (using bad names to demonize people), testimonials (using celebrities to endorse you), card stacking (using the truth conveniently in favor of your idea), glittering generality (using words that people like to get them to accept your idea), bandwagon (using the rationale "Everyone is doing it"), plain folks (using language to appear "of the people"), and transfer (using a respected institution to carry over its authority in favor of your idea). When reviewing the transcripts of interviews conducted with women of all ages at the Edwards rally in Hempstead, New York, I discovered that seven of them identified traces of propaganda in Edwards's speech. They came to participate in democracy; they left with an education about how the media work.

AP: You came here interested and wanting to learn more about the candidate, but you're leaving feeling what?

WOMAN #1: As lost as when I showed up. I came to find out more about the candidate and you show up and you still can't find anything out because you can't see—you're all the way in the back. It's all for the media, everything about the campaign is media. It's about getting that one sound bite on television. All the guy has to say is "Bush is bad, he is hurting our economy, cheating our future, damaging our country, he is not a uniter, he's a divider" [Technique #1: name-calling] and the crowd goes nuts.

AP: Do you feel like a prop?

WOMAN #1: When you show up, the cameras are in the way, he's so far away you can't even see him. I just feel like a second-class citizen, they don't really care about us. "Yeah, it's great that you're here, but we're going to shove you behind the press, because they're more important and I need to get the media, the media are number one." It's unfortunate, but that's just the culture we live in now. It's a media-driven society. It's not fair that they treat the media so much better than the rest of us. We are the people who came to hear you and want to know your views and if you have us behind the press, you're just treating us like we're not even here and that's not cool. The TV people have way too much power.

AP: Why didn't you just stay home and watch it on TV?

WOMAN #1: They're not going to show a complete presentation on television. They'll show a couple sound bites and that's not a good portrayal of who the candidate actually is.

AP: But you could watch C-SPAN.

WOMAN #1: C-SPAN is so boring. It's like watching the surveillance video at the mall.

AP: Are you getting disillusioned by the process here?

WOMAN #1: I think I was disillusioned to begin with and this was hope to find out that there are real candidates and maybe to find out something new, and my worst hopes are right there. I haven't been inspired by the political system at all and I'm a young voter. I know it's staged and you only hear thirty seconds of what someone has to say. I was hoping to hear a little bit more and I realized that they just pick the best thirty seconds—so it's not even worth coming here to show up. It's become a platform for the media, nothing but a springboard for the candidates to get noticed in the media for free.

AP: How was the experience live and in person?

WOMAN #2: Not what I expected . . . Because I'm stuck in the back, you can't even see the candidate, you don't even know what he looks like.

AP: Do you blame the candidate or the media?

WOMAN #2: It's a partnership. They are definitely working hand-in-hand. The media benefits by getting this candidate on TV, gets better ratings, and the politician gets free media, free publicity. I think politicians have learned how to manipulate the media for what they need, and it works both ways. If a candidate didn't use the media to their advantage, they wouldn't be elected. So, it's a lose-lose situation. One hand washes the other. I think it's interesting, it's a statistical fact that the taller candidate always wins the presidential election. So, I think we should just measure everybody up, see who's taller, and stop wasting millions of dollars on campaign funds and watching it on television for six months unnecessarily . . . Better yet, let's have a battle of the celebrities, let them fight it out, because all the candidates do is name-drop, like Edwards says, "My friend Glenn Close is with me 'cause she endorses my campaign" [Technique #2: testimonial].

AP: What's it like being here at an actual event?

WOMAN #3: I'm just trying to listen. It's really hard because you really can't see what's going on. You never know, everything's just made up nowadays. It is kind of frustrating. I really want it to be more personal. I really want to know what he has to say, not just what he's reading. Not what his speechmaker has made for him to say. But really what he feels in his heart. You know all of us are out here being optimistic that maybe something will be true. We keep optimistic, but a lot of times it doesn't work because you know that all that the candidate is going to tell you is what is good for him. He says something in his speech about how he's been fighting this fight his whole life, for twenty years he was winning cases in a courtroom. He says, "I beat them and I beat them again." He never says he lost a case. I am sure in that twenty years he must have lost a case, but he's never going to tell us about that one [Technique #3: card stacking].

AP: Now that you've been to your first political function, give me a report.

WOMAN #4: He's at a college campus, you'd think he would kind of touch more on the issues that affect us. At least, acknowledge our presence. It's early on a Saturday morning and he's just doing his speech and he doesn't really care, and he left the stage right afterwards and he's got the music and the banners and it was just kind of dull, I thought. Being behind the press was really irritating. What's more important to you, the press or the people who are going to vote for you?

AP: So, you're saying that this presidential candidate came to town and just told you what you wanted to hear.

WOMAN #4: Exactly, and that isn't what I wanted to hear. You know, I wanted details. And I wanted him to treat us a lot better. He stuck us behind the press and I couldn't see him. I saw his hand once. I think if he really wants to get my vote, he needs to treat us with respect and he needs to not treat me like I'm so malleable. Just don't tell me what you think I want to hear. Tell me what you really think because that's what I want to hear. Most of what he had to say was kind of "glittering generality" [Technique #4]. It was all things we had heard before, like freedom and democracy; he used all these catch phrases and grazed over all the issues, but he didn't really get to the heart of any of them. I wanted to scream out "Yes, we all know that, what are you going to do about it?"

WOMAN #5: You know, the fact that I was behind all the cameras just really put a bad taste in my mouth from the beginning. And the fact that he says something in his speech about the press being in the back of the room, when it was actually the press are in front and the people are in the back of the room. Don't lie to the camera, people know. People know it's press right there in front of you. It gave me a bad idea of him as a person.

AP: Don't you think all of the candidates do it?

WOMAN #5: Well, they shouldn't. I don't care if everybody does it, they shouldn't do it . . . I went to bed at three and I woke up at eight. And he spoke for thirty minutes. If he's running for president, he better have more to say than that. Also, he was two-dimensional. Everybody is two-dimensional. He's no different from anybody else, and that annoyed me. Because I was really hoping for somebody to jump out at me, but he didn't . . . He didn't tell me anything that I needed to know, he just bragged about how all these new people are coming out to see him and all these young people are excited about his campaign [Technique #5: bandwagon].

AP: Tell me about your whole experience.

WOMAN #6: I'm feeling like he wasn't even talking to me, he was talking to the cameras. And he wasn't even being real to the cameras. Like, at least be honest. But he wasn't, he was being completely two-dimensional. I would rather have somebody who I think was actually going to represent the American people. And not the American media, you know. I feel like he's just playing to the media and there's no substance.

AP: Don't you think John Kerry plays to media?

WOMAN #6: Okay, but they shouldn't play to the media. They should talk to the people, don't talk to the cameras. Don't act like you're talking to me if you're not. He said something about finding out what goes on in real people's lives, and as soon as he said that I was like, that's bull. He's not. He can't find out what's going on in real people's lives if he comes to a university on a Saturday morning and talks for thirty minutes and leaves again and the press is in front of you. How is he finding out what's going on in real people's lives? He gives just a general speech and then he leaves. We deserve more than a stump speech. All he had to say was that he's the son of a millworker, just to make us think that he's just like one of us [Technique #6: plain folks], but he is a millionaire trial lawyer now!

AP: So, you're a real live human voter who came to see a presidential candidate. What is it like?

WOMAN #7: Basically, what they do is they put all the people in like cattle and they squeeze them in to make it look really busy and crammed and it looks like there's hundreds of people there cheering for Edwards and the cameras are right behind. And it's set up. It's like a little stage with the American flag in the background trying to get as much of the American constituency interested through the television. When you walk in they are blasting the patriotic music and the first thing you see is the hugest flag I've ever seen. The whole scene is set up to make us feel patriotic and have warm and fuzzy feelings that will make us feel good about John Edwards [Technique #7: transfer].

John Versus John

San Francisco
FEBRUARY 26, 2004

AS THE CROWD CHANTED "We want John, we want John," I couldn't help but ask, "Which one?" To which John Edwards lashed out, "You are so obnoxious." It seemed like a perfectly good question now that the race is down to John Edwards versus John Kerry. You have to hand it to both Johns; the two who said the least went the farthest.

"We call this the No News Express," a member of the Edwards press corps explained to the newest reporter to join. "You will find your news needs will not be met here." Those are not the only needs that will go unmet. Ever since I decided to start following John Edwards again, after completely giving up on him back in New Hampshire, I have been starving. The only sign of food today was when the ABC off-air reporter offered to share her Tic Tacs; that was all she could scrounge up for lunch. Still, she was not complaining.

Just like dog owners who start looking like their pets, the traveling press corps eventually start to look like their candidates after being around them long enough. The Edwards press corps is the nicest and best-looking; everyone is friendly and well-behaved (even though the campaign is making it impossible for them to do their jobs). There are no schedules, credentials, or meals provided. Even if he ever did make news (which is highly unlikely), there is no time to file stories and no Internet connections to do so. We are lucky if we get a hotel room. The other day the campaign didn't book rooms and all day the reporters were worried about where they were going to sleep that night.

The Edwards campaign is operating on a shoestring. Since the race has gone nationwide, they had to ditch that überbus. The staff is down to the bare bones and the events are poorly advanced (by volunteers). Luckily, due to the large contingency of traveling press (thirty-two) now, they have upgraded to a press bus. Even though the other night we were riding in a school bus, it felt like first class compared to the dingy little van they were using in New Hampshire with a teenage volunteer driver with no local knowledge or sense of direction, who hit a moose on the road.

Over at Kerry Inc., the organization is run by experienced professionals. "I spent a month on the Kerry bus and there were no less than six meals a day," one reporter reported. There is a lot of talk about the difference between the campaigns, but usually the talk is focused around what kind of food they are serving or what disease the press corps is sharing (a mysterious eye infection has been making its way around the Kerry plane).

Kerry has the bigger plane, but Edwards has a mirrored airplane with '70s-style couches, Abba playing on the sound system, and a carpet in the pattern of a golf course (so that you can fantasize about your vacation when this is all over). Those who have served time on both campaigns claim the Kerry press corps has all the perks, while the Edwards press corps is slumming it (except for the Texas-shaped cookies we got in Houston with John Edwards's initials on them).

Ironically, the one thing that both press corps have in common is amazement that their candidate is still in the race. "Never has a candidate gone so far on such a thin résumé," a magazine reporter covering the Edwards campaign observed. "I thought this guy would drop out before New Hampshire," said a scribbler who covered all the candidates but is now stuck with Kerry. On the Edwards bus, a network producer kept saying the same thing on her cell phone that her colleague on the Kerry campaign was saying last week: "Can you believe we are still out here?" For some, these are the last two men expected to still be in this race.

Now that John Edwards is the only viable candidate left standing toe-to-toe with John Kerry, he is playing it safe. His campaign swings feel more like a victory lap around the country than a crusade to destroy the presumptive nominee. As Candy Crowley said on CNN, "Edwards's warm and fuzzy campaign has made him a hit, but all that sunshine has made it difficult for Edwards to rain on John Kerry's front-running campaign." As Edwards races back and forth to the Super Tuesday states that he hopes to win, huge crowds are coming out to hear him talk about the Two Americas.

There is only one problem. The voters are a little more intelligent than John Edwards thinks they are. "It was all mostly a 'well, duh' kind of speech. It sounded like he was reading a speech that I have seen in the movies," a college student in Hempstead, New York, complained. "If he's running for president, he better have more to say than that." Another college student in the crowd said, "When he talked about how racism was bad, of course racism is bad, that's all he said about it. He was like, 'When I was a kid, people were racist and it sucked.' No kidding." Another young woman in the crowd said, "I wasn't inspired to vote for him. He's saying, 'Well, I'm not gonna be the guy who makes enemies with the other candidate' and at the same time, you kind of want him to, because you want him to make the point, 'Why should I vote for you over the other guy?' " Her friend was also not impressed: "He does not deserve to be in the highest level of national politics."

Others in the crowd were more satisfied with their John Edwards experience. After getting his autograph, an older lady squealed, "We've got to frame it." Her husband reasoned, "Let's see if he wins first." Another woman marveled, "His speech sounded like a speech from the movies." (Again with this movie line. Why does everyone think that they have heard this speech before?) She continued, "He looks like a president, especially with those Secret Service agents all around him." The agents are the perfect prop, they make the entourage look legit.

The two Johns are the only two candidates who lasted long enough to get Secret Service protection, and by now they really need the structure to provide a way to get from point A to point B, without the mass chaos that you have with the twenty-three-year-olds running the show. You can just tell how much this son of a millworker loves having the Secret Service around him. The journalists are not as happy to have the men in black on their backs. Maybe it's because the agents are always barking out orders and searching us. The press agent explained that the reason they have to search us every time we get on and off the bus is in case we sneak off to see our "Lebanese cabdriver friend who hands you a machine gun." (Hearing this, the Lebanese cameraman from ABC in the front seat was not pleased.)

The Secret Service are not the only ones on board who are oversuspicious of the press. On the airplane, a campaign staffer hung up a bedsheet so that the reporters could not spy on the senator's activities in the front of the plane. In an attempt to look accessible, Edwards has press conferences on the airplane, but only right as the plane is taking off, to make sure they are as short as humanly possible. The last time he had one, the plane was physically lifting into the air as all of the drinks and snacks were flying off the tables. The senator was trying to stand up straight and hold on for dear life. A college kid on a democracy field trip observed, "He only talks to you guys in the time that the flight attendant has to teach you how to put on your seatbelts."

For those promised one-on-one interviews, the senator waits until the flight attendant makes the announcement that we are landing until he grants them, just to blatantly limit them. Yesterday he gave ABC News their exclusive interview right as the flight attendant announced that we were "making our final approach." After the fresh-faced correspondent asked a tough question (about Saudis buying the senator's house), he received an angry phone call from the campaign press secretary threatening his access. He held his own, but he has been getting the persona non grata treatment ever since.

John Edwards's in-flight press conference.

Every now and then the senator comes back on the plane to schmooze with reporters off the record. In the chitchat, he reveals that when he is on stage, he notices everything going on in the back of the room (which reporters were falling asleep and who was on their cell phone the whole time). Like a southern gossip, he tells us things we aren't supposed to know about other people. In his off-the-record mode, John Edwards tries to act natural, likable. Some find it totally phony; others who have not spent as much time around politicians think this is as real as a politician can be.

Without violating the rules of the secret society of journalism, which dictate that the public is not welcome to join the exclusive off-the-record club, the one thing I learned from John Edwards (without telling you anything John Edwards said off the record) is that if you want to succeed in presidential politics, you cannot take a stand. Senator Edwards made it perfectly clear that if he took a stand on certain issues, he was going to get burned and so is avoiding taking a position.

Take, for example, the biggest losing issue for the Democrats, gay marriage. On his swing through California, the Super Tuesday jackpot state, John Edwards had a scheduled trip to San Francisco at the same time that gays were lining up to get married and the gay marriage controversy was in full swing. "Doesn't he get credit for going into the belly of the beast?" his press person asked us (implying that it was an amazing act of courage to cross into gay town).

At his rally in the hotbed of political activism, on the day that Rosie O'Donnell was getting married at City Hall, he did not mention the words "gay marriage," "civil unions," or "equal rights"; he just talked about the Two Americas. In a town that loves to protest just about everyone for everything, no gay rights activists showed up to protest the senator's position against gay marriage (perhaps this is a sign of how irrelevant John Edwards actually is).

In his press conference, the *New York Times* reporter asked Senator Edwards why he "came to the epicenter of this big fight and did not mention gay marriage." He responded by explaining that he "came to spread my basic message of hope and opportunity for everybody." A local reporter followed up by asking how much gay marriage will be an issue once the courts get a hold of it. Edwards said, "If you look at what George Bush is doing, he is trying to make it a political issue, he is doing very little to help married couples."

Nick Lee from KRON-TV yelled out, "How do you define marriage?" But just as the rhythm of the questions got going and the senator was going to be forced to go on the record against the gays, some funny-looking European reporter yelled the loudest and changed the subject: "What do you say to those who say you don't have enough foreign policy experience?" The Euros are well-known for ruining American press conferences this way. Usually they ask totally Eurocentric questions.

Again Nick Lee tried: "How do you define marriage? It's a big issue in San Francisco!" Instead, the senator answered the question from a young student reporter from *Scholastic News:* "Where would I travel if I were president? Europe, because they are hungry to have that relationship be strong."

At this point Nick Lee was giggling and saying, "Who cares?" Then he tried out his question about the issue du jour one last time: "How do you define marriage?" The senator ignored him. As the senator walked away, reporters asked Lee if he really thought Edwards would answer him and he replied, "I hoped he would. It's a big issue in San Francisco; he owes San Francisco voters a definition. Politics is politics. I was not expecting any great revelation, but I tried. That's my job."

This country is heading for a showdown between the gays in the blue states and the evangelicals in the red states, and by forcing same-sex marriage into the spotlight in an election year, the mayor of San Francisco may turn out to be the Ralph Nader of the 2004 election. But John Edwards managed to get out of town without having to take a stand on the issue that the Republicans are using to try to destroy the Democrats this year.

Dodging the issue doesn't mean it will go away. Back on the bus, one of Edwards's staffers tried to explain the difference between sincerity and authenticity, admitting that his boss had one and not the other. But I can't remember which he was claiming Senator Edwards has. Personally, I think he is perverting the process by smiling his way through it all. How far does this guy think he is going to get if he doesn't face issues head-on?

After spending a week on the Edwards campaign, which cost HBO over $12,000, I still have not gotten one good scene that will ever make my movie. The difference between me and the other people here is that I don't have to write a story just to justify the cost of taking the trip (when their editors pay this much for them to travel, they have to come up with a story). So it is time once again to give up on John Edwards. On my last flight I told a member of the Edwards press corps that I was leaving because Edwards is a one-trick pony. He asked, "Really, what's the trick?" Talking about how much time and money I wasted here forced me to conclude, "Being here makes me wonder: What am I doing with my life?" To which my fellow journalist replied, "You think the man in the front of this plane isn't asking himself that right now?"

Candy Crowley Explains It All!

AP: How are all of the cameras affecting the candidates?

CROWLEY: I think what we've lost with the dominant presence of all the cameras is any sense of honesty or reality. If you are on all the time, you are on all the time. The candidates are aware of it. There's the un-

Edwards and the mob.

certainty principle in physics, and it's basically that "an experiment watched is an experiment changed." Well, we are watching this experiment, and it changes. The biggest way it changes is that I don't think we have gotten a single element of truth as to who these people are in this entire campaign.

AP: Have you ever seen an honest moment on any of these campaigns?

CROWLEY: I'm not saying these candidates are lying, what I'm saying is that the minute you turn the camera on, it's not truth anymore. It's a natural human instinct and it's a supernatural human instinct, when you're running for office. This lens makes everything so big that they become not who they are. It's never an honest moment when the cameras are on, and the cameras are on all the time. And I have not seen in this entire time an honest moment.

AP: You've covered so many of these campaigns, are you seeing anything different this year?

CROWLEY: I don't know if anything different is happening or if I'm seeing things differently. There's a nuance there. Is it because I have done so many of these and now I'm four years older? In the private moments, there's a lot less truth than there used to be. You know, I think the media takes a big blame for that, but it seems, and this has been going on for some time, candidates are just so ultimately packaged that it's difficult. You just wish the window would open up so that you would get a peek at their soul, but they're afraid to show us because they're afraid of what we do with it, so there's a standoff. And I think that over time that's gotten worse or over time I've become more reflective, one of the two.

AP: When I watch *The Daily Show* with Jon Stewart and they are making fun of reporters and this whole circus, I wonder, "Do you get it?"

CROWLEY: Yes, we get it. We understand that this is a part of the process. This is silliness, this is a part of a kind of elaborate show, but this isn't the totality of what we do. A lot of it is on the phone . . . It's not valueless to follow a candidate day by day because the candidate hits good days and the candidate has his really bad days, and watching how the campaign and the candidate deal with that gives you a measure of who the guy is . . .

There is a part of me that loves the theater of the absurd part, and then there's a part of me that thinks: This is democracy and it's about who has the best banner and who has the most words written. And I look and I see this and I think: This is our fault. This is television's fault because it's all about how it comes across right there. I have a love-hate relationship because it's silly, and I love to see it unfold, but then I think: This is democracy, and the leader of the Western world. Who did this? We did this. Television did this.

Who Has the Power?

Los Angeles
FEBRUARY 27, 2004

AS THE LAST MEN STANDING in the Democratic primaries assembled for yet another boring, old, nonnewsworthy debate at the University of Southern California in Los Angeles, something was very different. Everywhere you looked you could see Secret Service, bomb squad teams and their canines, LAPD, sheriffs, motorcycle cops, campus cops, and emergency vehicles of every make and model. Overhead, helicopters were circling; on the ground, the debate site was under lockdown. Standing guard at every entrance were teams of security men. Apparently some important people were inside.

For the first time since the beginning of this election, there was a feeling that these men we have been following are somebody (except for Sharpton and Kucinich; apparently their lives are not valuable, as they were not granted Secret Service protection). For the past eighty-two debates, you could walk in side-by-side with the candidate of your choice and escort him to his green room. Now that the Secret Service has been assigned, you are not allowed within fifteen feet of the protectee.

The press now has to go through the magnetometers and get sniffed down by the guard dogs just to get into the filing center to be around the other reporters. Outside the debate hall, politically active (young white) students protested—not the war, not for gay rights, not for the choice issue, but the fact that they couldn't get tickets to the debate on their campus.

Next to them, some African-American students were protesting a cross burning by students at a college in the area. Cross burnings in California—what year is this? When I asked the one white woman in the group what she was doing here she said, "I'm taking a racial integration course and my professor is giving us extra credit for this."

Nearby, a group of college students were performing some street theater without an audience. It was a mock debate, with one man dressed up like John Edwards, the other like John Kerry. A pretend moderator asked them each the same question and while the puppeteer hovering over them with a sign reading CORPORATE MEDIA was pulling their strings, one John would say, "The answer is six"; the other John would say, "No, John, the answer is half a dozen."

Waiting to see if they could sneak into the debate, a college hottie said to her friend, "Did you notice that the only two candidates that got better-looking during the race were Edwards and Kerry?" Her friend responded, "It's funny that the last two men in this race are the two richest and best-looking." The ladies then discussed what they would do if they were unsuccessful in their effort to woo the agents into letting them in. "I want to go to the Beverly Center to buy some Juicy Jeans."

After the ninety-minute debate in which no news was committed, I broke out of the security barricade and rushed across town to see some friends at the *Starsky and Hutch* premiere party. Seeing the string of stretch limos, the red carpet, the rugged handsome-looking doormen (there to enforce the dress code), all the groupies and autograph seekers standing behind the ropes waiting for someone famous to show up, you could tell that some really important people were inside. (The rope line is an institution of both political rallies and Hollywood functions—but here they have nice velvet ropes to keep the unbeautiful people away.)

Entering the party, all you could see were scantily clad beautiful women. On the bar and in cages around the room there were almost-nude dancers with glitter smeared all over their bodies, erotically gyrating to disco classics. Based on the looks of it, there was not one person in the room over forty. The horny '70s music was so loud you couldn't even talk (which wasn't such a bad thing; my suspicion was that those in this room had little to say).

Warner Bros. is spending millions of dollars to launch this movie with Owen Wilson and Ben Stiller as two hot streetwise characters with good hair firing jokes back and forth at each other with the help of a funny black pop star as their wingman. Sounds similar to, but much more fun than, the debate I was stuck watching.

Watching the guests swarming around to kiss the ring of Owen Wilson (who, if you can believe it, looked better in person than in the movies), it struck me how different it feels to be at an event with real celebrities. Owen Wilson had no security detail, but he is still the most powerful man in the world tonight. Every woman in the room wants to sleep with him. Hollywood beauty is so much more powerful than anything you can see on the campaign trail. Despite the Secret Service and the trappings of power, nobody really loves John Kerry. They like the idea of touching a powerful man, but they don't love him personally. And if he loses, they will never admit they ever liked him at all.

Standing there, watching my male friends gawk at the hot sexy Hollywood babes, I could not help but think about how different this whole scene would look in different lighting. What percentage of the Hollywood mystique is lighting? At campaign events the lights are so bright it makes everyone look drowned out. There is no glamour in presidential politics. Looking around the room, all I see is the challenge that John Kerry has ahead of him. This is what he has to compete with.

What would you rather watch: a Hollywood blockbuster or C-SPAN? My office at HBO is on the "porn floor"; while we screen footage of John Kerry's foreign policy address, we can hear the sounds that adults (who just met on the Internet) make. When the mailmen come to pick up or drop off packages, they inevitably end up taking a seat outside of the Pornacopia edit room and watching the editor work. They never sit outside my door to hear John Kerry talk about what he is going to do in Iraq. This is the reality of the television business: More people want to watch porn than a movie about the process of running for president. Despite what anyone says they prefer, the ratings prove that America watches more porn than news or "educational programming." Those porn producers keep the documentary unit in business.

Back on the dance floor, dancing between a topless model and a bottomless go-go dancer, actress Juliette Lewis was telling her admirers, "Ben is the greatest actor ever!" Get a grip, sister. Ben Stiller is goofy and entertaining, but he is no Marlon Brando.

After a while, watching this whole scene started to feel so hollow that it made me want to run back inside the campaign bubble. On the way out, we were each given a gift bag loaded with campy '70s items, including Breck shampoo, which I brought back to give to my friends in the Edwards traveling press corps, since John Edwards's nickname is "the Breck boy."

Back at the Century Plaza hotel bar, where the Kerry and Edwards press corps were mixing it up, a bunch of balding, disheveled, poorly dressed reporters with dandruff and credentials around their necks were talking about the ramifications of the gay marriage debate on this election. My people. Oh, how I missed them. Say what you will about these creatures that look like they just crawled out of the swamp. At least they talk about things that matter.

In the same hotel where Arnold had his election victory party just a few months ago, the bartender confessed that even though he is a Democrat he likes the idea of Arnold being governor because it is good for tourism. As Al Sharpton said, "A guy who couldn't even win an Oscar won the role of being California's governor." This is why Michael

Moore argues that the Democrats should just draft Oprah or Tom Hanks to run for president, because everyone loves a celebrity! Celebrity will always beat out knowledge and experience. But why would a celebrity want to tarnish his reputation with a campaign when we are living in a culture that values fame more than public service? We lingered at the bar late into the night debating: What is America's greatest export, democracy or Hollywood?

Super Sucky Tuesday

AFTER A YEAR AND A HALF of listening to these candidates every day and dreaming about them at night, it is finally Super Tuesday, the mother lode of all primaries, with 1,151 delegates up for grabs. Tonight there will be a nominee! It's time for all the votes to be counted. Or not. When I got to the polls, the non-English-speaking poll worker and her highly incompetent coworker told me (exactly what all those voters who got turned away in Florida were told four years ago) that my name was not on the voter rolls. After physically waking up another sleeping poll worker to prove that my name was on the list, I was granted permission to vote. Ah, Democracy.

It took a long time to get into the polling booth because the man ahead of me was taking so long in there. When he came out he apologized. "I didn't want to vote for any of them. They should have added the choice: none of the above."

Inside the booth, I was reunited with all of the names of my old friends from the road trip: Joe Lieberman, Dick Gephardt, Howard Dean . . . But on the day that California and New York got to weigh in, the race was already over. Who winnowed them down? A few small states? The media? By now we only had two options: Kerry or Edwards. The rest had given up. Seeing on the ballot the names of the candidates I liked who are no longer in the race gave me a feeling of helplessness. But seeing Howard Dean's name made it clear what is wrong with the system.

The only real loser in this primary is the Democratic Party. By front-loading their primary calendar so that they could have a nominee early in the year, they ended up denying their voters the right to be heard. We all walked in to vote with a bad taste in our mouths from the Florida recount, and Super Tuesday reminded us of this feeling that our votes don't matter. Again we feel cheated. Didn't the Democrats learn anything from the last presidential election? They had all of this time to mobilize their party; now Democrats are leaving the polls saying they felt cheated? The one thing that really bothers me about the Democrats is that if they were so angry after the 2000 post-Florida fiasco and they had four years to come up with a strategy to beat George Bush, why didn't they come up with a better plan than this?

Outside my polling place, a news organization doing an exit poll asked me whom I voted for. (Isn't that tacky? It's just like asking someone to kiss and tell.) When I told them, a young woman informed me, "He's no longer in the race" as if I hadn't heard. Then she asked, "What was the point of even coming down here?" Exactly. Go ask Democratic Party Chairman Terry McAuliffe that, would you?

"How could a Jew drop out of the race without getting to New York and California?" my Jewish friend Allen, who didn't vote for Joe Lieberman, asked. Another neighbor, who voted for Dean, complained, "My vote is meaningless, I am not a part of the process. It sucks. This is Super Sucky Tuesday. I feel like a vegetarian in the back of the airplane when the meals are being served. By the time the flight attendant got to me, all that was left was beef." This is not the feeling you want the people in your party to have.

Another angry Dean supporter declared, "I feel a deep outrage towards the Democrats because they let this happen." Then he went on a rant about how Katherine Harris should be hanged because she didn't allow the ballots to be counted. The one thing we all seemed to agree on today is that we believe our candidate did not get a fair shake. "We have no influence. By the time it got to us, it was over. This election was only a spectator sport," my friend Bob in California, who voted for Sharpton, said. "I did not vote for John Kerry, and that felt really good. Voting for Kerry is a wasted vote." The only neighbor I know who voted for Kerry said he did it because "I guess he's all we have left." When I asked him if he felt the process was unfair, he said, "Hey, this is not children's soccer, not everyone gets a trophy at the end of the season."

My neighbor who worked her heart out for Dean said, "I will not give money, I will not volunteer, I will not wear a button, but I will vote for Kerry in the general election because we have to beat Bush." Another Deaniac left the voting booth in tears, feeling the system didn't work. "Dean lost his place and there was no time to regain his footing because of the front-loaded schedule. It was unfair. The entire state of New Hampshire is the size of a big city. We give them way too much influence."

This election cycle proved that New Hampshire no longer deserves to hold the first primary. What do the voters of New Hampshire know? They had two years to size up the candidates and all they did was follow Iowa in lockstep. For two years I went to house parties and listened to Howard Dean win over supporters; the polls showed that he owned New Hampshire. Then, in some perverted form of peer pressure, when the moment of truth came, everyone just jumped on the Kerry bandwagon. They all chickened out and second-guessed their guy. So much for their independent reputation and that state motto "Live free or die." New Hampshire should be stripped of its title as first in the nation for ignoring their research and voting for the guy they never even paid attention to last year. In their keeping-up-with-the-Joneses mentality, they did not vote for what they wanted, they voted for what they thought someone else wanted.

Here are some suggestions for how to do it better next time. After we move the New Hampshire primary into the summer, we should make all of the primaries regional so that candidates don't have to fly across the country back and forth like chickens with their heads cut off.

Better yet, the results of all the primaries should be secret; we should not release them until all the states have voted (and we should ban the media exit polls). Most important, the candidates should not be allowed to drop out, they should be forced to stay in until the bitter end so that every state has their say.

Today, for the men at the Democratic Leadership Council who invented Super Tuesday to stop liberal candidates from rising too quickly, the system worked. But for those of us in New York (with our 236 delegates) and California (370 delegates), the process failed miserably. There is nothing I can do to stop my friends and neighbors from voting for Ralph Nader, or not voting at all. Everyone assumes that people don't vote because they are ignorant; the truth is many stay home out of protest.

An NYU student told her friend at the ATM machine, "I know that I should vote, but I don't know anything about those candidates. I'm not paying attention for a reason. I've got my priorities, I have a paper due today." A local in my coffee shop explained, "Why should I vote? Bush is going to win because the Democrats made him the strongest candidate in the race. The only winner of the Democratic primaries is George Bush because every time the candidates attacked each other they said things like, 'Bush is so strong, the only way to beat him is to get a general' or 'I am the only one who can beat him 'cause I am a conservative Democrat.' This reinforced the idea that Bush is so strong that none of them can beat him."

Those guys talking on TV all project that John Kerry will win the nomination with one of the lowest turnouts in history. At the end of this whole primary season, only 10 million voters will have participated in picking Kerry as the nominee. That is only 11 percent of the eligible electorate.

After I fulfilled my civic duty of voting today, I fulfilled my professional responsibility by jumping on the Amtrak and heading down to Washington for John Kerry's victory celebration. On the train, a man who voted for Kerry was telling his friend, "He may be an asshole, but now he's my asshole."

———————————

Here in D.C. at the Old Post Office just down the street from the Capitol, in the heart of the belly of the Beltway, was Howard Dean's worst nightmare: a solid inside Washington establishment crowd. Every working political journalist, many congressmen, and lobbyists gathered to watch the coronation of the compromise candidate.

One congressman there who endorsed Dean admitted, "There were three reasons why I didn't endorse Kerry: He puts people to sleep when he talks, he voted for the war and then regretted it, and he is not energizing the base like Dean did." Another who endorsed Clark confessed, "I didn't care who won, I just needed a horse." But maybe it was one of the warm-up acts who said it best. While we were waiting for Senator Kerry, one of his supporters was on stage praising him, but every time he said his name it came out as "Senator Scary."

How did we end up here, with this lukewarm candidate? The answer is simple. Only ten people tried out, and only half of them had a real shot. When you are running for president, you are not competing against every eligible American over the age of thirty-five; you only have to beat a handful of people who get into the race. This time around, one was too old, one was too young, one was too green, one did not have the fire in the belly, one was not liberal enough, and one was typecast as the angry liberal. John Kerry won the nomination because he was in the right place at the time Dean fell. It is that simple.

If you want more than that, you must remember that there were no great candidates this year, just as there were none four years ago. George Bush explained to me why he was going to be our president: Very few people actually wanted the job, and of those who did, none had the money, name recognition, and family connections. George Bush was not a great candidate in 2000 and John Kerry is not the dream candidate for 2004. There is no such thing as a great politician or a perfect candidate; they are all just men. As Ted Kennedy often says, "Don't let the perfect be the enemy of the good." In other words, picking a candidate is all about settling. It may be sloppy and imperfect, but that's democracy!

Top Ten Lessons Learned

After each of the candidates dropped out, I asked him what it takes to run for president. Let's recap some of the lessons they learned:

1. You never want to be the front-runner: It gives the media the license to pick apart your personal psychology and break down every word that comes out of your mouth. Eventually they will lose interest in you and go looking for a new story.

2. Timing is everything: You have to pace yourself. The burnout factor is high and he who gets the most sleep wins. As the French say, the Tour de France is won in bed.

3. Define yourself before the media define you. You need to differentiate yourself, but don't try to sell your "experience" because nobody is buying it. You need to have a good story. Everybody's looking for a Seabiscuit.

4. You need money. It would be good if you could mortgage your own home.

5. You need a good team. The first question you should ask yourself is, "Where am I going to get the staff?" The execution is the hardest part.

6. You have to be shameless. You have to do a lot of begging and it's not glamorous. It's like competing in a beauty contest but you never feel pretty, especially when you are eating off your lap.

7. You have to have the look. Kerry looked the most presidential. You have to be able to perform on TV. It was a victory for the guy who knew how to use the camera.

8. You have to be egoless. People like it when you say things like "I don't care about being president." Take your ego out of it and act like a populist. You have to not need it. Nobody likes desperation. They can smell it a mile away.

9. You have to be able to switch gears instantly: You go from making fund-raising calls, to television interviews, to giving your stump speech, and you never have time to sit alone in a room to think about your positions on the issues.

10. You've got to have skin thicker than steel. People say terrible things about you, most of which are not true, which makes running for president what Thomas Jefferson called "splendid misery."

And remember, no matter how many times the reporters promise, there is no such thing as off the record.

P.S. Even though none of them would admit it, personally, I think the hardest part about running for president is having to be nice all the time.

ACT III

"The press has let the country down. It's taken a very amoral stand, in that essential issues are often portrayed as simply one side says this and the other side says that. I think that Fox News and the Republican right have intimidated the press into an incredible self-consciousness about appearing objective and backed them into a corner of sorts where they have ceded some of their responsibility and righteous power."

—BRUCE SPRINGSTEEN, *ROLLING STONE,*
SEPTEMBER 22, 2004

The War of the Photo Ops

New York City
APRIL 1, 2004

SITTING ON A BUS watching a campaign every day is like watching a child. If you are there every day, nothing changes, but if you show up every few weeks you can notice the growth. A little distance is a good thing. From a distance, everything looks better than when you are up close. So for the next phase of this election, I have decided to start covering the race from my "home office," where my boyfriend does all the cooking and our friends come over to watch anything other than C-SPAN. Here we are having lots of spirited conversations with regular people (aka nonjournalists) and this is what I have found out: Nobody is excited about John Kerry right now (not even the lesbian barista in the Village coffee shop with the "Not my president" tattoo).

It is amazing how much more I have learned with my remote control than I did from being in all those remote locations. From the comfort of my purple couch, I get to see how the rest of the world is going to receive the biggest decision of John Kerry's week: to ski or snowboard, that is the question. Cascading down the slopes with a camera crew in tow made me wonder: Did he invite them to come along on his family vacation thinking that this would make a good photo opportunity, or did the networks insist on being there, making the candidate just another victim of the paparazzi? I asked the candidate this at the Unity Dinner and he defended his press corps, saying that they were not stalking him; he invited them to ride along. (Next thing you know they are going to be following him into the shower!)

You mean that you actually staged that shameless photo op? This is not the image that the world needs to see during wartime. It's a good thing we aren't at war. Or are we? Even though the newspaper headlines say that our soldiers are dying on a daily basis and Americans are

207

being beheaded in Iraq, we are coming up on the one-year anniversary of the day when Bush jumped around on an aircraft carrier with the MISSION ACCOMPLISHED sign behind him, declaring that the war was over.

So we aren't at war and John Kerry has gone snowboarding. Party on, dude! But then, why is George Bush visiting the troops? I saw him on CNN at a U.S. military base in Fort Campbell, Kentucky, eating in the mess hall and delivering a speech about how "the war continues" and we must act in "this time of war" and we have "to fight and win the war." The next day, in the East Room at the White House, the president gave a speech "reaffirming his resolve to war" and he visited the soldiers at Walter Reed. He's not a war president, but he's playing one on TV. And the performance you put on TV is the only one that counts.

That is why the psychological operations team of the U.S. Army staged that elaborate photo op of the statue of Saddam being toppled. With what was supposed to look like a jubilant crowd of Iraqis cheering them on, U.S. Marines smothered Saddam with an American flag and took him down. The truth is, that was a carefully orchestrated publicity stunt: The Marines sealed off the empty square across from the Palestine Hotel (where all the reporters stay), and there were only a few dozen Iraqis in attendance; all the rest were reporters. But that is how the war is won, with symbols.

George H. W. Bush said it best: "In politics, you have to remember that it isn't what is actually happening—it's the perception that's out there." Bush 41 remembers fondly the two defining moments in the 1988 campaign that sank his opponent: when Michael Dukakis played soldier, riding around in a tank with an oversized helmet on, and the Hide Your Daughter ad (aka the Willy Horton ad), which implied that Dukakis would open up all the American prisons to let dangerous black men out so they could rape all the white women. Was it true? Who cares; it worked.

In this game, who you are doesn't matter, it's who people think you are. It seems like voters are looking for someone who is a blank slate onto which they can project their own ideas about who the candidate is and what he stands for. The one thing Bush has going for him is that he has the myth on his side. He has the heroic story line of being the illegitimate president who rose to the occasion after 9/11 and made us all feel good with his "I can hear you, the rest of the world can hear you, and the people who knocked these buildings down will hear all of us soon" comment. He is having one propaganda victory after another.

On Sunday, the Bushmen don't go to church, they go on the talk show circuit to preach the Word of Rove. They are on a crusade to meet and beat the press. Tim Russert is their tool, they prepare for his show as if they are going on trial to defend their lives. By the time they get there they have rehearsed so much that they don't even need a moderator, they could grill themselves. As one of the administration media coaches put it, "We do more preparation for those shows than the cast of *Cats*."

By sending his little minions out to repeat a few catch phrases with Iraq and al Qaida in the same sentence, Bush has the circuit wired—he has managed to make people think that he is the "wartime president" and it's all going according to his master plan. But it is all a game of smoke and mirrors that affects people's perceptions. The Republicans are just much better at selling themselves. They know how to manufacture and slant information to their advantage; they are P.R. geniuses and the product they are selling is "freedom."

While Kerry was fulfilling all of his extreme sports fantasies, George Bush saw more military men than he did during his service in the Air National Guard (but we all know that wasn't too difficult). You have to hand it to those Republicans: They really know how to win the war of the images. At the end of the month, in the same week that Kerry had surgery on his arm, George Bush threw out the first pitch at the St. Louis Cardinals season opener. The Bush strategy is all about the pictures and a limited number of words. This president has had fewer press conferences than any president since 1913; even Nixon, the most famous press-hating president there was, had twice as many news conferences (as the Vietnam War was raging).

As Pixie the Fed Ex lady explained it, "The Republicans are in the sales business. They know how to sex it up and sell it. They know how to manipulate the images. If only the Democrats packaged themselves and their issues better, they would win." Or as Jesus, the cable guy who came to fix my DSL line, explained it, "This whole country is run by advertisers; it's not the candidates, it's the campaign managers who make the man. Just like Hollywood, it's the agents who place the stars."

He's right. When I covered the Bush campaign in 2000, the campaign knew how to use the candidate wisely. They "event-ized" everything, Ronald Reagan–style. He had a big event in the morning, went for a run, took a nap, had a rally in the afternoon, and flew off to the next town. He never came off as a guy who liked to work. Candidate fatigue was never an issue. My cameraman (who has covered every campaign since Carter) told me that of all his campaign experiences, 2000 was his favorite because he didn't have to work that hard. He said he "never shot so little" on a campaign before. He rarely shot more than one or two thirty-minute tapes a day, and the home office was always surprised at how rarely we needed new tapes.

In 2000, one of the Bushies explained his philosophy about feeding the media: "On a campaign, there are hundreds of decisions to make each day, but the only decision that matters is: What is the news of the day? What do we want on the 6 o'clock news? When you're running for president, the question is not what am I going to do for the country? It's what should I do for the nightly news? All we have to do is water and feed you guys and that will shut you up."

Say what you will about Karl Rove and the boys, it is brilliant and disturbing how they manipulate the media. By holding the White House press corps captive and making them eat out of the hand of the administration, all the president's men enforce the rules by threatening to cut off access, turning established journalists into subservient little girlie men.

At the White House, the trains run on time. Bush doesn't let his day job interfere with his summer vacation. You can't blame the guy for wanting to run away and hide. These days, all we are hearing is bad news. Four Americans were burned, mutilated, and dragged through the streets of Iraq. This is the worst possible scenario imaginable for humanity, but it's good for John Kerry. The creepiest part about election season is how crass the partisans can get. In their lust for victory, they root for the worst. On MSNBC one "Democratic strategist" pro-jected that "the doom and gloom in Iraq is good for Kerry." The econ-omy is still in bad shape, but on CNBC the pundits say, "that is so good for Kerry." Gas prices are up; "that is very good news for Democrats." As we await news from the 9/11 commission about how our govern-ment failed us, one of the many pundits (whom I've never heard of be-fore) is on cable right now guessing that "it's all good for Kerry." It seems the worse the news gets, the better it is for the Kerry campaign. In the same way that the Republicans were praying for the stock market bubble to burst, do Democrats want Iraq to implode? What may be good for America may be bad for John Kerry.

Back Inside the Bubble

Pleasureville, Kentucky
MAY 2004

THINGS SURE HAVE CHANGED since the primaries. On the ride in from the airport in Los Angeles, they shut down rush-hour traf-fic for John Kerry! At the hotel, people were waiting in the lobby for hours just to get a glimpse of the man. One woman said she waited three hours just to see him with her own two eyes; the only other per-son she would wait that long to see is Brad Pitt. Outside an event in San Bernardino, a congressman's daughter spontaneously serenaded the senator! These kinds of things never happened in Iowa.

In my first full week back on the bus since Super Tuesday, I am re-minded of how much time and money I wasted following John Ed-wards. If only I had known. That was a news paradise compared to the Kerry campaign. Even though the election is still six months away, Kerry and his press corps are breathing the rarified air of a general election campaign bubble. I remember in 2000 when my cameraman came to terms with this phase: "We no longer have freedom of the press. They are controlling us so tightly that everything we shoot of George W. is flattering."

After surviving 2000, how could I have forgotten how painful the emotional roller coaster of traveling in the bubble is? Signing up to travel with a presidential campaign is like volunteering to go to prison. As soon as you check yourself into the Kerry boot camp, they take control of your whole life. The minute they issue you your credentials with your Secret Service ID number and hand you the schedule of where you will be in the next week, you have surrendered your identity. From now on they will tell you when and what you will eat, when and where you will sleep, where you are allowed to stand, and what you will write in your notebook. Life on the road is like being stuck on flypaper.

The routine is so ritualized and predictable that you quickly become a slave to the rhythm, with your melatonin levels swinging up and down with every flight. You can just feel how the longer you sit on the bus, the less you know about what is happening in the outside world.

If you want to cover a campaign, you have to get used to being roped off in the back of the room like cattle. You are constantly getting poked and prodded by Secret Service agents who are always making these arbitrary perimeters around the candidate. You never have a hard time finding people telling you what you are not allowed to do. Since this is the first presidential election post–September 11, the Secret Service is over the top. Wherever you step, there is always some guy you have never seen before barking orders at you and telling you, "You are not allowed to videotape this."

The worst part about getting back inside the bubble, besides the sleep deprivation, is the initial hazing process. The first day everyone asks you what you are doing here and how long you are staying. Everyone is very territorial. Are you getting an interview? What is your movie about? Who has talked to you on camera? By the end of day two, you find yourself asking the new people the same questions.

Whether it is fueled by competition or boredom, the regulars often interrogate newcomers to the point that it sends the interlopers home with the sense that the press corps is in bed with the campaign. One local reporter told me how, when she first got on the bus, a guy asked her so many questions about the story she was writing that she thought he was working for the campaign; later, she was surprised to find out that he works for the *New York Times*.

The strangest part is how everyone talks in the "we" form. Are we going to Los Angeles next week? Since the press goes everywhere Kerry goes, technically we are going to Los Angeles. But the question really is, "Is John Kerry going to Los Angeles?" But like birds of a feather, we are all stuck together, and our social calendars revolve around the candidate's campaign schedule.

In a traveling press corps, the candidate sets the tone. The pack will make jokes only if he makes jokes; they will laugh only if he laughs. Which means that Kerry's plane is just as dry as he is. The best observation that I heard one of the reporters make is, "This campaign has no cool, from the top down."

Of course, I have heard complaints that the senator never asks the reporters questions about themselves, but he has developed a faux intimacy with them. For example, in a (rare) press conference, the senator said he was going to take a question from one reporter "because it was her birthday yesterday." That reporter told me earlier that the candidate usually ignores the women reporters—she thought he didn't even know they existed. Apparently he does when it is in his interest.

Being in proximity to power makes everyone on board feel like they are actually somebody. One of my friends said without irony, "I have the greatest job on earth, this is the center of the universe. Unfortunately, my rise and fall is linked to his. If he wins I could go to the White House; if he loses I have to go back to writing obituaries and being a nobody again." This is the perverted relationship that journalists have with their subject: Their fate is tied to his and covering a successful presidential candidate is a career stepping-stone. For example, the *New York Times* reporter who covered George Bush in 2000 was rewarded with the post of Rome bureau chief, and the MSNBC correspondent is now the host of NBC's *Weekend Today*.

Just like junior high, there is a cool clique; they are the gang of six who were the first to cover Kerry, who don't allow you to sit in their section of the campaign bus. They call themselves the Champagne Lounge, which is what they called the back section of the Real Deal Express bus in Iowa, where only they were allowed to sit. A Fox News correspondent once made the mistake of sitting in the Champagne Lounge for a fifteen-minute ride to the airport and the *New York Times* reporter kicked him out. Needless to say, they do not make others feel welcome. Just like the movie *Mean Girls,* they say things out loud, like "It was so much better before Felix and Sasha came on board." What they do not realize is that when the general election starts, most of them are going to be kicked to the back of the plane.

An American Legion reporter who was on the Kerry press charter for only one leg of a flight concluded, "I had no idea that the press corps would be so cliquey. They seem to be giving off this vibe that 'We are insiders, we have our inside jokes and our inside language and you don't belong here, you're an outsider.' "

When you travel with a presidential candidate, it is hard to see the big picture. It is easy to completely lose touch with reality. You live on an airplane flying from airport rally to airport rally. You are watching the world from an airplane window and there is a cultural disconnect at 10,000 feet. When you hit the ground, every town looks exactly the same, with its Wal-Mart, and McDonald's. After a while, every place and everyone looks familiar. It seems like you keep seeing the same people at every event. You have to resist the urge to ask everyone, "Do I know you?" Or are the mass media and the Internet turning us all into clones. (In 2000, Bush's check writer used to take pictures of guys with mullets in every town. That was his way of documenting where he'd been. He had the largest, finest collection of mullet photos you've ever seen.)

Standing at a rally waiting for Kerry to arrive (the candidates are never on time), one local asked, "What time is the twister touching down?" implying that campaigns are like tornadoes the way they tear in and out of town. We come and go so quickly that we rarely even have to engage with the locals. We are insulated and isolated. We go from the door of the bus, to the door of the plane, to the door of the high school gymnasium, to the door of the hotel. It could be 2 degrees or 102 degrees; we can't tell because we are never exposed to the elements; we never have to take more than ten steps outside.

You can never stray too far from the pack because if you lose track of time or get stuck on the wrong side of a security line, you are going to miss the bus. So when you are talking with the locals, you always find yourself looking over your shoulder for a fellow bubble dweller, and if you don't see one, panic sets in that you got left behind.

The candidates gave me an excuse to see America. They have taken me to almost every state in our union, but I could not tell you a defining characteristic of one of them. Whether we are in a boutique town or a thriving metropolis, it all blends together. Eventually, the two parties avoid states they have no chance of winning, so the entire country gets reduced to a few swing states. We are just going around in circles to places that you would never choose to visit on your own. Nobody has these towns on their list of vacation destinations.

When a candidate comes to visit, people try to hide the color of their town; they clean up for the occasion because they don't want their town to look bad on the national news. They sweep the homeless, winos, and protesters off the streets. When I was traveling with Bush in 2000, I don't think he ever saw one protester. As far as the candidates can tell, this country is on a journey toward yuppification and mediocrity.

In a campaign, appearance is everything. The goal is to make Kerry look "presidential." So the aides are constantly watching out for things that will hurt the candidate's image. For example, this morning the senator was holding a bagel in his hand while he was talking to reporters and an aide ran over and took it from him, because it doesn't look presidential for a man to be holding his own bagel. And everywhere we go, they are looking for black kids to have photo ops with. This has become so common that one of the wire reporters calls Kerry's photo ops LBKs (which stands for Look, Black Kids).

At every airport there is a posse of veterans waiting on the tarmac to shake the senator's hand. As we deplane, the photographers are placed in shooting distance so they can get the intimate shots of Kerry getting a hero's welcome. The funny thing is how, when you are there, the event feels like a nonevent, but when you see the photos on the front page of the newspaper, it looks so real. For example, the other day when John Kerry landed in Connecticut he was greeted by six veterans; they made some small talk and posed for a photo. The whole event lasted five minutes. Being there, the whole event was meaningless, but when that photo of John Kerry with those vets was on the front page of the *New York Times,* it looked like a real moment.

But few are paying attention these days anyway. We all have parts of the newspaper that we choose to ignore, and most don't read the stories about the election until it's time. When I was done reading that *New York Times* in the hotel restaurant, I asked the guy at the table next to me if he wanted to read it. He took one look at it and said, "Who cares about John Kerry campaigning in May 2004? It must be a slow news day. And besides, when was the last time you actually read any news in the newspaper?" He has a point.

On the trail, Kerry is not saying much. There seems to be a total disconnect between what people are talking about in the outside world and what Kerry is talking about on the campaign trail. For example, when the pictures of U.S. soldiers abusing prisoners in the Abu Ghraib prison were released in public and everyone was talking about whether Donald Rumsfeld will be forced to resign, Kerry didn't make any statements about Rumsfeld in public. He played it safe, so safe that you could say he is running a cowardly campaign.

"As the leader of the party he should be calling for Rumsfeld's resignation. That is what a leader does, he leads," yelled one of the instapundits on the bus. The campaign spokesman disagreed: "John Kerry doesn't want to talk about Rumsfeld, he wants to talk about education." But no one in the country wants to listen to Kerry talk about education. Since there are no press conferences and the reporters aren't going to get close enough to ask any other questions, that is all Kerry will be heard talking about.

The reporters want Kerry to talk about what is happening in the news. If he doesn't talk about Rumsfeld, he (and, more importantly, they) won't get in the newspaper. The campaign has made a conscious decision not to engage. The handlers are telling the candidate to stay on message, don't let them get you to say anything other than the message of the day: Today is education day and Kerry is proeducation (now that takes courage).

Behind the scenes, the staffers argue that if he wants to win, Kerry has to keep his mouth shut and hide, let Rumsfeld and Bush self-destruct. Why should the candidate say anything? If he opens his mouth, no matter what he says, he can't win. After all, this election has nothing to do with John Kerry; it is a referendum on George Bush. It is not the most courageous route, but they think it is the road to victory.

The campaign argues that the reason they have to keep the candidate away from the press is that reporters ask stupid questions like the ones they have been asking recently about a group of angry Swift Boat veterans who are out to destroy the senator. He would rather not discuss them. For weeks, the Swift Boat Veterans for Truth have been running an ad accusing Kerry of fabricating his Vietnam record, but he refuses to respond to their allegations. The reporters want to ask whether Kerry threw away his war medals thirty years ago (as the Swift Boat vets allege), but Kerry does not want to answer questions like that. So the Kerry haters' side of the story is all we are going to hear. The *Boston Globe* reporter admitted that he was not proud of these stories: "The stuff I am writing is all bullshit." If the press knew where Kerry stood, they would report it, but he will not let them know where he stands.

Because the candidate doesn't want to talk about the things that the reporters want to talk about, he doesn't want to be anywhere near them. He is saying nothing, the reporters are getting nothing, and it's the campaign staffers' job to keep the press away from the candidate to make sure he doesn't say anything other than what they planned to serve up today. This is the dance that goes on in every campaign between the candidate, his staff, and his press corps.

Because the senator doesn't trust the pack of unwashed snarling dogs at his heel, he acts like a scripted cardboard cutout when he is around them. He can't tell them how he really feels about what is going on because they would not know how to use it. In the current political climate, words are like bombs, and so the chance of ever seeing an unguarded moment on this presidential campaign is gone.

You want to know what happens when a candidate speaks off the cuff? The most recent example is when Senator Kerry had a spontaneous moment and instantly it ended up on the *Drudge Report*. The senator was at a party at his headquarters with a bunch of his supporters. A reporter told him that President Bush fell off his bike. Kerry said, "I didn't know the president rode a bike." The reporter said, "He doesn't," and the whole room laughed. Then Kerry said, "Can I make an off-record comment on that?" The *New York Times* reporter and a few others said yes, so he joked, "Does it have training wheels?"

Since the pool camera was rolling when Kerry made the comment (and the pool producer said that she never agreed to go off the record), the whole incident set off a huge controversy of whether airing the comment was fair game. The conclusion that all the networks came to was: We'll use it if someone else does first.

Within the hour, the *Drudge Report* had it up. (He actually had the quote wrong; he quoted Kerry as saying "Did the training wheels fall off?") The *Washington Times,* the *New York Times,* the *New York Observer,* and the *New York Daily News* all printed Drudge's quote of the incident. Of course, then the *Chicago Sun-Times* had a story about the mayor of Chicago "scolding" Kerry for the wisecrack. So there you have it: There is proof of why you can't make jokes with your press corps.

Even when a reporter asks him the simplest question, the senator overthinks his answer. One reporter asked him what his favorite drink is and he couldn't say. Another asked him who his three favorite presidents are, and he named five, just to cover his bases and make sure he didn't leave out a politically popular one. One of the reporters told me the most frustrating part about talking to Kerry is that he often answers a question by saying "What?" "He wants us to think that he has a hearing problem, but he really just wants more time to think about the answer he is going to give." He is living by the golden rule in politics: You have to have strict message discipline.

This is how Bush does it and Kerry hopes to have the same success. But Bush has some of the most skilled media manipulators working his press corps. Kerry has Bob Shrum (who has never advised a successful presidential candidate) and a tag team of amateur spin men and that makes me wonder if they have any clue what they are doing. They don't trust reporters around their man and they don't trust their candidate to hold his own with reporters. They are so paranoid about the candidate's image that they keep him tightly locked up, and the only image we get of him is at a podium in a suit. And then they wonder why people think he comes off as pompous and aloof.

The campaign staffers are a bunch of stressy taxpayer-funded babysitters who always have that suspicious look in their eyes. They often joke about how the press are the worst-behaved people in the world. It is true that by nature journalists are an unruly bunch who do not have the reverence for the candidate that the staffers feel they should. Reporters notoriously do disrespectful things, like talk on cell phones while the candidate is speaking or question the truthfulness of something the candidate says.

Obviously, inside the press corps there is not a lot of trust of the campaign. Reporters are constantly complaining about how the campaign staffers are lying to protect their candidate and they treat reporters as if they are the enemy. The *New York Times* reporter covering Bush in 2000 explained it like this: "We are all involved in this unholy relationship whereby we can't always be honest with them for simple reasons of etiquette and also because we have to live harmoniously with them and they can't always be honest with us, and they aren't always honest with us, nor probably would anyone be in their situation. So you never know when you are interacting with them whether they are deferring to the influence your paper has or whether they have respect for you as an individual."

If you aren't working for the paper of record, the campaign doesn't have to be that politically correct with you. Once I asked the man in charge of controlling the press corps on Kerry's campaign who he thinks is responsible for making the American people hate politics. Do you blame the media for not acting responsibly? Do you blame the candidate for not always telling the whole truth to the media? Or is it the handlers, whose job it is to spin and mislead reporters? He blamed me. "Documentaries are what make people cynical because they look at the process. Process pieces are bad because they make people more cynical about the process." I tried to explain to him that all I am trying to do is shed some light on how the system works, but he accused me of trying to screw up what he orchestrates. "My goal is to keep up the appearances. Your goal is to deconstruct them."

Someone on the Kerry campaign told me that if I came out for the first week in May, I would get five minutes with the candidate. All I have gotten is a series of not todays. And so I march along with all of the other members of the traveling press corps. Eat. On the bus. Eat. Off the bus. Eat. On the plane. We eat again. It's 9 A.M. and I've already had three chocolate chip cookies. Love that campaign diet! It is a rolling dinner party. At the end of the day yesterday a reporter declared, "I had seven meals today," and the campaign staffer told her, "You are only supposed to eat every other meal we feed you." Like freshmen in college, campaign reporters gain at least fifteen pounds in their first few months on the trail.

Unlike 2000, this time around, I am experiencing a new humiliation: begging for access, getting led on, but ultimately getting rejected. Why is the war hero acting so guarded? He is a U.S. senator, he should be able to hold his own. The best reason the Kerry staffer gave me for why they don't want to give me time is, "We are afraid you are going to ask him some question about pop culture that he doesn't know the answer to." To which someone on the bus remarked, "They aren't worried about the rest of us because they know we don't know anything about popular culture. We are stuck on this bus, totally cut off from the rest of the world."

Probing further, I found out that the Kerry campaign is worried that I am going to do what VH1 did back in February. They gave all the presidential candidates a pop culture quiz and Kerry was not amused. Even though Wes Clark and Joe Lieberman failed the quiz miserably, they laughed about it; but Kerry said, "I hate when you guys do these things," and he acted annoyed the whole time at the kid asking the questions. Strangely, he knew all the answers. He knew Justin Timberlake was a member of *NSYNC, he knew about the breakup of Ben Affleck and Jennifer Lopez . . . The thing I don't get about this is why wouldn't a candidate say "Who cares?" I personally don't know anyone in the world who cares if the leader of the free world knows what's up with Bennifer. Regardless, the Kerry campaign seems scared that I am out to reveal that John Kerry doesn't read *Teen Beat* magazine, so they won't let me near him.

I asked the *Time* magazine photographer who just shot pictures of Kerry in the front of the plane, "Why do you think they only let the photographers up there and they won't let me shoot any video?" He said, "Because we don't talk. You have a mouth that makes you a threat. Maybe you should shut your mouth." With that kind of encouragement from my colleague, I decided to sit back and take in the scenery.

If you look around the plane, it is interesting that all you see is a handful of journalists from the nation's leading newspapers and networks. These are the only organizations that can afford to pay thousands of dollars a day for the privilege to ride along. And what are they getting out of this? The only original thought I had this week was that we should have a running scroll in the movie of how much it cost for HBO to get a five-minute interview with John Kerry. Ten thousand dollars? Twenty thousand dollars? My guess is that in the end I will probably spend more than $20,000 to get it. What could he say that would be worth spending that much money to hear?

I don't know why I believed them when they told me I was going to get my five minutes. Each day when I woke up, I thought, today is the day I'm going to get my five minutes. Or so I was told. Looking over his schedule, I could see them making time right before the San Bernardino High School newspaper or after *American Legion* magazine. Every day he does at least a half hour of local interviews and then has a few hours off. Heck, he took hours to do a photo shoot for *Ladies' Home Journal,* surely they can squeeze in HBO. But inevitably, after the last flight of each day I was told, "He wanted to play cards" or "Not today." So I sat on the bus all day for nothing.

At the end of these kinds of days, alcohol really helps. On the plane, a glass of red wine spilled on my camera and it no longer works. Luckily, I brought a backup camera just in case, but wine got inside the second camera as well, so now I am functioning without any equipment. Why am I still paying to sit here if I don't have any tools to make the video? Because the traveling press secretary promised me an interview and even though I know that I am never going to get it, if I go home now, they will assume I give up easily. I will sit here until election day if I have to, with or without a camera that works. Hey, there is some fun to be had.

The other night in New Orleans we all went out on Bourbon Street, where the smell of vomit was in the air along with lots of girls' nipples. There is nothing like the Hurricanes at Pat O'Briens. Although I never ordered one, everyone was sharing theirs with me. Somehow we ended up rolling around town with our flight crew from the Kerry charter plane, and one of the flight attendants kept threatening me, "Behave or I'll put you in a middle seat." (There are no middle seats on the charter.) Needless to say, everyone was dry-humping each other on the dance floor at some cheesy dance club at 4 A.M. On the walk back to the Fairmont Hotel, a young man exposed his penis in exchange for beads, while his friend was puking in the gutter next to him. The kids are all right.

At the end of a long and empty week, we ended up in Pittsburgh on Mother's Day with no events on the schedule. So the press corps went out to a baseball game. I tagged along (what else was there to do on a Sunday in Pittsburgh?), but since my interest in baseball is limited, I ended up sitting in the bleachers interviewing the drunken hecklers who were spontaneously screaming "Kerry is a pussy." They philosophized about gas prices and George Bush. This ended up being the best political discussion I had all week.

That night John Kerry invited the press corps over to the Heinz family farm for an "off the record" cocktail. Put the plastic on those couches, the press corps is coming over! As we marched off the bus like school kids on a field trip to the zoo, Kerry, wearing his dirty old Asics sneakers, a blue Oxford shirt, and tan khakis, approached us with his dog in tow. Just like in the Purina Puppy Chow commercial, he threw a tennis ball and the loyal dog ran after it and returned it to his master.

As we walked into the home, the first thing we saw was a delivery of fresh flowers with a note sticking out that even the least nosy of reporters could not ignore. A warm and fuzzy Mother's Day note to

Teresa from her stepdaughters. It was clear from the portrait of her late husband and all the old photos: This is a haunted house.

The candidate invited us out into the garden, where there was a table with a bowl of chips and guacamole next to some jalapeño-stuffed olives that must have been a gift that sat in their pantry for years waiting for the day that guests of our caliber came over. The senator offered us all Bud Light or red wine. Teresa took a few of us for a tour of her garden, where she demonstrated her knowledge of the things that are growing in it, while the other reporters sat with the senator and asked inane questions about policy and politics. As Kerry tried to make small talk with the pack, I was fixating on a piece of old snakeskin that was right next to where he was sitting. Literally, a snake had shed his skin right there in their yard and the old skin was sitting right next to him. It seemed like the perfect metaphor.

That is all I am allowed to say about the off-the-record Mother's Day rendezvous we had with the candidate. Although if the affair were on the record, there still was not much more to say than that. The reporters asked questions that might as well have been on the record, proving that they do not know how to behave around politicians. Those on the bus who were there in 2000 when Bush had the press corps over to the ranch for a barbecue agreed: George was a much better host because he barbecued burgers for us and let us use his bathroom.

On the ride home from Chez Kerry, one of the reporters (who was uncomfortable with the whole off-the-record cocktail hour) ranted about the night, "What was the point of that? Schmooze them, use them, and defuse them. I feel so dirty. It seems like the media doesn't understand their role in our society. They are not supposed to get invited to the cocktail parties, they are supposed to be exposing the politicians for having them."

The next morning I was told that they don't have enough seats for members of the press and I have to give up my seat. So after spending eight days and $14,000 with Club Kerry, I got kicked off the plane.

There I was stranded on the tarmac in Louisville, Kentucky, in 100 degrees with two broken cameras and no clue how to get to the terminal, watching the traveling press corps load through the rear end of the plane, while an army of Secret Service agents with John Kerry and his staff who lied to me all week reload the plane through the front door. I'm going to miss those guys.

Hunting George Bush.

Hunting with the Pack

Destination Unknown
MAY 12, 2004

COVERING THIS CAMPAIGN, I have met some of the best journalists in the business. I have also met a lot of total buzzards. In the real world, there are both. Like the good America and the bad America (of which George Bush spoke in defense of the crimes committed at Abu Ghraib prison), there are always going to be a few rotten apples that spoil the whole lot.

Like Abu Ghraib, reporters covering a presidential campaign are far from home, sequestered on a bus, living in surreal circumstances that make them act with a strange groupthink mentality. It is only a matter of time until one of the journalists in the campaign press corps starts behaving badly, and their actions influence the entire bus, which in turn affects how the outside world views the Kerry campaign. When you are sitting on the bus with the press corps, individually they seem decent and well-intentioned, but together as a pack, they are dangerous. "This press corps is a monster. Being cooped up here makes me feel like I'm going to suffocate from the peer pressure," remarked one visiting journalist who felt excluded.

Needless to say, the campaign bubble is not a healthy work environment. As the *Dallas Morning News* reporter said about being in the Bush traveling press corps in 2000, "It's a prison. We are all captives to these kidnappers, who happen to be the Bush campaign. We are competitors, but the bubble builds a bond. We have developed a friendship; we are all in this together. There is a 99 percent chance of something happening here, and if it doesn't, we will make it happen." Some might say that boredom is the root of all evil.

Campaign buses are intense, surreal, artificial, claustrophobic, incestuous microcosms. On the road, there is no such thing as a private moment. One full-time bubble resident explained, "All these brilliant, egomaniacal, neurotic reporters are my family. Sure they can be uptight and righteous and humorless, but they are all I've got." The longer you stay, the more comfortable you start to feel living among them, and you realize that they have their own internal wars going on. "You know how it is, everyone knows my business, and I know theirs," explained one of my old friends from 2000 who covers Kerry. "They aren't all that bad. That hyperaggressive reporter is not indicative of the whole group. We aren't all like that."

Many reporters drop in for a day or two and feel like they had a full campaign experience. They don't get the luxury of being able to stick around long enough to understand the complexities of the place, so they go home with a distorted and disturbing impression of the traveling press. Those who live inside the bubble don't seem to realize how many reporters come for very short stints and then go home telling their friends about the odd and alienating behavior of the press corps. "This place is an orgy," observed a college student who was covering the election for his school paper. "When I came on the plane, it was just like walking into a dorm, they were all talking about how much fun they had in New Orleans. They made it seem like covering a campaign is just one big frat party rolling around the country."

Presidential campaigns are expensive, exclusive, mostly white fraternities. All you have to do to belong is get some media conglomerate to sponsor you. That is it. As long as your employer pays the bill on time, you will be able to ride along on the costliest year-round summer camp for journalists. Once you get here, there is no currency required; everything is provided for us. The campaign takes care of all of the logistics. It's like being the Queen of England: You never have to sit in traffic. We are immune from the responsibilities of adult life. I can't remember the last time I had cash in my hand. They make us feel spoiled and cared for, but all they are doing is breaking us down, making us fat, lazy, and dependent.

As my seatmate said in 2000, "This is like going on a field trip every day. That is what it is like: Someone says we will get up at 6 A.M., you get a little pack lunch, and you make a lot of new friends." He was the one who coined the term "instamacy" to describe how on the bus we were forced to instantly become intimate with perfect strangers. In this kind of environment, there are always those who are nurturing friendships for professional reasons. We used to call them "frienemies" because we knew the people we lived with were our friends but also our competitors and enemies.

My favorite quote from the NBC correspondent in 2000 was, "Most of these reporters are self-centered, insecure, and untrustworthy leeches. That is why we get along so well. I know why they want to be my friend, but I can't remember why I want to be theirs." Just like being stuck in an elevator together or on the *Love Boat,* relationships are bound to develop, and those are known as "locationships."

Regardless of what they are called and why they are formed, just like on the reality TV show *Survivor,* you have to forge alliances so that you will not be eating alone at night or making the mistake of transcribing the speech (before someone tells you that the hard copy is available on-line). But if you want to fit in, you better know your place. Of course, there is a hierarchy on the bus.

In a traveling press corps there is a caste system that lets everyone know where they fit into the complicated little ecosystem. The *New York Times* and *Washington Post* get front-row treatment. Where you are assigned to sit on the plane is the clearest indication of your value. Behind the *Times* you will find the wire services, followed by the television correspondents. In the midsection, you will find the news magazines and second-tier newspapers. The rear end of the plane is reserved for the photographers and TV crews who are there to service those sitting in the forward cabins of the plane and obviously do not share their Ivy League pedigree.

If you really don't matter, you will get shifted to the zoo plane (the second plane that follows behind the candidate's plane). Without the restrictions of having the candidate on board, the zoo plane allows grown men and women the freedom to slide down the aisles on plastic trays during take-off and have drinking contests between campaign stops.

Back on the civilized plane, if Senator Kerry dared to mix and mingle in-flight (and that is a big *if*), he wouldn't dare wander past the first-class cabin. Candidate Bush in 2000 was quite the opposite; he went straight to the back of the plane to visit the people he called the "working-class people," knowing that they would never ask him any questions other than "Can you sign this baseball for my kid?" Once, when I tried to explain to my cameraman why journalists aren't supposed to ask for autographs (because it could be seen as a conflict of interest), he reasoned, "Isn't that what journalism is? Journalism is the intellectual form of asking for an autograph . . . reporters just want to be near famous people. They are all just a bunch of star fuckers; they just hide behind their notebooks."

The reporters are always treated with more respect than the photographers, even though the most important factor in a presidential campaign is how it looks on TV, and the men in the back of the plane have a

You have to give good plane.

lot to do with that. (Ironically, my NBC cameraman in 2000 helped the Bush campaign so much with their stagecraft that after the election he got the job as head of the White House television department.) The candidates assume that the photographers don't pay attention to what is being said (and they usually don't, when it comes to politics), but when it comes to getting the dirt, the shooters always have the best campaign gossip.

On every campaign plane there is a debate about whether the plane is on or off the record. Every four years the press has to reinvent the wheel. Some candidates want to be able to come back on the plane and build a relationship with their press corps in hopes that their coverage will be more sympathetic (like Bush did so effectively in 2000). While some media outlets insist that every word that comes out of the candidate's mouth is for public consumption, others feel it is good to nurture a relationship with the candidate so that they can see where he is coming from. Without any off-the-record moments, there is no reason for a working journalist to leave his own home; he could cover the whole campaign by watching C-SPAN.

After his first trip with a presidential candidate, a college student writing for his campus paper asked, "Why do you pay $2,000 a day for this? If you travel with the candidate, you don't get anything more than you would if you followed in a rental car." I explained to him that logistically, you couldn't keep up with the campaign if you went on your own. You have to pay to play with the boys on the bus (so that one day you, too, will become one of that kind of journalist that Bush in 2000 called a "major league asshole").

The reason each media outlet needs a representative in a traveling press corps is that each news outlet needs someone there to act as a liaison or goodwill ambassador between the network and the campaign. In 2000, when I was the on-the-bus producer for NBC News, my job was to request interviews for the network, deal with booking Bush on the morning shows, ask questions at press conferences (if the candidate had any), and act as the in-house librarian (they need an expert on everything that comes out of the candidate's mouth). Who would catch contradictions in his speeches? Who would know the last time the candidate spoke about gun control? The job was excruciatingly boring, but because Bush won, everyone thinks it must have been the most exciting job on earth.

In 2000, the decision about whether the plane was on or off the record reversed weekly. Not every news organization agreed on the subject, so the question was never resolved. My network told me never to agree to going off the record; after all, I was not there to make friends with the candidate. Anything he said could and would be used against him by the network if they saw fit. (Even if the airplane were to be declared off the record, we all wrote up memos to the home office about what the candidate said and those notes got e-mailed around the newsrooms for everyone to see.) All of the footage I collected with my camcorder was shown to the news executives in New York, but they did not want to air any of it for fear of jeopardizing their relationship with the candidate.

In 2004, the campaign plane is mostly off the record. And Senator Kerry and President Bush rarely even come back to schmooze the media. So the question remains: What is the point of paying $10,000 to $20,000 a week to travel with the campaign? The concept of a traveling press corps seems obsolete. Campaign reporters have been reduced to nothing more than stenographers, documenting every scripted word that comes out of the candidate's mouth.

While the debate lingers on about whether the candidate's words are on or off the record, there is no question that the banter on the bus between the reporters is not for public consumption. In what could be seen as a strange double standard, the same people who print anything about the people they are covering feel entitled to restrict what is written about them.

Most reporters argue that their words are private; they are not public people and if they thought what they were saying would ever end up in print, they never would have said it. Every time someone new joins the group, one of the news nuns barks out, "Hey, new kid, everything we say on this bus is off the record." (This disease has even spread to the staffers. In a casual conversation, one told me, "Off the record I'm twenty-three. On the record I'm nineteen.") But as a rule, you should assume that if you say something out loud on a bus full of journalists, it will get repeated, if not printed.

On a number of occasions, I had a conversation with the reporter sitting next to me on topics ranging from my mom to what I really think of my employer, only to find out, much to my surprise, that they published what I said in their newspaper. One guy even went so far as to offer me a ride to the caucus and recorded our entire conversation on the way and published it. When my friends asked me how I could be foolish enough to talk to a reporter, I said I thought I was just making small talk with a colleague. I didn't know that he was recording it!

Which leads to the most obvious lesson I learned from living among and getting burned by journalists: Never say anything to a reporter that you do not want to read in the paper. I don't care if that reporter is your best friend, because I know some who have burned their best friend for a story. The only person I know who has never betrayed my confidence in this regard was that college kid writing for his school newspaper. The last time I saw him, he told me that he didn't quote me in his article because "I didn't want to burn you." Now that's a first.

Every so often, a journalist shows up to write about the press corps and the whole bus freaks out. The reporters argue that if you are there with the intention of writing about the press, you have to disclose your intentions up front. But lots of times, reporters who are not there to write about the press hear something they think they can turn into a story, so they call it in to the home office.

The funny thing is, I never thought about quoting a reporter until I was sitting on the bus talking to the *New York Times* reporter and he asked, "Is this off the record? Are you going to quote me?" When I joked with him about the size of his ego, he said, "A lot of people show up and find out there is nothing to write about, so they start writing about us because we are so quotable and the candidate isn't quotatious."

In honor of all those who have published my words without my knowledge, I would like to share with you my top ten favorite quotes overheard on the Kerry press bus. I think it will help you understand what you can expect to hear on a presidential campaign trip:

1. "Don't steal my idea."

2. "I am the most connected political reporter on the market."

3. "Damn, he is focusing so much on the issues I am never going to make air" (correspondent talking to his boss).

4. "What is going to be our news today?" (reporter asks campaign spokesman).

5. "I focus on the campaign strategy, I can't tell you anything about the issues."

6. "I hate sunshine, my job is to look for the rain."

7. "What day is it today? I write the news of the day even though I never know what day it is."

8. "My parents never would have paid for college if they knew that I wouldn't find a husband here" (a thirty-year-old news nun).

9. "Does anyone know what the president said today? How could we be so ill-informed?"

10. "From the road, I can only see about 10 percent of what is going on in this race. Is there any meaning whatsoever in what I do?"

Why Can't Aunt Zon
Come to the Party?

Phoenix
MAY 17, 2004

"I WANT TO GO FIND MY MOM," my seven-year-old nephew Alexander insisted. "Aunt Zon, come with me." I can't. "Why not?" he demanded to know. I am not allowed to. "Why not?" the kid persisted. Those are the rules. "But why?"

While my older sister Nancy and her husband were inside the Kerry fund-raiser in Phoenix, I sat outside in the hallway babysitting their two children, Alexander and Madeleine. Having spent the past week on the road traveling with the Kerry campaign, spending at least $12,000 of HBO's money without getting one piece of video that would ever go on TV, this is the only worthwhile part of this trip. I'm getting some quality time with the youngest members of my family. And all they want to do is ask questions.

"How come John Kerry has so many police officers with him?" Alexander asked. Because he is a very important person. "He's not the president, is he?" No, but he could be. "What happens if he loses?" Then he will not have any policemen with him. "So he is not really important but he could be?" That's right. If he loses, no one will care if he lives or dies.

"Did John Kerry give you this new camera?" Alexander asked as he played with my new toy. No, HBO gave it to me. "Has John Kerry ever given you a gift?" No. "But George Bush gave you that Scooby-Doo doll. Remember?" I didn't remember until he reminded me that four years ago, when I was on the trail with Bush, a member of his staff gave me a stuffed animal for my birthday, which I then regifted to Alexander when he came to visit me at the hotel. When we bumped into George

Bush in the lobby, someone tried to take a picture of Alexander with him, but the kid was crying the entire time. Needless to say, his mother is raising him Democrat.

"Where is my mommy?" my five-year-old niece Madeleine whined. Your mommy is inside the party. She will be out soon. "Why don't you go in there and get her?" They will not let me in. "Why not?" Because you have to pay to go in and I didn't pay. "Why don't you just pay?" I can't afford to. "How much does it cost?" Two thousand dollars. "Is that a lot or a little?" That's a whole lot. "Why does it cost so much?" You get to listen to John Kerry. "But I can hear him from right here." Well, in there, you get to see John Kerry. "You can see him on TV." You are paying to help elect John Kerry president.

Interested in seeing what all the fuss is about, Madeleine took her ticket, walked over to the security checkpoint, and asked the Secret Service agent, "Why can't Aunt Zon come to the party?" The agent ignored her completely. So she walked up to the door to ask another guard; there she spotted men with cameras. "Did they pay to get in?" she asked the man standing in the doorway, who stared at her blankly.

"Aunt Zon, I see cameras in there. You can come in now!" Madeleine announced. No, I can't. "But there are other cameras in there." That is the pool. Sometimes the campaign lets a few cameramen in because the room is not big enough for all the cameras, so one guy goes in and shoots the event and he has to share his video with everyone. "So it's like adult swim, when only the grown-ups get to go in the pool?" Alexander asked. Yes, it's kind of like that. "You are kind of like a grown-up. When do you get to go in the pool?" I am never allowed in the pool because I do not work for one of the big TV networks. "So they don't ever share with you?" Nope. "That's not fair." Hey kid, feel my pain, it's an unfair world.

Feeling charitable (and desperate to get out of this place), Alexander reached into his mother's bag. "Here is my mom's wallet. I am sure that she wouldn't mind if you took her money to buy a ticket." I can't do that. "Why not?" As a member of the traveling press corps, I am not allowed to buy a ticket. "Why not?" Instead of explaining FEC laws, I suggested we go see if there were any cookies in the filing center.

After we ate all the cookies, rode the escalator backward, and crank-called my boyfriend on their mother's cell phone, they were back to asking questions. "Do you sleep in the same hotel room with John Kerry?" No, everyone has their own room. "But didn't you share a hotel room with George Bush?" No, we stayed in the same hotel but we all had separate hotel rooms. "But you slept on the same airplane with Bush!" Yes, we all rode and sometimes slept on the same airplane.

"Go get Mommy and tell her that it's time to go," Alexander demanded. But I can't. "You can use my ticket," the little boy offered. Why don't you want to go to the party? "Because there are no kids in there and the grown-ups are all talking about boring stuff." But you can get your picture taken with John Kerry and if he becomes president that will be really cool. "I want John Kerry to be president," Alexander declared. Why? "Because my mom likes John Kerry and I voted for him."

Ever since my sister took her kids to vote with her in the Arizona primary, they have been bragging about how they voted for John Kerry (even though I told them to vote for someone else). As we sat there on the floor outside of his fund-raiser, Madeleine started telling everyone who walked by that she voted for John Kerry. The rich old ladies found it adorable, but the other traveling journalists thought I brainwashed the kid to kiss up to the campaign. I only wish that I was smart enough to think of that, because when the Kerry staffer whom I have been begging for access all week walked by, Madeleine informed him, "I voted for John Kerry, but she didn't."

After that I had to tell the little troublemaker not to repeat that to anyone else here. That opened up a new series of questions. "Why not?" Because I am trying to get an interview with John Kerry but his staff won't let me talk to him. Alexander was having a hard time understanding all of this. "You got on a plane to come to Arizona with John Kerry and he didn't talk to you?" Yes. But it is more complicated than that; it is not a regular airplane, it is his campaign plane and we are not seated together. "How many rows are there between your seat and John Kerry's seat?" Probably five. "Why didn't you just walk up and talk to him?" That is not allowed. You can only talk to John Kerry if he comes to talk to you, and he doesn't want to talk to me because he is afraid I will ask him a silly question.

"John Kerry is afraid of you?" I guess so. "But why?" I have no idea. "But didn't he see your movie with George Bush? George Bush wasn't afraid of you . . . he always talked to you." Well, John Kerry doesn't like me and he does not want to talk to me. "Why don't you tell Mimi to make him to talk to you?" (Mimi is what they call their grandmother, my mom, who has been campaigning for Kerry.) Someday they will learn that Mimi can't solve all their problems.

"If he doesn't want to talk to you, why does he let you fly on his airplane and sleep in his hotel?" Because I am paying a lot of money and he can't really say that I am not allowed on the plane. "Why don't you go buy a ticket and then go in the party? That way you can talk to him." I think that is against the law of journalism. "But aren't you paying to be on his airplane? How is that any different than paying to get into his party to talk to him?" the seven-year-old asked. While I tried to come up with an answer to this question, Madeleine declared, "They should make a law that says that anyone running for president should have to talk to everyone, even kids, without having to pay money." I couldn't agree with you more, kid.

"Aunt Zon, I know how you can get him to talk to you," Madeleine announced. "Bake him cookies," she suggested, "everyone loves cookies." Alexander came up with another idea for how I could get time with the senator. "Why don't you hide in the bathroom and then when he comes in you could jump out and ask him questions?" I don't think the Secret Service would like that.

While Alexander was demonstrating how I could jump out of the bushes and surprise Kerry, the partygoers started filing out of the room. That was how we knew that the speech was almost over. When my brother-in-law came to get the kids to go back in and meet John Kerry, Alexander went, but Madeleine didn't want to. She preferred to stay and braid my hair into dreadlocks.

Minutes later Alexander came running out. "We met John Kerry and I had my picture taken with him and he told me that he loves you."

Now it was my turn to ask the questions. What did you think of John Kerry? "He was boring . . . but I liked it when he talked about security." What else can you tell me about the party? Did it look like people were having fun? "That party was lame. It was no fun." Then he gave me his own theory for why they would not let me in. "I think they don't want you in there because if people see how boring it is, no one will ever pay to go to one of these parties again," he concluded.

My sister confirmed her son's account of the event. She introduced herself to the senator and he said, "Your sister is traveling with us. She is so much fun." Fun? How would he know, he hasn't said one word to me the entire trip? But Alexander assured me, "Aunt Zon, John Kerry really likes you, he told me so. I am sure you will get to talk to him to-morrow." Happily we all went home, where Alexander baked chocolate chip cookies for me to bring to the interview they were sure I was going to be getting with the senator.

In the morning, when they dropped me off back at the hotel, I asked Alexander what he thinks I should ask John Kerry in the interview. "I would ask him why he was so afraid to give you an interview," the boy

Alexander with John Kerry.

suggested. "And ask him if he liked the chocolate chip cookies." Not surprisingly, John Kerry never got to taste Alexander and Madeleine's chocolate-chip cookies.

Stakeout

Boston
MAY 21, 2004

ACCORDING TO THE SCHEDULE, Senator Kerry will be at home in Boston with no events for the next three days except a fund-raiser at Paul Simon's house in Connecticut that is closed to the press. So we are getting a long weekend, unless something comes up. In the meantime, the cool clique is going to a Red Sox game, while the others take in the sights, go shopping on Newbury Street, or just sit in their hotel rooms watching porn.

I ventured over to Jasper's Summer Shack with the un-cool crowd, which includes CNN, Fox, and the NBC correspondent and his producer. As we were sipping a flaming scorpion bowl, we heard a rumor that things were bubbling over in the Champagne Lounge. One of the reporters got a tip: Senator Kerry is having a private meeting at his house tomorrow with someone (we don't know who) about something (we are not sure what). When you get a scoop, you are never supposed to share it with the competition, but in the Champagne Lounge they share everything, though they wouldn't tell us, the dork clique, any more than that.

Even though the campaign staff denied that there were any meetings on the schedule, the journalists representing the *New York Times,* NBC, the *Boston Globe,* ABC, and CBS didn't believe them, so they made a pact to stake out the senator's house without telling CNN and

Fox. This posed a dilemma because it violated the protocol of the network pool arrangements. Officially, NBC and CNN are corporate partners and ABC, CBS, and Fox are in bed with each other. But that was not the real problem; the bigger issue was that this whole episode was a breach of the unwritten rules of the bubble.

This is the politics of covering the politics: The networks pay millions of dollars to keep someone on the road with the candidate at all times, just in case he ever "makes news." They are paying for access. If the senator should have a spontaneous urge to leave his front door and go get a cup of coffee, a local camera could ask him a question, and if he said something, the networks would be screwed out of a sound bite. So they assign one person to be as close to the candidate as humanly possible every single minute of every single day, just in case.

The networks all used to have their own camera crews out shooting film and then video of the campaigns. Then one day some number cruncher figured out that if all of the networks pooled their resources and took turns shooting the events, all the networks could save lots of money. This is really convenient and cost-effective for them, but it is dangerous to reduce an entire presidential campaign to one set of eyes. As we all know, the same event can be seen differently by whoever is watching (or filming) it.

Besides, the networks get to decide what gets shown on TV. It could be a five-second clip or the entire event, but there is a good chance that you won't get to see everything that happened at that event. (This is why, in 2000, I used to go in with my camcorder to interview the individuals that were not hand-picked by the campaign to shake hands with the candidate. They always had off-color things to say, which is why they never made it on the evening news.)

The networks still have a monopoly on campaign coverage. If you are not in the pool, you are not allowed into an event. Despite the fact that HBO paid for me to join the Kerry traveling press corps, there are plenty of events that I am excluded from because I do not work for the network. So if a president and/or a presidential candidate walks into a bar, only one network cameraman is authorized to record it, and you as the viewer get only one view of how it all went down.

It is the network pool producer's job to give the campaign grief if their camera misses any move the candidate makes. For example, the other day John Kerry walked across the street to shake hands with spectators, and the pool camera wasn't there to catch it. The pool producer had it out with the campaign staff—it was her position that the campaign violated their pact with the networks. Why are they paying so much money for the crews to be there if they are going to miss out on things? In theory, someone could have thrown a pie in the senator's face. Yeah, you never know. And that is what the networks are paying for: a guarantee that they will get video of everything that happens in a day. Therefore, the relationship between the networks and the campaign guarantees that spontaneity is forbidden on a presidential campaign.

At this point in the campaign, the arrangement the press corps has worked out is that whenever the senator goes out in public, he has to take the press pool with him—whether he is going to ride his bike or buy a jock strap, they are there. It is all on the honor system: It is up to the campaign to tell the press what the candidate is up to; if they say he isn't doing anything, the press can either take their word for it, or stake him out to see for themselves.

John Kerry has made it perfectly clear that he doesn't want press loitering near his property. But he is running for president; he should not assume that he can have any privacy. Since the only news that will come between now and the convention is the selection of a vice president, reporters are bound to stake out the candidate's house because it is their job to know who he is meeting with. And they have every right to stand outside of his house, but for those living in the bubble, staking him out is risky business because they don't want to upset the man they have to live with.

When the CNN producer found out that the Champagne Lounge was planning to stake out the senator's house, she managed to get herself (and her network) into this ersatz pool rotation, agreeing to take the 8 A.M. shift with the NBC producer. Since I have no pool privileges, I tagged along just for the fun of it.

So there we were at 7:57 standing on the street corner outside of John Kerry's Beacon Hill home waiting to see who was or wasn't coming or going. As discreetly as we could, we stood there talking on our cell phones, sipping Starbucks, and taking pictures of each other, just praying that the senator wouldn't look out of his bedroom window and spot us. If he did, he would not have been happy. He doesn't want to see his press corps lurking outside of his house; it only proves that they don't trust him when he says he'll call the pool if something is going to happen.

There was a lot of movement in Beacon Hill at eight o'clock in the morning. Ladies on their power walks, mommies with their strollers, a few men who walked straight out of the L.L. Bean catalogue. There was one guy wearing a pink polo shirt with a sweater wrapped around his neck carrying two squash rackets. Something tells me that we were sticking out. Everyone was eyeing us suspiciously; somehow they knew we did not belong in this upscale community.

"This is the only street in Boston with private parking," the CNN producer informed us as if we were on a walking tour. "John Kerry lives in an old convent. His kitchen used to be the chapel and the room on top was where they made altar bread." "I got to pee," the NBC producer complained. "Then go ask John Kerry if you can use his bathroom," Ms. CNN suggested.

8:43 A.M.: "Someone's going in! Let's make a note of it." The CNN producer started typing on her BlackBerry: "There is a woman appearing to be on the older side with short cropped gray hair, blue blazer, I would almost say it was black, navy to black blazer, picked up the newspapers, and entered the house, she had her own key." Yep, that's going in the pool note.

8:45 A.M.: What are you filing now? "I was telling my mom that I am standing outside of John Kerry's home at 8:45 in the morning and isn't she glad she spent thousands and thousands of dollars to send me to college so I can do this."

This led me to wonder aloud: "Is this the bottom of my career? We went from all-access in the primaries to staking out the senator's house?" The NBC producer reminded me, "You weren't even invited.

You are staking out our stakeout. And yes, the fact that you are here proves that your career is dying. I suggest you get that boyfriend of yours to marry you soon so you can start knocking out some puppies."

8:53 A.M.: "Someone's coming out! It's the old gray-haired lady leaving. And it's navy, that suit is definitely navy. Correct the pool report!" NBC demanded. "I have to say Teresa or whoever does their gardening has done a lovely job on those window boxes," CNN observed. Are you going to put that in the pool report?

"We are getting the evil eye from that Secret Service agent. He's coming to bust us!" "No he's not, he's going to give parking instructions to that dry-cleaning van," Ms. NBC noticed. "Maybe that's a decoy. Is that John Edwards getting out of the back of that dry-cleaning van?" the CNN producer joked. "No, that guy is Chinese."

9:05 A.M.: "Here she comes again!" The old gray-hair reentered the house with two grande cups of Starbucks coffee.

That was all the action we got on our stakeout. Just like the Secret Service has shifts, at 9:08 A.M., our replacement showed up and we changed shifts. It turned out that a Secret Service agent told our replacement that he saw three women hanging out drinking lattes and he could not figure out why they were standing there for so long. We did it! We blended right into the Beacon Hill community; we are the Charlie's Angels of presidential stakeouts.

So here is what we've learned on this stakeout (besides the fact that John Kerry lives in the kind of neighborhood where you don't have to pick up your own dry cleaning): There is a deep mistrust between the campaign and the press. The press corps don't trust the campaign staff to keep them in the loop about everything the senator is doing. As the CNN producer put it, "There is definite tension between the press corps and the campaign—the guy could be president of the U.S. We need to know what he is doing, what kind of coffee he is drinking—private moments are gone." It goes without saying that this problem exists on every campaign, but every four years it seems to only get worse.

At the end of the day the Fox News producer returned to the hotel with this report: The senator was glaring at her from his second-story window. Moments later, two of his staffers came out the front door and waved at her and she waved back. At which point Kerry appeared at the front door, saw Ms. Fox News waving, and assumed she was waving at him, so he waved back. He was not happy to see her. She ended her stakeout just before the senator left to go to his fund-raiser in Connecticut.

At the same time, the news was breaking that Kerry might not accept his party's nomination at the convention. Will the Democrats leave Boston without a nominee? All the local TV stations decided to stake out Kerry's house while all the traveling press headed to the airport to be on the flight to Connecticut for a fund-raiser they would not be allowed into.

When Kerry got to the airport and loaded the plane, reporters on the tarmac asked about the convention, but he pretended that he couldn't hear them. All he said was, "We'll do something on the plane."

He boarded the plane and went straight for the food spread, where he was asked how he felt about looking out his window and seeing the reporters staking him out. He said, "I figured, boy, they've become an untrustworthy group." The *Boston Globe* reporter asked, "Are you going to tell us about this delaying the nomination?" All Kerry said was, "The campaign will have a statement about it. I think they do already, I hope they do," and he retreated to his seat.

In flight he came back and scolded the reporters for not playing by his rules. "I want you to know I had five local cameras outside the house, I protected you. Okay? So I kept my part of the deal, now why were you all staking me out? You're not keeping your part of the deal. I didn't tell them anything. I didn't comment." What Kerry was saying is, "Since you guys weren't there, I didn't talk to the cameras. Therefore, you did not miss a sound bite."

While he sounded like he was protecting his press corps, he didn't really have a sound bite to give. When a reporter asked him about his convention plans he said, "The office is going to tell you." Will you tell us? "The office is going to tell you." Will you tell us if you are going to accept the nomination in July? "The office is going to tell you." Why won't you tell us? "Tell you what?" Then he walked away.

At the fund-raiser in Connecticut, the press pool was trapped like pets in Paul Simon's basement, where they rummaged through old Simon and Garfunkel memorabilia and took pictures next to a painting of the Simon family, while the rest of the press corps ate dinner at a restaurant near the airport.

When the plane landed back in Boston, all the reporters and camera crews took their usual position on the tarmac awaiting the Kerry arrival shot. But the senator snuck out through the back of the plane and walked up behind the press and said, "Gotcha. You guys were sneaking around me all day, I thought I would sneak up on you."

Media Culpa Redux

Reston, Virginia
MAY 24, 2004

I FINALLY GOT IT. It took thousands and thousands of dollars, fifty-seven varieties of no, and a promise that I would not "make fun of him." Just when the flight attendant made the announcement to prepare for landing, I got time with John Kerry.

While three aides hovered nervously overhead, I got to ask John Kerry the one thing I really wanted to know: "Why you? What did you do right that the other guys didn't?" His answer was "luck." I tried to probe deeper, but it just turned into a photo op. As I was trying to get him to reflect on the modern media environment, he took the camera and gave the same performance that Bush delivered in 2000.

When all was said and done, the whole experience felt like cruel and unusual punishment. He tried to be cool, but you could feel that he was self-conscious and out of character.

I wanted to say to him, "You are a U.S. senator and the nominee of your party. You don't have to do this! This is not who you are. You don't have to perform like a standup comedian for my camera!" But he does. Because this is what modern presidential campaigns have become. And whether we like it or not, it is only going to get worse unless the networks find a new way to cover elections.

So what if Senator Kerry isn't a warm and fuzzy teddy bear and he doesn't have what it takes to be a great television personality? That's not his fault. It's our fault for expecting these serious men to act like morning show hosts. Who was it that concluded that we all want a president that we can have a beer with? We'd all like to have a beer with Homer Simpson, but we wouldn't want him to be our president.

Whether you can see it or not, people like George Bush because they can relate to him. In America, we like the life of the frat-party-boy-turned-redeemed-sinner more than the overachiever who made all the right decisions in his life.

For the good of the country and of mankind, we have to stop asking our candidates to be likable guys. The future of Western civilization is at stake!

I am sorry for playing any part in this. In 2000, I provoked Bush because I could; we had the luxury of being able to fool around on the campaign trail. It was pre-9/11 and there was plenty to laugh about. We can't afford to goof around like that anymore. These deadly serious times require more than just a cute little tap dance from our presidential candidate. With the weight of the world on his shoulders, he should not have to be "fun" (a word that Senator Kerry used fourteen times in our conversation).

I learned my lesson from 2000 and this time around I came to discuss serious topics. When I asked him what it is like to live in this kind of unforgiving media culture, he just told me, "We are having so much fun." When I tried to talk about why he can't be honest in front of reporters, he claimed he was "having a lot of fun." When I asked if he agreed with the conventional wisdom that you are not allowed to change your mind in your lifetime (if you haven't thought the same thing since you were eighteen years old, you're labeled a flip-flopper), he made yet another joke about how much fun he was having. So I shared my theory with him about how the press oversimplifies and reduces things and makes caricatures out of the candidates, but he defended their right to have "fun." I get it, the candidate is on message: He is a *fun* guy.

This seems to be the goal of the campaign: to make their senator look cool. They are on the talk show offensive, trying to encourage people to come see the softer side of John by booking him on all those shows that lonely housewives watch while they wait for *Oprah* to come on. Still, even the housewives are having a hard time getting excited about Kerry. As one said after *Oprah,* "I think John is still trying to decide if he's a Democrat or a Republican. He doesn't take any positions, he just wants to win." Another said, "He doesn't deserve to win because he is not challenging our way of life. He is trashing Bush because it's trendy, but no original thoughts have come out of his mouth." The last woman to step up to the mic said, "I am a diehard Democrat, but I am not sure that I am going to vote for Kerry because you can say what you want about George Bush, but he seems like a real person, he doesn't make me feel uncomfortable." That seems to be all people want—comfort—and Kerry can't deliver.

The Republican scriptwriters know that we are afraid of the unknown and that despite all of the Dr. Phil and Oprah we watch, we are too scared and lazy to make a change. The administration has boiled this entire election down to this one talking point: "Are you comfortable changing horses midstream?" Americans are insecure, weak, and don't like to be challenged; we will stay the course for continuity's sake, no matter how badly our president treats us. For the same reason that some women live with domestic violence, people usually stick with what they know. Like a battered housewife, our country is the traumatized giant who is dependent on our nurturing president who is exploiting the sacred fact that, in America, it is our God-given right to be "comfortable." After September 11, Bush told us that he was going to protect us. We haven't gotten attacked since, and so he is going to get another term.

Everyone has their own way of measuring the candidates. After seeing all the footage I shot, Sheila Nevins, my boss at HBO, decided to put my movie on the air before the election because she thinks that

Kerry is not going to be president, and since he is not an interesting TV character, there will be no interest in him the day after he loses. I suspect she is right. Here is how I know that John Kerry is not going to be the president: At the gym when people are on the treadmill watching CNN, they always seem to change the channel when John Kerry comes on. Despite how much fun he thinks he is, few can see it.

George vs. John: Who can perform better for the cameras?

Catching Up with George

Washington, D.C.
MAY 29, 2004

AS A STUDENT of American history and a huge fan of Bob Dole, my boyfriend begged me to take him to the World War II memorial dedication ceremony. Since he's Dutch, I thought it would be good to take him to remind him that America has not always been the evil empire that Europeans think we are today.

We arrived in Washington, D.C., hungry on a busy Friday night: There were college graduation parties, bachelor parties, thousands of summer tourists, and veterans from all across the country here to see the new memorial. The only place where we could get a table without a reservation was Nathan's in Georgetown.

While we were eating dinner (the early bird special), an old man who was by himself walked by our table on his way out of the restaurant and my boyfriend thought he looked familiar. He said, "That man looks a lot like George McGovern. But it can't be him, that man has no pleats in his pants." No, that couldn't be him. The war hero, U.S. congressman for twenty-two years, and former nominee of the party could not be having dinner by himself on a Friday night in the nation's capital. Or could he? I went to investigate.

By the time I got to the door, he had gotten into a taxi and was pulling off into the sunset. When I asked the eighteen-year-old maître d', she told me that in fact that was our old friend George. I asked her, "How did you recognize him?" She said, "I didn't. He introduced himself to me as Senator McGovern and said he used to be a regular here. He asked me if we still serve his favorite dish and I had to ask what that was."

The German waitress who served him told us that he was telling her about his combat missions in World War II in which he dropped bombs over Germany (luckily he did not go into the details of how many of her countrymen he killed). She told us that he was reading a book during his dinner and he fell asleep. They had to wake him up to make sure he was okay. She said he told her, "I am the John Kerry of yesterday."

She also told us that she has been asking around and so far, we were the only ones in the restaurant who knew who he was. Scenes like this remind you that in the high-stakes poker of presidential politics, the winners are immortalized and the losers are completely forgotten and discarded.

At the end of our meal, as we were walking out of the restaurant, a motorcade was on its way down M Street. Since this is Washington, D.C., a town known for motorcades, heads barely turned, but being the political tourists that we are, we stopped to see who it was. Traffic was backed up for blocks. A black guy who came to cruise down the strip in his pimped-out Mazda, but ended up stuck on the side of the road, shouted out of the window, "It is a good thing that they don't put their names on those sedans because I'd never vote for a guy who made me wait in this traffic." When the entourage came speeding by we realized it was John Kerry! I hope he is enjoying this ride.

The next day at the memorial dedication, Senator Kerry saw George Bush for the first time since this race began, but George didn't have to see John. When you are the incumbent, you have the luxury of keeping your opponent as far away from you as possible. The volunteers doing the seating told us that George Bush wanted John Kerry in the bleacher seats, but the seaters fought to get him in the VIP section with the Cabinet members and other members of Congress, which was still a long way away from the action.

Sitting in the VIP section with my parents, I got to spend some quality time with my old friend Don Evans, the secretary of commerce who was on the road in 2000. I told him not to take it personally that Kerry wasn't coming over to say hello to him. I gave him the old "It's not you, it's me." He asked, "What is wrong with him, doesn't he know how much fun you are?" Those around me were amused by this. Kerry never did come over to greet any of the Cabinet members or members of Congress seated in his row.

When the program began, we could barely see a thing. On the Jumbotron, we saw Bob Dole standing next to his former rival, Bill Clinton. Looking out at the crowd of more than 150,000, Dole started off his speech by saying, "Never had a crowd like this when I was running." Former president George Bush laughed aloud knowingly. Poor old George McGovern was nowhere in sight (and he didn't even get a mention).

When the president was introduced the crowd rose to their feet as the president's own Navy Band played "Hail to the Chief." As the president came out with the color guard, Kerry rose to applaud, and he clapped along politely when the president gave his speech. For the rest of the two-hour ceremony, Kerry, the Vietnam War hero who has made his combat experience the theme of his campaign, just sat and watched the AWOL president command all of the attention.

Panning from the Washington Monument to John Kerry, I had to wonder: Will John Kerry be written into the history books as one of the great leaders of our time? Or will he disappear into oblivion like all of those who have tried out for this job and failed?

Good Guys and Bad Guys

New York City
JUNE 20, 2004

The political theater is a contest between good and evil, and if you don't find some evil to contest, you often find yourself (cast as) the evil that somebody else is contesting.

—FORMER PRESIDENTIAL CANDIDATE
JERRY BROWN

LIKE ANY GOOD HORROR MOVIE, every campaign needs a villain. In the 2000 election, George W. Bush recognized that anti-Clinton backlash was his most effective weapon. He followed the script—"I will swear to uphold the honor and dignity of the office to which I have been elected, so help me God"—casting Al Gore as a horrifying new monster, the Son of Clinton. And the sequel died.

If Bush wants to fulfill the Hollywood storyline of going where no Bushman has gone before (into a second term), then he is going to have to beat off those evil Democrats in the movie industry. And if you are looking for a preview of what he is up against, this was the week to see it!

Monday night was the New York premiere of Michael Moore's *Fahrenheit 9/11.* The celebs came out in full force to celebrate one man for having some balls. The gang was all there: Leonardo DiCaprio, Tony Bennett, Richard Gere, Tom Brokaw, Brian Williams, Ed Bradley,

Mike Myers, Martha Stewart, Al Franken, Tim Robbins, Yoko Ono, Al Sharpton, Glenn Close, Kurt Vonnegut, Lauren Bacall, Lauren Hutton, John McEnroe, Patti Smythe, Vernon Jordan, Carson Daly, Macaulay Culkin, Sandra Bernhardt, Philip Seymour Hoffman, Kyra Sedgwick, and Linda Evangelista.

During the film, the A-list booed and cheered in all the right places (Condi got her own special sinister hiss). When it was all over, the adoring crowd gave Moore a standing ovation. He came out (with bodyguards on either side) and gave an inarticulate speech about how Bush is destroying America (but the words Democrat and Kerry were not spoken) and how he hopes his movie will take down this evil regime. This is the great thing about America: You can make movies about how evil your government is and become rich and famous doing so!

Now that Michael Moore got me in the mood to hate Bush, it was the perfect time to go back to the White House to see him, which is what I did on Tuesday night. Before I could tell the president about how much trouble he is going to be in when America sees Michael Moore's movie, he laid on some of that old Texas charm by making jokes with my boyfriend about how patient he must be for putting up with me. Is this supposed to be endearing?

When I told Karl Rove about how evil he looks in the Moore movie he responded, "The problem with the filmmakers in the world is that they have no idea what it's like to have a seat at the table." A Republican congressman referring to Moore as "that big marshmallow slacker" showed no concern about the film. "Anyone can get thrown out, who cares what an outsider thinks? . . . Our voters don't go to the art houses to see those kinds of films." He predicted that this movie will not be seen by those outside of the underground film world, but what he doesn't realize is that *Fahrenheit 9/11* will be playing in real movie theaters all across the country because of all the publicity Moore has gotten from the Republicans attacking his film. Every time someone goes on TV attacking Michael Moore, calling him un-American, he sells more movie tickets. If they really want to hurt Moore, they will ignore him.

Many Democrats are afraid that Michael Moore's movie is going to undermine them and help Bush. One senator said, "The reason I don't appreciate Michael Moore is because he doesn't live by the rules of journalism—he's just as bad as Fox News. His movie may hurt more than it helps." Another joked that if Moore wanted to help, he ought to "take a shower."

But the Democrats have bigger problems on their plate right now: That pesky well-sponsored group of Kerry-hating vets, calling themselves the Swift Boat Veterans for Truth, are hijacking this election! They keep running dubious ads disputing Kerry's version of what happened in Vietnam. Initially Kerry ignored them, waiting seventeen days to respond to their attacks against his character. That was just enough time to make people think there was some kernel of truth in what they were saying. Even though the content of the ads has been discredited based on Kerry's official military record and testimonials from his boat mates, the media refuse to flat-out call the Swift Boat Vets for Truth a bunch of liars, and the news stories about what they said versus what he said are keeping the anti-Kerry Swift Boaters' stories alive! In the politics of television, the truth is irrelevant; the only thing that matters is the impression that people get. Because Kerry waited so long to respond, it created enough doubt in everyone's head to damage his image.

There is a lot of noise from Democrats that Kerry is not stepping up. He hasn't grown from the late primary level and there is no energy coming from his campaign. As one congressman put it, "He is having a problem with his message; rather, he has no message." Another complained that their candidate is "saying nothing." But one congressman who spent the month of January campaigning for Kerry in New Hampshire assured me, "It doesn't matter what Kerry is saying. Bush is going to kill himself with this war of his."

Speaking of presidents who are still fighting their own wars, Wednesday night was the New York premiere of another political film, *The Hunting of the President,* starring Bill Clinton as the victim of a witchhunt. After the film, Slick Willy came out to talk about how he was "persecuted by the vast right-wing conspiracy." (The question remains, if it all went down while the whole world watched, is it still a conspiracy? And if he knew all along they were hunting him, why was he so recklessly fooling with his destiny?) By now we all know that the Republicans wasted $73 million of our tax dollars to prove that Bill got a blow job, diverting the nation's attention from things that really matter, like those terrorists who had already bombed the Twin Towers in 1993. You have to wonder if we would be in Iraq right now if our Congress had been taking care of business instead of obsessing over what base Bill and Monica got to. Damn you, Ken Starr!

Since we are on the topic of partisan warfare, Thursday night offered a screening of *Outfoxed,* a new documentary about how Rupert Murdoch is destroying American television. But if you didn't already know that, then you must be living in a cave somewhere in Afghanistan (then again, even there I am sure they know that Fox is partisan and deceptive). Fox News may be bad, but the reason I watch it is because Hannity and O'Reilly are so much more fun to watch than those guys on the other networks that are so much smarter than us mere mortals!

This week was all about preaching to the converted. Friday night brought us to *Bush's Brain,* a documentary about Karl Rove, the evil genius who made Bush the statesman he is today. You already know the story: George Bush was this total loser who couldn't hold a job until Rove came along and started pulling the strings. Probing deep into the sinister forces behind the throne, this film serves as a retrospective of all of Rove's finest work—portraying him as the kind of guy who would cheat in a game of Monopoly against his own son. All the evidence is there to prove that Rove is the master of the dark arts of getting his candidate elected! That bastard! Oh, to be liberal, it's all so simple: Bush is the bad guy, we are always right about everything, and we always lose.

Man, it sucks to be a Democrat these days. It seems like the only people we have on our side are the lefty documentary filmmakers, and while everyone keeps saying that "political docs are hot," the box office receipts prove that the only thing that is selling is partisanship. The Republicans are already running ads grouping Kerry with Moore, Clinton, and all the other left-wing weirdos (even Howard Dean made the cut!) because, in our two-party system, you aren't really voting for one person, you are voting for the party.

Who can think of a more perfect way to wind up this week than snuggling up on the couch on Sunday night to watch Bill Clinton on *60 Minutes* standing on his mother's grave in red, white, and blue Nikes with Dan Rather sharing secrets from his childhood. The only thing I learned from this episode is that the president is still wearing that blue dress! He wants to be loved and is fighting for approval and not even *60 Minutes* cares about anything other than hearing the dirt on Monica. All of the teases for the show talked about Monica, and Dan Rather had to feign interest in Bill's childhood, just waiting to get the part about "couch time" (when Hillary made him sleep on the couch).

So all we are going to see on TV this summer is Michael Moore selling tickets to his movie or Bill Clinton pimping his paperweight-size autobiography. And the questions that all of the political analysts on Fox News will ask are will Michael Moore be good or bad for Kerry? Will Clinton help or hurt Kerry? There is only one person missing from all of this: the Democratic challenger!

The Number Two

Pittsburgh, Pennsylvania
JULY 11, 2004

DESPITE WHAT THE *New York Post* cover story said, John Kerry did not pick Dick Gephardt to be his vice president. He made the easiest and most obvious choice: Mr. Cutie Pie. Kerry did what the polls and the donors wanted him to do. Deep down we all knew that this was going to be the ticket, but many speculated that Edwards would never get the job because of the animosity between the two men. But then again, who else was there?

John McCain? Sure, there was a lot of noise that Senator Kerry would pick the beloved right-wing Republican. The two were spotted having secret meetings in their secret Senate hideaway. But eventually McCain rejected Kerry by saying "I spent several years in a North Vietnamese prison camp, in the dark, fed with scraps. Do you think I want to do that all over again as vice president of the United States?" He followed his misguided sense of loyalty back home to the president who has always treated him like dirt. You have to hand it to those Bushmen: They can accuse you of having an illegitimate black child and a doped-out wife and still get you to go out and do their bidding. (Poor John McCain, this time he really has sold his soul.)

It is a good sign that Kerry didn't take a conservative Republican as his running mate (even though the word on K Street is that Kerry offered McCain half the government to join the ticket). If he did, it would have been a blow to the people in this business who dedicated their entire lives to defending their Democratic principles. When hearing about the speculation that McCain was in the running for the running mate position, a former candidate who was campaigning for Kerry (and wanted the job himself) said, "See, all he wants to do is win and he doesn't care about the consequences."

After the inevitable announcement that the media had been waiting months for, the "Dream Team" (a term I heard on TV fourteen times in the first two days) could be seen touching and tickling each other so much that all the Internet chatter was buzzing about how they "can't keep their hands off each other." All the heavy petting, hair jokes, and talk about how much "fun they are having" couldn't fool those of us who had heard the two men speak about each other off the record before this holy union.

The Dream Team sat down with their wives on *60 Minutes* and even Leslie Stahl commented that Teresa "makes it sound like they're on a double date—not in the midst of a campaign." But there was one moment in that interview that revealed everything you need to know about this ticket.

LESLIE STAHL: How do you think the honeymoon is going?

ELIZABETH EDWARDS: I think we are in for—we need to start looking right now for silver anniversary gifts. This is a marriage that's working. Yes.

TERESA HEINZ KERRY (SINGS): We are getting to know you. We are about four days in and all we've done is laugh and have a good time.

STAHL: What are you laughing about? I've heard you say that out loud even in front of crowds . . .

JOHN EDWARDS: Now, don't tell everything. This is the one we have to worry about telling everything.

STAHL: I know. That's why I am interviewing her.

Even though he has only been on board the Kerry train for ninety-six hours, John Edwards is already trying to rein in Teresa? Go easy, tiger. Leave that woman alone. On that note, isn't it sad how we are still living in a time when everyone wants the independent-minded woman to shut her mouth? Even the most liberated New York woman I know put it like this: "If your man told you that for one year he was going to pursue his lifelong goal, wouldn't you blow your hair out and keep your mouth shut?"

In between the primaries and this big announcement, I saw the movie *The Candidate,* the story of Bill McKay, the senatorial candidate with hair as good as John Edwards's. When McKay (played by Robert Redford) spoke, the ladies had the same look in their eyes that they have when they watch John Edwards. During the film, I couldn't help but notice that McKay's speech sounds eerily familiar:

I think it's important to note which subjects we haven't touched. We completely ignored the fact that this is a society divided by fear, hatred, and violence and until we talk about just what this society really is, I don't know how we are going to change it. For example, we haven't discussed the rot that destroys our cities . . . we haven't discussed race in this country, we haven't discussed poverty. In short, we haven't discussed any of the sicknesses that may yet send this country up in flames. And we better do it, we better get it out in the open and confront it before it's too late.

After McKay delivers his speech the TV executive tells him, "That was quite a show." Who does this remind you of?

When I saw John Edwards's traveling staffer Miles Lackey (yes, that is his real name), I asked him if he plagiarized the McKay speech and he told me that I was not the first person to ask that question.

While many in the party are happy to see their Southern boy back on the trail using that social lubrication gene to attract voters, others are worried that he doesn't add any gravitas to the ticket. Those who are skeptical about Edwards's ability to be president said this of Kerry's choice: When making their pick, candidates always think of living, not dying. Unless the president dies, all the vice president does is go to state funerals. Which is why FDR's vice president John Vance Garner said, "The vice presidency isn't worth a bucket of warm spit."

These days, the job still may not be worth much, but the selection is the biggest public relations decision a candidate can make, and Kerry gave the media the Dream Team story line they wanted. Evan Thomas from *Newsweek* admitted, "The media, I think, wants Kerry to win and I think they're going to portray Kerry and Edwards—I'm talking about the establishment media, not Fox—but they're going to portray Kerry and Edwards as being young and dynamic and optimistic and all. There's going to be this glow about them that . . . is going to be worth, collectively, the two of them, that's going to be worth maybe fifteen points."

The Summer of Hate

New York City
SEPTEMBER 2, 2004

WHO DOESN'T LOVE A CONVENTION? With all the cheer-leading, and the fanfare, and the party favors, and the propaganda, and the prostitutes, and the cheesy Americana music, and the $9 hot dogs, and the stinky Porta Pottis, and the kind of security you would expect to see at Armageddon, and the never-ending speeches about how much we love America, and the best balloon drops ever (as long as the director isn't yelling for the "fucking" balloons to drop), and the celebrity sightings (Bono, John Cusack, and Sarah Jessica Parker all in one night?), and the highest concentration of credentialed media ever assembled under one roof, all sitting in the press box complaining that there is no story here!

My favorite convention was in the summer of 1984; my mom was in charge when the Democrats came to San Francisco. The first thing she did when there was a glitch in the convention schedule was order more food and alcohol for the reporters. She said that as long as they are eating and drinking they won't be writing bad stories. That was when I knew I wanted to be a journalist.

That was the same convention where my sister Jacqueline had her magical encounter with Warren Beatty. She was sixteen in her floral Laura Ashley *Little House on the Prairie* dress. He asked her to get him a Coke: She gave him his beverage; he said, "Thank you." To this day, she still thinks there was a real connection between them. I am sure he remembers the whole affair fondly.

But I digress.

The best part about the Democratic Convention in Boston in 2004 was being reunited with all of our old candidates from the primaries. Some had more closure than others. At a party for the California dele-

The Summer of Hate ~ 257

gation Howard Dean said, "If California voted sooner, I would be speaking Thursday night instead of Tuesday." When John Kerry took to the stage on Thursday night, I had to salute him for all of the shitty days he had to endure to get here.

The highlight of my Boston convention experience was when I was walking down Newbury Street and the motorcycle cops came whizzing by, sweeping the cars to the side of the road and lining up all of the people gathered on the sidewalk to see who was coming. The crowd was murmuring with anticipation, "Can you see anything?" "Is it John Kerry?" "Maybe it will be Bill Clinton?" "It could just be Hillary." "I want to see Jimmy Carter!"

Alas, there was no motorcade and no political stars to be spotted. The police were clearing the streets for the smallest parade of protesters ever assembled in the history of American demonstrations. There were more camera crews than protesters. The ringleader was banging on her drum shouting, "Free Tibet Now." "Who is Tibet?" a young girl asked her mother. Mom explained, "Like disco and leg warmers, Tibet was one of those things I was into when I was a kid. But that was a long time ago. Not even Madonna cares about Tibet anymore."

That small collection of protesters, with hundreds of thousands of their unwashed friends, took to the streets of New York City a month later to protest the Republican National Convention. In what looked suspiciously like a Halloween parade, hundreds of thousands of out-of-towners took to our streets to make a statement against this administration, and the war, and Blood for Oil, and global warming, and Falun Gong, and hate crimes, and white-collar crime, and the death penalty, and AIDS, and breast cancer, and the draft, and abortion haters, and electronic voting, and religion being taught in schools (to name just a few of the signs I saw). There was also a large collection of slogans like "No more French Fries," but we couldn't determine if this was anti-European sentiment or just a bunch of McDonald's haters.

Here is what else I figured out from reading the signs at the protests: Bush is Satan, Bush is Hitler, Bush is evil, Bush is a terrorist, and the only bush many women trust is their own. Signs were visibly lacking for John Kerry—his supporters seemed to be few and far between. In one hour, my boyfriend counted three Kerry-Edwards posters and twenty-eight animal rights signs (not including the one that asked, WHO LET THE DOGS OUT? because that could have been a political statement). There were a number of signs that read "No love for Bush" on one side and "No love for Kerry" on the other. Needless to say, Bushwhacking has never been so fashionable. Every other marcher seemed to be wearing the same black T-shirt with a big red X over Bush's face. (Isn't it strange how Osama, the guy who engineered 9/11, is getting a free pass? No one has a T-shirt with his face crossed out.)

The Bush haters are camped out in our local park, Union Square, so whether we like it or not, everyone in my neighborhood is going to be spending a lot of time with them this week. It seems no one is a big fan of the guy marching around chanting slogans on his Mr. Microphone at all hours of the night. He seemed to have only three things to say: "Hey, hey, ho, ho, George Bush has got to go"; "Racist, sexist, antigay, George Bush go away"; and the oldie but goodie, "No justice, no peace." (These are the same chants they were using when I was in college. Shouldn't we get a new protest chant every generation?)

There was one woman who was advertising the fact that she spent two weeks in prison during the Republican Convention in 2000. She was here, prepared to go back to jail for two more weeks, "just to send George Bush a message." By nightfall her wish came true; as she was getting dragged into the police wagon she was shouting, "Punish Bush." I am sure that George Bush didn't hear a word of it. I bet he doesn't even know anything about these protests. I am sure they hide those stories from him. And I bet he didn't hear the one-legged vet at Union Square screaming at the top of his lungs, "Half the country hates you, Mr. President, did you know that?"

The city was under siege and it was hard to figure out who there were more of: police, protesters, or press. On my walk to work I saw cops lined up in a straight line from 14th Street to 42nd. There were thousands of them. And it didn't take much for them to take out their orange nets to rope up and arrest an entire city block of those practicing their right of free speech, along with any unsuspecting innocent bystanders who happened to be in the wrong place at the wrong time. The

NYPD had all of downtown under total surveillance, with helicopters and blimps monitoring our every move. The combination of police and news choppers made it sound and feel like we were living in a war zone. And we were.

There was a lot of activity in Union Square all week: puppet shows, poetry readings, street performances, anti-Bush dance troupes, antiwar art exhibits, protest bike rides, a soapbox that was open all day and night, candlelight vigils at which the group formed a group hug and sang "Kumbaya." Over by the statue of Mahatma "icon of protest" Gandhi, demonstrators were being offered free food! A homeless New Yorker (who usually lives in this park) asked for a sandwich, but he was denied because he could not show any proof that he was against anything. Gandhi would be ashamed; he was a showman who understood it was all about public relations. His memorial here makes it clear what is missing from this scene: a leader and strategist who could organize these people to create an event that would capture the imagination of the public and actually have some impact.

Watching the young men streaking through the park naked with NO BUSH painted on their chests made me wonder how many came here to make a political statement and how many were here just for the theater of it all. The whole scene reminded me of the time I went to the Federal Building in San Francisco to pick up my mom from work. There were protesters outside chanting, dancing around, and getting their groove on. When my mom walked out, no one seemed to notice. When I told her that I was afraid that they were going to confront her, she told me, "They are here all the time, this is what they come for; they are here just for this."

This doesn't seem to be about taking political action. Few seem to have any interest in the political process. If they did, we would have seen them during the primaries. If they care so much about getting rid of Bush, how come they weren't out there back then trying to do something about it? Maybe some were for Dean, but many here are wearing their support for Nader on their sleeves. Of course, not everyone participating in the protests is a caricature of the counterculture, but the potluck of Greenies, lefties, tree huggers, and granola eaters are the ones who stick out to the tourists. Watching the red double-decker buses pull up to Union Square full of sightseers taking pictures and videotaping all of the tattooed, pierced, angry rebels, I couldn't help but think that this scene is the best commercial for the GOP. They will go home to their swing states telling their friends and family about all the weirdos screaming in New York City against Bush, and they will have a great laugh at our expense.

It is fashionable in press circles to complain that the conventions are nothing more than a spectacle, staples of American political iconography that don't produce any news. But fifteen thousand credentialed journalists are here (three per delegate), and you know what they all show up for: those political parties! One of the old-school newsies bragged to a political figure he was sucking up to, "In all my years of covering conventions, I've never been inside a convention hall." It is fun to watch the journalists brown-nose the politicians because you can tell instantly which politicos want media attention and are opening themselves up to be used as a source in the future and which won't give a press hound the time of day, and therefore inevitably will get burned.

Even though the networks have cut back on their coverage, the gang is all here. Rather, Brokaw, and Jennings got together in Boston to complain about their networks' unwillingness to show more of the convention in prime time; they blamed it on their entertainment divisions. (Those poor anchors have no pull, even though their title is managing editor?) At the Harvard Club in New York, the media elite gathered to discuss their failures and to bemoan the fact that the Swift Boat Veterans for Truth have set the agenda in this election. Joe Klein of *Time* blamed cable television for airing and reairing the swift boat charges: "The more we talk about swift boats, the less we talk about George W. Bush's remarkable decision to go to war preemptively in Iraq. That's what we should be talking and writing about." There was no explanation for why the media let Bush's distortions go unchecked.

Since I know Democrats, I got to go to all the big donor events in Boston, but I assumed that when the Republicans came to town, I would be persona non grata. Ironically, during the Republican Convention, I was invited to "do lunch" at some of the finest restaurants in the city—Daniel, Le Cirque, Le Bernardin—places that I have never been in my eight years in Manhattan. Dressed up in my Nancy Reagan power suit, I walked to the subway at Union Square to catch the subway uptown, to see how the other half lives. There, waiting on the platform with all the other locals dressed to go to work, a gang of outcasts who were squatting in the subway station yelled out at us, "Republicans go home." To which a cop replied, "They must be out-of-towners, they don't know that Republicans don't ride the subway."

On my journey deep into the belly of the RNC, here is what I learned. Republican men wear really nice, expensive socks and have impeccable table manners, but all they talk about is the markets. They have heavy, extensive discussions about "the ramifications of the capital gains tax holding periods" and "midcap stocks in your allocation" and "leveraging a proprietary stock rating" and "the fully indexed rate in a softening market" and "up-tick in performance numbers." Without an MBA, you can't really talk to them; they are speaking a whole other language.

In Boston, at every breakfast, lunch, and dinner there was a deep discussion about how schoolchildren are going to get their milk money, and how senior citizens are going to get medications, and how college students can get loans. After attending a week of cocktail parties with both political parties I can tell you that the clichés fit. The Republicans care about how the markets are performing and the Democrats care about solving the country's social ills.

A caterer who worked at both conventions compared her experiences: "The Republicans drink more expensive wine, the Democrats tip better, but neither look like they are having much more fun."

The strangest part about the Republican Convention coming to town was how alienated the protesters made many New York Democrats feel. Every time I walked by the park and heard them singing a '70s revolutionary anthem, it inspired me to go home and stay locked up until the circus left town. Inside my Greenwich Village apartment building, many seemed to agree with me. "I vote with them, but I did not identify with them," said the guy from 3D. The guy from 1A explained why he didn't want to go anywhere near the park: "I think they are hurting our cause. Whatever they are doing out there is all so foreign to me." The gal from 7D said, "All that noise makes me uncomfortable because it isn't coming from the right place." Perhaps this only shows how gentrified the Village has become, or it shows a real problem for the Democratic Party.

The one thing both conventions had in common was that they were unwanted. Bostonians and New Yorkers (who rarely agree on much) were all complaining about the disruption and inconvenience that the conventions brought to their towns. One NYC Sanitation Department employee said as he was sweeping up after the elephants, "They made a lot of noise and left a huge mess just to tell us that it's Bush versus Kerry." Everyone (except for those who got serenaded by John McCain at Cipriani's) seems to think that the $100 million spent on the DNC and RNC pep rallies was a colossal waste of money that didn't bring any money to the people in the towns that hosted them.

Except for the entrepreneurs out on the street. Still, of all the paraphernalia that was being sold—the bumper stickers with Bush wearing a swastika on his forehead, the "Bush is an evil moron" coffee mugs, the refrigerator magnets with Osama having sex with Bush, the "Fuck Bush" underwear, the anti-Bush song books, the children's books with titles like "Bush Is an Ass" and "Watch Cheney Burn in Hell," the "Give Bush a Brain" board games, the nudie calendars encouraging women to "Show your bush against Bush," and all the varieties of T-shirts with crude and unoriginal vagina puns (they really got a lot of mileage out of the whole Dick and Bush thing)—the only item I was tempted to buy was the one that said, "Elect Better Actors."

One thing is for sure: Despite how the election turns out, the big winners this election year are the capitalists selling the T-shirts with Bush's face crossed out.

Why Does Everyone Love Celebrities and Hate the Media?

Napoleon, Ohio
OCTOBER 31, 2004

"CAN YOU BELIEVE ARNOLD CALLED ME?" a lady squealed at Loser's Deli. "How did Arnold Schwarzenegger get your phone number?" her friend asked. I knew what these women were talking about because it happened to me. There I was, fast asleep on a Saturday morning at 8 A.M. and guess who called and woke me up? Arnold! He said, "Vote Republican. Hasta la vista," and then just hung up. (He is not the first celebrity to crank-call me this week: Laura Bush, Rudy Giuliani, and Bill and Hillary all have, too.) But these women actually believed that a campaign robocall was Arnold himself calling, and from the excitement that her story generated it was clear that people love getting woken up by celebrities!

With the countdown to the election, the stars are coming out. It's Puff Daddy versus Bill Clinton: Who can deliver a bigger crowd? Springsteen or Schwarzenegger: Who will draw more camera crews? Which celebrity do you want to listen to: Britney Spears, Kid Rock, Billy Ray Cyrus, Wayne Newton, and Lynyrd Skynyrd, who are all singing Bush's praises? Or Madonna, Justin Timberlake, Ozzy Osbourne, Willie Nelson, Leonardo DiCaprio, and Missy Elliott, who are all out for Kerry?

The cult of infotainers are all here! We are in the phase of the campaign that has nothing to do with politics and everything to do with entertainment value. Even *The Insider*, a tabloid Hollywood gossip show, is getting in on the act. They are advertising that they are "leading the way in election coverage." Some blow-dried bimbo who usually stalks celebrities is going live right now "reporting" that "Ashton Kutcher is in his hometown campaigning for Kerry," to which the ladies in the diner asked, "Can you turn that up?" The wall between politics and entertainment has been breached.

Just ask any of the cool kids, "Why are you voting for Kerry?" And don't be surprised when they say, " 'Cause Puff Daddy told me to!" The young crowds are in Cleveland, waiting for Puffy's charter to land, screaming "Vote or die!" But the kids of today can't actually be trusted to show up on election day. (Most of them will do what Paris Hilton does: wear a T-shirt that says VOTE but won't.) That is why the Kerry campaign is leading people who showed up to see Bruce Springsteen straight into a voting booth. One of the young tarts at the concert refused to go along with the pack because Kerry did not meet her criteria: "Kerry turns me off because of that goofy face. Like, do you want to have to see that face for four years? I won't apologize for it. I only care about how they look." Her drinking buddy disagreed. "I can't stand looking at Bush, he is so lame, the way he walks is so funny, it's like he has a turd in his pants." These are the kinds of informed choices that voters are making. They are tuning out the news and listening to their favorite celebrity. But what about all those trusted experts?

As the networks are getting their full election team coverage going 24-7, the talking heads are falling in love with their microphones and the sound of their own voices, but few are happy about the media takeover of their town. As one local complained, "We were really excited about the election until all of the camera crews started showing up and turning this into a big soap opera. Why do the networks have to do this to us? They take a good thing and suck all of the joy out of it. I just can't wait 'til this whole thing is over." Everyone wants to see Leonardo DiCaprio, but they don't want the smelly journalists that come with him. You can't get one without the other. If there were no media, how would you get celebrities? We all love Hollywood because it fulfills our fantasies, but we hate the people who deliver us that fiction.

The candidates are now bona fide celebrities and they don't even pretend to talk to the real people anymore—the events are set up so that they are speaking directly to the cameras. Across from the stage there is a bank of more than one hundred cameras, while the locals are shoved over to the side of the stage so that they will not be in the way of the working press. Usually these things are staged, but this is 100 percent made for TV. One of my fellow road warriors from 2000 observed, "I am remembering why I hate this phase in presidential campaigns. All of the cameras make it a circus."

Every working journalist in America (from *Good Housekeeping* to *AAA Club Magazine*) is getting in on the election action and everyone is an expert! All the newspapers and magazines are pushing their reporters onto the TV screens to promote their publications. Most of what they are talking about is predictions, and it is clear that nobody knows what they are talking about. All of these so-called experts are just reading tea leaves and crystal balls. We are all experts on the future because it hasn't happened yet.

What would happen if there were no polls? What would the chattering cheeseballs talk about for the month leading into the election? We all know that there is nothing left to say, but the news organizations have a lot of space to fill, so what do they do? They commission pollsters to run polls so that they can make their own news. "A new *Newsweek* poll today says . . ." And then the candidates are forced to respond to this poll. This is not news—it is just filling dead air and everybody knows it.

At a rally in Philadelphia, a man who was being asked about the latest *Newsweek* poll said, "I got news for *Newsweek:* Not one person on earth cares about your poll. I'll tell you what I am going to do. I will wait and see who *Newsweek* says is going to win and I'll vote for the other candidate." His friend chimed in, "We can think for ourselves, we don't need the media to tell us what to think. Who elected them to think for us?"

When a spectator saw Chris Matthews walk by he screamed, "Chris Matthews, go home!" When asked why he felt this way he said, "He thinks his show has some cachet, but what is the point of it? Just to see people scream at each other like on *Jerry Springer*? There is a reason why WWF wrestling is the most popular sport on cable. Sure people like car crashes and natural disasters, but it is not good for them to see. Those shows are just jerking off the public."

Nearby, a young man was holding a sign that said ANNOY THE MEDIA, DON'T VOTE. He explained to the few who would listen to him that he is not going to vote in this election to protest the media. "I have disdain for Tim Russert. He is always telling us what to think and predicting how we are going to vote. He and all those fat old white men that he talks to on TV make me hate politics. I am not voting in this election out of protest. I don't want to be a part of it." It seems that not everyone votes, but they all watch television.

Another fellow in the crowd had this to say: "It's too bad that the media is so out of touch with the country they live in. Ah, to be enlightened, that must feel so good. But we hate all the pretentious intellectuals who write for publications with 'New York' in the title, preaching to us about what's right for us . . . I canceled my cable because I got tired of all the noise it brought into my house."

At the Dunkin' Donuts, I asked a woman why she was not going to listen to Kerry speak and she made this observation: "All that politics is just entertainment, it doesn't really mean anything to me. The candidates come to town just to get on TV and to give the people on TV something to talk about. How much of it is real? How much of it will affect real people?" Another donut eater suggested, "There are no real reporters anymore, no one in the middle, no one wants even-handedness; people want to hear from their own kind. All they want is the ammunition for their own ideology. I don't know who to believe anymore. They are all full of shit. Just look at Dan Rather." Using the example of CBS airing inauthentic documents to impugn President Bush's National Guard service, many point out that the networks are so out of touch with mainstream America that they have to "make up stories to get attention."

It is not news that so many people no longer trust the networks, but it is interesting to ask why, because everyone has their own opinion. One guy will tell you that the TV folks "rush to air" without doing their homework (like CBS). Another guy will complain that those newsmen make million-dollar salaries but are always trying to sell us something (like Brokaw's book series). Some other guy objects to how the newsmen have become a part of the news story (who will win the Tim

Russert primary?). And you will always find someone who is tired of looking at those saccharine smiles and hearing that pompous protocol ("Back to you, Tom"). It is impossible to list all of the reasons the man on the street resents the Fourth Estate, but this we know for sure: People do not appreciate it when the media interfere in their personal decisions.

The Guardian, a British newspaper, launched a letter-writing campaign to beg Americans to vote against Bush. Americans have been writing back to the Brits telling them, "Mind your own business. We don't need weenie-spined Limeys meddling in our presidential election. If it wasn't for America, you'd all be speaking German."

The more people I talk to, the more it seems that "real people" don't know the difference between the politicians and the press. They see them sitting all cozy, side by side, in the television studios, so they put them all in the same category. And since the presidential candidates are keeping the networks in business with all of their ad-buys, some see democracy as nothing more than a way to keep capitalism strong. An old man sitting in a lawn chair in downtown Philly holding a sign that read STOP GOVERNMENT-SPONSORED NEWS said, "You know what I hate about those types of people? They aren't talking to us, they talk at us." When asked who "those types of people" are, he replied, "You know, all them whities you see rapping on the tee-vee. They either work for the government or the media, they're all the same—those men who own this country are all in business together. Why do they call it free press? There is no such thing, the corporations own them and they are in business with the politicians, and we are the ones who are paying the price."

The thing that everyone seems to resent about the stories in the newspapers is that they reduce everything to a simple "he said, she said" street fight. Instead of focusing on the issues, they obsess over the mistakes people make. The truth requires an explanation, which makes for a boring story, so in the interest of time it gets cut. Talking about what is actually true in a news story would be like going into the emergency room and telling them that you aren't in any pain—no one would pay attention. One of the campaign reporters pointed out that his goal is to make some noise: "It's only news if it gets picked up and echoed all over the place." Like when Teresa Heinz Kerry told that reporter to "shove it."

In this hypercompetitive climate, the reporters sit on the sidelines and dissect everyone's words, trying to provoke a fight. Like scavengers in a junkyard, the newsmen are picking apart every new line that comes out in a desperate attempt to make a story out of it. There seems to be no explanation for what they choose to pick up on.

For example, when asked if she would be different from Laura Bush as first lady, Teresa Heinz Kerry told *USA Today*, "I don't know that she's ever had a real job." Even though what Teresa said is true, Laura hasn't worked since the 1970s, except for being a mother (like many women in America), the partisan pundits squawked about it to the point where Teresa was forced to apologize (because there is no political gain in attacking a beloved first lady). Laura said the apology was not necessary, making the point that, "actually I know those trick questions," implying that this is a nonissue, just another example of the media stirring the pot.

Similarly, when asked about the "War on Terror" on the *Today* show, President Bush said, "I don't think we can win it." Finally, an honest assessment of how long this struggle will be instead of that simplistic propaganda that we usually get. These are the most honest words to come from the president's mouth, but of course everyone had to spoil this moment by jumping all over Bush for being defeatist. Mr. Sunshine Edwards was sent to the cameras to say that this war is "absolutely winnable." Who is responsible for perpetuating this conflict, the campaign operatives or the media?

And let's not forget about John Kerry's infamous statement, "I've met with foreign leaders who can't go out and say it publicly, but boy, they look at you and say, 'You've got to win this. You've got to beat this guy. We need a new policy.' " The Republicans exploited this by demanding a list of names. Grow up, we all know that most of Europe hates Bush because he takes pride in making fun of old Europe. Bush knows that the whole world doesn't love him, but he never seemed to

Waiting for news to happen.

care. Now, ironically, he is insisting, "He should not say things without backing it up." Why not, Mr. President? You told us that Saddam had weapons of mass destruction and you can't back that up.

We all say that we want our politicians to be honest and tell it like it is, but when they do, they get punished. Those who don't choose their words wisely will get burned and we are all going to be tuned in to see it. Because even though we say we hate that trashy television, we are watching it (and not PBS), and that's all that those self-anointed gods of the newsroom care about. As long as we are watching, they can defend what they are airing.

Election Night!

Washington, D.C.
NOVEMBER 2, 2004

SO HERE WE ARE AGAIN. Four years ago on this night, the networks were so desperate for attention that they called the election early and often. The outcome of 2000 shamed them into promising to Congress that they would hold back on their projections until actual results come in. But if they are going to wait until they get the facts before they report this time, how on earth are they going to fill in all those endless hours of live television?

NBC News is talking more about Brokaw's retirement than the race. Fox is reairing the three most embarrassing photo ops of the campaign: Kerry snowboarding, windsurfing, and hunting (these are sure to be the only lasting images from this campaign). On CNN, Paul Begala is espousing the virtues of negative campaigning. His argument is that negative ads are good because they arouse emotions in people and that passion inspires them to go vote. So lying, deception, and obfuscation are good? And you were offended when Jon Stewart came on your show and asked you to stop "hurting America"? No wonder *Crossfire* was canceled and people are looking to comedy shows for news.

Even though Bush has been ahead in the polls all along, all the newscasters have convinced us that this race is a dead heat. They have spent so much money on campaign coverage that they need to hype this whole "closest election ever" story so that we will keep watching. How else can they justify the costs of those expensive high-tech sets? The only way they can sustain any interest in their product is by perpetuating the "dead heat" story line. Everyone likes a close game; it keeps the viewers glued to the screen.

The coverage would be a lot different if all those who called themselves experts had to put their money where their mouths are. Here is how you know that this race is not going to be that close: Bush has always been ahead in the most accurate indicator of all, the University of Iowa electronic futures market, where people have been betting that Bush will win this election. When people put their own cash on the line, you know you can trust them.

Of all those who fancied themselves as experts and pundits and spent the past year preaching to us about how it is all going to go down, the only person I trust is the homeless guy who panhandles on Sixth Avenue with a sign that says VIETNAM VET, PLEASE HELP. When I asked him for his prediction he said, "Vietnam was a loser, it fucked everyone up. Anyone who tries to use it will lose."

Now for the good news: After tonight we aren't going to have to listen to those unctuous creepy buffoons pontificating about polls for a while. Like roaches they will all scurry back to wherever it is that they hide for the next four years. The media built this election up for months. Now it will disappear. Don't expect them to be there for you after the election to make sense of it all when you may actually want to hear their insights. They will have moved on to the next story.

Looking back on their performance covering Campaign 2004, I predict that the race for the Democratic nomination will go down in history as the one the media got all wrong. They prematurely anointed Dean and wrote Kerry off completely. If a weatherman were wrong this many times, he would be fired. But this is one of the few professions in which you can be wrong and there are no consequences. Reporters often make mistakes but never have to pay the price. One of these days someone is bound to file a media malpractice suit.

There was some really irresponsible journalism committed in the 2004 election and much of the news coverage provided a disservice to the American people. In their rush to get it first, they got it all wrong. And they never apologized for their miscalculations. This is the disease of the twenty-four-hour news culture. Does anyone care about content anymore? In today's hypercompetitive news media, the reporters don't report what happened, they predict what could happen. They would rather guess and take the credit for getting the story, instead of waiting for it to play out naturally.

The thing that doesn't make any sense is why all the news organizations spend so much time and money chasing the campaigns and then, like indentured servants, just parrot their stump speeches. They jump in their news vans and chase the candidates like tornadoes, but they fail at providing us with any perspective. The flood of coverage provides so much information without anyone to sort it out for us. The networks are abdicating their educational responsibilities.

Here is what I learned from watching TV: Bush is a terrible president who dodged the draft and John Kerry is the war hero who flip-flopped on the issues. Both sides should be ashamed of their commercials (and the commercials they claimed they had nothing to do with). Both should apologize to the other for their immature, rude remarks about the other.

Despite how many times both candidates have told us that they are looking out for us, most people don't believe either one of them. As the Amtrak conductor (who did not vote) told me on the ride into Washington, D.C., on election night, "A majority of the people that ride this train every day don't know the difference between Republicans and Democrats—they hate them all the same. Presidential elections are overrated. It doesn't really matter who wins. The truth is, regardless of the results, America is going to feel like we lost either way."

He confirmed something that many people I have met over the past few years have been saying: Despite the fact that we all pay taxes and our tax dollars are sponsoring the actors in this political reality TV show, to most living outside the Beltway, politics is something that is happening on television and means nothing to those without a professional stake in the game.

George Is in the House

Washington, D.C.
JANUARY 20, 2005

NOW THAT THE PEOPLE HAVE SPOKEN and half the country agonizes over the results, it is time to celebrate our democracy! Sitting at the U.S. Capitol waiting for the president to show up and get sworn in for his second term, I couldn't help but think about the $1.7 billion that were wasted so that Bush could keep his job. This was painfully clear when the crowd laughed out loud at the sight of John Kerry appearing on stage (the man got 59,028,109 votes, which is more than any of us will ever get and today he is nothing more than a punch line).

Speaking of losers, you can't mention Howard Dean. He is the only Democrat who will be getting anything out of all of the effort he put in the last two years. Soon the blogosphere's most famous outsider will be joining this exclusive club here in the nation's capital as chairman of the Democratic National Committee.

As I sat in the "friends of Cheney" section in what felt like the "hell-freezing-over" cold with a bunch of white Republicans in mink coats (and every possible fur accessory) who paid top dollar to be here on this "glorious day," I managed to camouflage myself as one of them by singing along to all our American anthems, including the hit "Let the Eagles Soar," which John Ashcroft wrote (and performed in *Fahrenheit 9/11*).

When the emcee announced the arrival of any Republican who ever served in any public office, the crowd went wild. But when Jimmy Carter or any other Democrat was introduced, they did not make a sound. When Bill and Hillary were announced, the guy sitting in front of me wearing a Stetson hat, snakeskin cowboy boots, and a George W. Bush inauguration jacket joked, "Did he bring Michael Moore, Osama bin Laden, and Gavin Newsom with him?" When asked what that meant he replied, "Those are all the people that helped us win."

I talked with a lady wearing red-, white-, and blue-dyed rabbit fur boot toppers about how great it is that rich people aren't the only ones voting against their self-interest. It has always been fashionable for rich liberals to vote against a tax cut in the name of all of the poor slobs out there who need that money more than they do. Now the Bible Belt is catching on; they are not voting their pocketbook, they are voting to protect their guns and their Bibles. All us blue-staters ask, Why do they vote against their self-interest? Working-class people are entitled to screw themselves. Amen.

A woman who described Dick Cheney as a "god" and refused to put on a scarf because she didn't want to cover up her pearl necklace said she "almost feels sorry for the Democrats." It is now very in vogue to talk about the grave peril that the Democratic Party is in. Don't believe the hype; this is just a classic case of lazy journalists repeating what the winners are saying. (They say that history is written by the winners. It is more like journalists only want to talk to people in power, and therefore theirs is the only side of the story being told.)

When the president finally made his grand entrance, the guy next to me (wearing a button with George Bush's face next to Mount Rushmore) had tears in his eyes. Earlier he told me, "George will be added to Mount Rushmore . . . he will go down in history like Caesar, Charlemagne, Churchill, Lincoln, and Washington, because our civilization just peaked."

At high noon when Bush took his oath, a protester stood up and started screaming "No war," but no one onstage seemed to notice. Every working journalist with a camera ran over to capture the moment, at which the fox-fur-clad woman behind me expressed her disgust. "How pathetic: 250,000 guests showed up and behaved properly, but the minute one man stands up and yells 'no war,' all the camera crews pay attention to him." (From seats with this price tag, you could not see the thousands of protesters who came from all across the country to protest this party.)

During Bush's inaugural address another man started voicing his dis-approval of the war; this time, Bush must have heard it. As the protester carried on, the crowd started chanting "USA, USA" to drown him out. My parents, who were seated onstage three rows away from the presi-dent, did hear that protester and the USA chant, but they said it was hard to tell what to make of the sounds coming from down below. They assumed it was delayed enthusiasm for the president's speech.

All of this reminds me of the most obvious thing you need to remem-ber about the media. Your experience of any event depends on where you were sitting. When you are reading the paper, all you are getting is one perspective. Your reporter is just one person telling you what they saw from their seat. If you were there, you would have seen the whole scene differently depending on where you chose to look. Like viewing an accident, everyone has a different view and there are multiple inter-pretations of every event. Everyone wants their view of the world to match what they see in the media—but it rarely does.

If you were in my seat, what would you have been watching during the final benediction? As the reverend prayed for peace and "clean fi-nancial records," would you focus on the few who were praying along with him? Or would you have been watching all the people rushing to beat the crowds out of there? Or would you have been observing all the people mobbing flamboyant boxing promoter Don King? (King is an admitted killer who took the fifth when questioned by a Senate sub-committee investigating corruption in boxing.) In the final moment of reflection at the fifty-fifth presidential inauguration, people were lining up to have their picture taken with him. Even in this faith-based right-wing crowd, celebrity trumps prayer.

It was only fitting that on this "historic" day, everything was tele-vised, from the minute the president left his house at the crack of dawn to go to church to when he arrived home at 10:08 after the last ball. Even though there was no actual "news," the events went on as sched-uled, we got to watch every single thing Bush did *live*. Including eating lunch! Throughout the meal, the eyewitness news teams gave us the play-by-play: "They are about to eat Missouri quail." They included the details of how each course was prepared and the history of steamed lemon pudding. After they exhausted every possible trivial detail about the menu, they started exchanging their own recipes, and then started guessing what Bill Clinton could be talking to Karl Rove about at the table nearby. "Now that is a powerhouse conversation I would want to be part of!" While we voyeuristically watched the powerful men eat, we were forced to listen to the anchors' verbal diarrhea.

As the newly sworn-in president made his way home down Pennsylvania Avenue, camera crews were positioned all along the parade route to capture five hundred different angles of the motorcade driving by. It seemed appropriate that the White House press corps got to ride along with the president in a bandwagon. Live on Fox News, a newswoman was talking about the people who came out to salute the president. When the anchor asked her what the people behind her were chanting, she reported that they were saying, "Hey George Bush, how are you feeling today?" In fact, they were chanting, "Hey George Bush, what do you say, how many soldiers did you kill today?" Details, details.

Over on CNN Wolf Blitzer was talking about how "there are a lot more people who have gathered along Pennsylvania Avenue who love this president," while signs that said FOUR MORON YEARS flashed across the screen. The latest buzz inside the Beltway has been about a journalist who accepted government money to promote Bush's programs, but on days like this, it is hard to see how the coverage could be any more flattering toward the administration.

From his Inauguration Headquarters, Chris Matthews had former Dodgers manager and Slim-Fast spokesman Tommy Lasorda giving his expertise. And to pander to the powers that be, NBC had two creepy-looking preachers with ambiguous religious affiliations providing commentary, proving that the biggest myth that came from this election is that "faith-based values are altering the face of politics." That is just what Karl Rove wants you to think. This election was not a victory for all the homophobic, evangelical, Bible-thumping bigots. Just because the exit polls said that moral values were important doesn't mean that we should be listening to all those crazy Christian capitalist preachers who want to start a holy war in this country. If someone asked you a multiple-choice question about what was important to you, you would say moral values, too. (You wouldn't want to look like a heathen now, would you?) And besides, those exit polls also said that Kerry was going to be the winner. They are meaningless.

The cameras stayed fixed on the first family the entire time they sat in the viewing stands watching the parade. As we watched them watch the parade, the anchors babbled on. When they ran out of comments like "I'd sure like to be in there listening to what Karl Rove is saying to Arnold," they started gossiping about how the president's daughter put on her lip gloss. This was a clear indication of how desperate they were to fill airtime, but at whose expense? On this day on which we are celebrating the "price of freedom" and all that comes with it—including a free press—you can't help but wonder: What would the Founding Fathers have thought about the live coverage of Jenna Bush applying lipstick?

In a discussion about the Bush twins on CNN, a female magazine editor was saying that everything they do and say is scrutinized because the press "loves to be hard on people in the public eye." But "scrutinizing everything" is not a necessary part of democracy; it is what sells magazines. Don't disguise your need for content and excuse your exploitation as a necessary part of democracy.

The live inauguration coverage went late into the night, with the celebrity profilers talking to Cabinet members about who designed their outfits. (There is nothing worse than journalists, who are notoriously dressed inappropriately, judging other people's fashion.) The remarkable part of this television event was how the anchors managed to combine frivolous details with deadly serious comments all in one sentence. How many minutes Bush spent dancing at the Freedom Ball was mixed in with talk about when the soldiers in the room will be shipped off to Iraq.

Larry King juggled talking to designer Oscar de la Renta about Laura Bush's winter-princess look and asking Bob Woodward about the ramifications of spreading freedom all over the world. In the discussion about the first lady's wardrobe, de la Renta was credited for "changing Laura's image." (Isn't it gross how Washington forces people to succumb to their standards? Fashion and otherwise.)

Throughout the day all we heard from the voices coming from our televisions was how much "Bush has changed" and "grown into the role of Leader of the Free World." But when they are talking about Bush's evolution, they are merely talking about their own. If you spent one minute alone with George Bush you would see he hasn't changed. Only the elitist press corps' impression of him has. They finally figured out that he is not as dumb as they said he was and that he is more than that caricature they made of him.

In this day-long infomercial glorifying the new and improved Bush presidency, all the reporters seem to be saying the same thing: This is George Bush's world and we are just happy that he let us into the party.

Acknowledgments

THANK YOU TO ALL of the rich and famous and poor and un-known strangers who invited me into their homes, dorm rooms, trailers, diners, bars, and VFW halls to discuss this crazy little thing called democracy. I appreciate everyone who kept me awake on those endless plane, train, bus, or RV trips across America.

Sure, I missed a flight (or two) and a few speeches thanks to my elastic boyfriend who taught me to let go. Thanks, Michiel, for saving me from the life of a news nun.

My grandfather, who served in public office for three decades, used to say that this business comes with a free head clipping. Anytime you try to reach above the pack, they will cut your head off! For my family and my HBO family (especially Sheila Nevins and Lisa Heller), I will not let the dream killers break my spirit. On that note, thanks to my homeboys Drew Fellman, Trent Gegax, and Bob Calo for making sure none of the sourpusses pissed their vinegar on me!

I am grateful to my agents, Jon Liebman and Sandy Wernick at Brillstein Grey, for encouraging me not to give my thoughts away on a blog, but to get them published!

Which brings us to the most important thank-you of them all. Thank you to everyone at Free Press: Martha Levin, Dominick Anfuso, Wylie O'Sullivan, and Nicole Kalian. I sincerely appreciate all their efforts on my behalf.

Index

Page numbers in *italics* refer to illustrations.

CNBC, 211
CNN, 69, 136, 139, 155, 169, 187, 208,
    246, 271
  Bush's second inauguration and,
    277, 278
  in stakeout at Kerry's house, 237–41
college students, 183, 188, 189, 195,
    228–29, 230
comfort requirement, of U.S. public,
    245
Concord High School, 91–92
Concord Monitor, 142–43
"Confederate flag controversy," 111–12
Congress, U.S., 113, 142, 176, 252, 271
  see also House of Representatives,
    U.S.; Senate, U.S.
Congressional Christmas Ball (Dec. 9,
    2002), 3–6
Connecticut, Kerry fund-raiser in, 237,
    242–43
conspiracy theories, 107
corporations, 75
Cross, David, 89
cross burnings, 195
Crossfire (TV show), 271
Crowley, Candy, 169, 187–88, 192–94
C-SPAN, 181, 197, 228
Cuomo, Mario, 12–13
Cyrus, Billy Ray, 264

Daily Show, The (TV show), 193
Dallas Morning News, 225
Dean, Charlie, 92
Dean, Howard, *8,* 11–15, 21–26,
    27–31, 83–90, 146, 164–69, 252,
    260
  background of, 49
  bloggers and, 51
  Clark contrasted with, 105
  Clark's alleged offer from, 105

  as coffeehouse candidate, 50
  "Confederate flag controversy" and,
    111–12, 143
  confidence of, 83
  demise of, 153–56, 160, 175–79, 202
  Democratic attacks on, 112
  at Democratic Convention, 258
  descriptions of supporters of, 45–47,
    49–51, *52,* 83–85, *86,* 113, 130–31
  DLC vs., 73–76
  as DNC chairman, 274
  at DNC winter meeting (2003),
    11–13, 14
  effects of rise and fall of, 50
  electability issue and, 75
  endorsements for, 59, 60, 87–90,
    119, 156, 178, 202
  family factor and, 27–31, 154–55,
    178
  foreign policy inexperience of, 60,
    71, 106, 112–13, 142, 177
  as front-runner, 86, 87–88, 105, 107,
    109, 112, 176, 272
  fund-raising of, 48, 49, 51, 76, 83,
    89, 114, 166, 178
  grassroots movement and, 45–47,
    49, 73–76, 153
  at Halloween party, 84
  handling problem of, 110–14
  hothead label of, 22, 30, 75, 136–43,
    169
  Internet used by, 21–24, 49, 50–51,
    137, 153, 156, 178
  introducers of, 46, 48
  in Iowa, 27, 35, 37, 45, 83–84, 112,
    118, 127–32, 136–43, 155
  Iraq war and, 11–12, 23, 107, 171
  Kerry helped by, 146, 178
  Kerry's views on, 71
  LaRouchie attacks on, 154

lessons from, 179
liberal label of, 22, 76, 156
media coverage of, 44, 46, 48, 49,
    51–52, 83, 86, 87, 98, 112, 118,
    119, 122–32, *132,* 136–43, 154–55,
    164–66, 168–70, 176–79
meet-ups and, 21–24, *26,* 27, 131
Moby's views on, 60
natural habitat of, 85
in New Hampshire, *8,* 27, 70,
    71–72, 84, 106–7, 155–56
people skills lacking in, 85–86,
    164–70
Perfect Storm concept and, 130–31
plane of, 129
in polls, 118, 133, 200
racism charges against, 111
religious views of, 106
scream speech of, 136–43, 146
Sleepless Summer Tour of, 45–52,
    86
speeches of, 11–12, 14, 23, 27, 47,
    74, 83–84, 111, 136–43, 146,
    155–56
staff of, 48–49, 110, 113–14, 130–31,
    133, 156, 165, 167
Super Tuesday and, 198–200
Vermont image of, 49
vice presidential running mate and,
    105, 142
Washington criticized by, 112, 113
at Women's Campaign Fund event,
    13–15
death penalty, 150
debates, 194–95
    Clark in, 56
    Kerry in, 70–71
Defense Department, U.S., xiii, xiv
Defense of Marriage Act, 150
de la Renta, Oscar, 278–79

Delay, Tom, *5*
democracy, 123, 162, 178, 180, 183,
    194, 274, 278
    effects of press-politician conflict
        on, xi, xiv
Democratic Leadership Council
    (DLC), 73–76, 79, 88, 201
Democratic National Committee
    (DNC), 58, 112
    Dean as chairman of, 274
    winter meeting of (2003), 11–13, 14
Democratic National Convention:
    of 1972, 80
    of 1984, 12, 257
    of 2004, 62, 82, 94, 257–58, 261–63
Democrats, Democratic Party, xi, 3
    activists in, 75
    at Bush's second inauguration,
        274–75
    centrists in, 74, 79
    Clark's running as, 70, 71
    conservative, 32, 76
    Dean attacked by, 112
    DLC vs. grassroots in, 73–76
    in election of 1960, 117
    in election of 1972, 75, 77–82
    in election of 1984, 81, 257
    in election of 1988, 10, 16, 68, 208
    in election of 1992, 74, 76, 85
    in election of 2000, 31, 42, 44,
        68–69, 76
    Fahrenheit 9/11 and, 250–51
    Iraq war and, 11–12, 16, 22
    liberal, 22, 75, 76, 150, 156, 160
    as loser, 199
    moderate, 76
"Democrats in Their Natural
    Habitats" (*Esquire* essay), 85
Des Moines Register, 111, 128, 143
DiCaprio, Leonardo, 264, 265

Dole, Bob, 30, 246, 248
domestic violence, Americans
    compared with victims of, 245
Dr. Dre, 64
"Dream Team", use of term, 254, 256
Drudge Report, 173–74, 218
Dukakis, Michael, 10, 68, 208

economy, U.S., 211
Editors, The (TV show), 142
education, 217
Edwards, Elizabeth, 39, 255
Edwards, John, 111, 114–18, 141,
    180–92, *192,* 269
  appearance of, 116, 133, 135, 171,
    195
  as "the Breck boy," 197
  children of, 29, 39
  endorsements for, 60, 182
  foreign policy inexperience of, 191
  in-flight press conferences of,
    189–90, *189*
  in Iowa, 39–41, 133, 135
  JFK compared with, 116
  Kerry vs., 186–89
  media coverage of, 141, 180–82,
    184–92, *189,* 211–25
  media problems with, 114–17
  in New Hampshire, 117–18, 187
  plane of, 187, 189–90
  propaganda identified in speech of,
    180–86
  "Real People, Real Solutions" bus
    tour of, 39–41, *41*
  Secret Service and, 188–89
  speeches of, 39, 40, 115, 180–86, 188
  staff of, 186, 256
  Super Tuesday and, 199
  supporters of, 104, 116–17, 171
  Teresa Kerry's relationship with, 255

Two Americas of, 114–15, 117, 188,
    190
  as vice presidential candidate,
    253–56, 259
Eisenhower, Dwight D., 34
electability issue, 72, 75, 109
election of 2000, ix–xi, 4, 13, 32, 54, 68,
    271
  author's coverage of, ix–x, 4, 13, 32,
    54, 97, 98, 99, 108, 167–68, 173,
    202, 210, 215, 226, 229, 234, 238,
    244
  Bush in, ix, x, 4, 28–29, 48, 54, 62,
    71, 89, 108–9, 110, 116, 129, 149,
    167–68, 173, 202, 210, 212–15,
    223, 225, 227, *228,* 229, 234, 243,
    244, 249
  in Florida, 198, 199
  Gore in, 31, 42, 44, 68–69, 76, 88,
    249
  Laura Bush's role in, 28–29
  Nader in, 74
  press visit to Bush ranch in, 223
  primaries in, 178
  Republican Convention in, 259
  Republican "event-ized" strategy in,
    210
  traveling press corps in, 225, 226,
    229
  vice presidential candidate in, 42, 44
election of 2004:
  ads in, 112–13, 273
  conventions in, 257–63
  debates in, 56, 70–71, 194–95
  electability issue in, 72, 75, 109
  election night in, 271–74
  foreign policy issue in, 60, 71, 106,
    112–13, 142, 177, 191
  irresponsible journalism in, 272–73
  polls in, *see* polls

Republican tracking in, 105
tactic of clarity vs. tactic of distortion in, 148
elections:
great losers in, 78–79
of 1948, 89
of 1960, 117
of 1972, 75, 77–82
of 1984, 81, 257
of 1988, 10, 16, 30, 68, 208
of 1992, 74, 76, 85
of 2002, 10
Elliott, Missy, 264
Elmendorf, Steve, 176
equal protection, 151
equal rights, 190
ESPN, 61
Esquire, 85
Etheridge, Melissa, 60
evangelicals, 191
Evans, Don, 248
exit polls, 199, 201, 277–78

Fahrenheit 9/11 (movie), 249–51, 274
fairness, 233
media and, 113, 123, 125, 126, 138–39, 218
family:
in political campaigns, 27–31, 154–55, 178
political costs to, 80
fashion, 163–64, 278–79
Filene, Ed, 180
"flash mob," 51
flight attendants, 20–21, 189, 222, 243
Florida, 198, 199
Flynt, Larry, 121
Ford, Gerald, 34

foreign policy, 75
anger and, 79–80
Dean's inexperience with, 60, 71, 106, 112–13, 142, 177
Edwards's inexperience with, 191
in election of 2000, x, 71
in election of 2004, 60, 71, 106, 112–13, 142, 177, 191
40/40, 64–66
Fox, Michael J., 61
Fox News, 15, 148–53, 175, 205, 214, 251, 252, 271
in stakeout at Kerry's house, 237–39, 241–42
Frank, Barnie, 3
"frienemies," 226
Frist, Bill, 3
front-runner status:
avoidance of, 203
of Dean, 86, 87–88, 105, 106, 109, 112, 176, 272
fund-raising:
of Bush, 49
of Clark, 64, 109
of Dean, 48, 49, 51, 76, 83, 89, 114, 166, 178
of Gephardt, 17
of Kerry, 232–34, 237, 242–43
funerals, 54, 256

Gandhi, Mahatma, 260
Garner, John Vance, 256
Garofalo, Janeane, 89
gas prices, 211, 222
gay marriage, 138, 148, 150–51, 190–91, 197
Gephardt, Dick, 15–18, 60, 85, 112, 118–20, 198, 253
experience as liability to, 135–36

Index ~ 289

Gephardt, Dick (*cont.*)
  family of, 29, 35, 135, 136
  fund-raising of, 17
  in Iowa, 35–36, 43, 112, 118–20,
    133, 156
  Iraq war and, 16, 112, 135
  lack of media coverage of, 15–16,
    118–20, 166
  loss of, 134–36, 160
  optimism of, 134–35, 136
  staff of, 119–20, 176
  Stop Dean Movement and, 113
  supporters of, 17, 119
Gephardt, Jane, 35
Gephardtpalooza, 118–20
Germany, bombing of, 247
Giuliani, Rudy, 264
glittering generality, 180, 183–84
Goffstown, N.H., 99–102
Gold, Judy, 89
Gore, Al, 11, 162
  Dean endorsed by, 87, 119,
    156
  in election of 2000, 31, 42, 44,
    68–69, 76, 87–90, 249
  media's relations with, 68–69
Gore, Tipper, 31
Graham, Adele, 42, 45, 58
Graham, Bob, 42–45, 58, 60, 68, 85
  children of, 29, 42, 45
  poor performance of, 94
Graham, Gwen, 43
Gramm-Rudman-Hollings, 150
grassroots movement, 45–47, 49,
    73–76, 153
Great Britain, 268
Green, Mark, 27
Green Party, 46, 50, 75
groupthink mentality, 225
Guardian, 268

Hair, Princell, 139
Harkin, Tom, 137, 156
Harper's, 77
Harris, Katherine, 199–200
Hart, Gary, 177
Hartford Courant, 159
Harvard Club, 261
Hastert, Dennis, 3
HBO, x, 192, 197, 221, 232, 238,
    245–46
health insurance, 111, 141
Heinz, John, 21
Heinz family farm, 222–23
Heyward, Andrew, 139
Hide Your Daughter ad, 208
Hilton, Paris, 265
hockey games, 61–62, *62*
Hoffa, James, 133
Hoffman, Dustin, xiii
Hollings, Fritz, 150
Hollywood, Calif., 32, 103, 196–97
honesty, 192–93, 219, 268–69
Hootie and the Blowfish, 60
Hoover, Herbert, 34
Horton, Willy, 208
House of Representatives, U.S.,
    Gephardt in, 16, 17, 18
house parties, 7–8, 65, 70–73, 157,
    200
Howard Dean Halloween party, 84
Hughes, Karen, 13
humility, 72
Hunting of the President, The (movie),
    251–52
Hussein, Saddam, 92–93, 114, 142,
    208, 270

Iggy Pop, 147
impeachment, 78
Imus, Don, 173

media (*cont.*)
  at conventions, 261
  Dean's coverage by, 44, 46, 48, 49,
    51–52, 83, 86, 87, 98, 112, 118,
    119, 122–32, *132,* 136–43, 154–55,
    164–66, 168–70, 176–79
  Dean's criticism of, 177, 179
  Edwards's coverage by, 141, 180–82,
    184–92, *189,* 211–25
  Edwards's problems with, 114–17
  front-runner and, 203
  Gephardt's lack of coverage by,
    15–16, 118–20, 166
  Kerry's relations with, 69, 86, 90–91,
    115, 121, 124, 141, 172–74, 187,
    211–24, 234–44
  as nasty and out of control, 101
  New Hampshire invaded by,
    97–104, *100, 104*
  perception and, 276
  regulation of, 176
  security and, 188–89, 194–95, 212
  self-definition vs. definition by, 203
  see also journalism, journalists;
    television; traveling press corps
Medicare, 89
Meetup.com, 21, 25
meet-ups:
  for Dean, 21–24, *26,* 27, 131
  for Kerry, 25–27, *26*
Michiel (author's boyfriend), 53–54,
  207, 234, 250
  at Congressional Christmas Ball
    (2002), 3–6
  job of, 15
  parents of, 143–44
  proposal of, 56, 241
  scream speech and, 137, 141
  at World War II memorial
    dedication, 246–49

Middle East, 72
Moby, 59–61
Mondale, Walter, 75
money, 15, 17, 203
  time vs., 20
  see also fund-raising
Moore, Michael, 109, 161, 249–51,
  252, 253, 274–75
Mount Rushmore, 275
MSNBC, 140, 142, 211, 213
MTV, 61
multilateralism, 12
Murdock, Rupert, 252
music, 274
  endorsements and, 59–61
  in Graham campaign, 42, 43, 45
  at political rallies, 46
Muskie, Edmund, 91, 177

Nader, Ralph, 11, 50, 74, 201, 260
Naderites, 88
name-calling, 180, 181
Napster, 21
Nashua, N.H., 99, 117–18
National Guard, Bush in, 267
National Public Radio, 142
NBC, 98, 213, 226, 228, 237–41, 277
NBC News, ix, 57, 58, 229, 271
Neel, Roy, 156
Nelson, Willie, 60, 264
Nevada, caucus in, 170
Nevins, Sheila, 245–46
New Hampshire, 6–10, 45, 53, 67–73,
  97–109
  Dean in, *8,* 27, 70, 71–72, 84, 106–7,
    155–56
  Edwards in, 117–18, 187
  house parties in, 7–8, 65, 70–73, 157,
    200
  influence of, 102

Redford, Robert, xiii, 255
Red Sox, 71, 237
Reed, Lou, 61
Reiner, Rob, 119
Reno, Janet, 13, *15*
Republican National Committee
(RNC), 4
Republicans, Republican party, xi, 46,
117, 205, 254, 269
campaign 2004 tracking by, 105
Clark's voting for, 70, 105
in election of 1968, 77
in election of 1972, 78
in election of 2000, ix–xi, 4, 13,
28–29, 48, 54, 62, 71, 88, 108–9,
110, 116, 129, 148, 167–68, 173,
202, 210, 212–15, 223, 225, 227,
228, 229, 234, 243, 244, 249
in election of 2004, 18, 25, 60, 68,
72, 74, 76, 87, 112, 148–50, 201,
208–9, 217, 218, 229, 249–52
Fahrenheit 9/11 and, 249–50
gay marriage issue and, 191
Kerry attacked by, 149, 152
Lieberman's relations with, 32, 158,
159
New York City convention of
(2004), 257–63
poor southern whites and, 111
vote switching of, 122
Rice, Condoleezza, 89, 250
Richard's, 101
Robbins, Tim, 61–62
rock and roll, 59–61
Roll Call, 87
Rolling Stone, 205
Roman Catholicism, 72
Rome, 56
Roosevelt, Franklin D., 78, 81, 111
Roosevelt, Theodore, 16

Rousset, Olivia, 128
Rove, Karl, 112, 129, 133, 210
Bush's Brain and, 252
at Bush's second inauguration, 277,
278
Fahrenheit 9/11 and, 250
Rumsfeld, Donald, 54, 105, 216–17
Russert, Tim, 48, 149, 209, 267–68

St. Louis Cardinals, 209
San Francisco, Calif., 12, 156, 190–91,
257, 260
Saudi Arabia, Saudis, 142, 189
Saunders, David (Mudcat), 87
Sawyer, Diane, 154–55, 169
Schwarzenegger, Arnold, 264, 278
Scooby-Doo doll, 232
scream speech, of Dean, 136–43, 146
Seattle, Wash., Dean in, 164–65
Secret Service, 69, 194–95
Bush and, 3–4, 5
Edwards and, 188–89
Kerry and, 188, 196, 212, 233, 235,
241
security, 236, 245, 257
at airports, 18–19
media and, 188–89, 194–95, 212
Senate, U.S., 276
Intelligence Committee of, 44
Kerry in, 10, 11, 59, 72, 92
Lieberman in, 74, 160
September 11 attacks, 31, 42, 71, 107,
209, 212, 245
investigation of, 142, 211
Moore's movie about, 249–51
Sharpton, Al, 111, 164, 195
birthday party of, 63–66, *65*
in polls, 91
Sheen, Martin, 119
Shrum, Bob, 86, 173, 218

Simmons, Russell, 64
Simon, Carly, 60
Simon, Paul, 237, 242–43
Sixth Sense, The (movie), 84
Sixty Minutes (TV show), 253,
    254–55
Slavin, Paul, 139
Sleepless Summer Tour, 45–52, *86*
South Carolina, 111, 164
Spears, Britney, 1, 264
special interests, 142, 150
Spratt Amendment, 12
Springer, Jerry, 266
Springsteen, Bruce, 205, 264, 265
Stahl, Leslie, 254–55
Stalkers, the, 22
Starr, Ken, 252
Starsky and Hutch premiere party,
    195–97
Steinberg, Judith, 28–29, 31, 154–55
Stevenson, Adlai, x, 78–79
Stewart, Jon, 193, 271
Stiller, Ben, 196, 197
Stop Dean Movement, 113
Sully's Supermarket, 99–100, *100*
Super Bowl, running for president
    compared with, 81–82
Super Tuesday, 190, 198–202
Swift Boat Veterans for Truth, 145,
    217, 251, 261
switching gears, 203–4

"Tale of Two Cities" speech (Cuomo),
    12–13
taxes, 150, 273, 275
Teamsters, 35, 119, 133
television, 33, 81, 92, 136–43, 167–70,
    181, 182, 252, 265–71
  in airports, 19
  cable, 138, 139, 211, 261, 267

Crowley's views on, 192–94
Dean's scream speech and, 136–43
importance of, 77, 141, 203, 227–28
Iraq war and, 208
journalists on, xiii–xiv
network monopoly and, 238–39
nuance and, 148–53
print journalism vs., 167–68, 227–28
real life vs., xi, 139, 141, 192–93
terrorists, 150, 252, 269
  see also September 11 attacks
Thomas, Evan, 256
Thurmond, Strom, 89
Tibet, 258
"Tide of Second Thoughts Rises
    Among Democrats" (article),
    130
Timberlake, Justin, 220, 264
Time, 44, 95, 112, 155, 221, 261
Today show (TV show), 269
Tour of Duty (Brinkley), 143–45
transfer, 180, 185
traveling press corps, 97–98, 211–31,
    237–44
  alliances in, 226–27
  campaign bubble of, 207, 211–24,
      238
  caste system of, 227–28
  cost of, 226, 228, 229, 232, 235, 238
  with Dean, 127–32
  in election of 2000, 225, 226, 229
  good vs. bad apples in, 224–25
  groupthink mentality of, 225
  hazing process and, 212–13
  as liaison or goodwill ambassador,
      229
  network monopoly and, 238–39
  odd and alienating behavior of, 226
  off-the-record comments of, 230
  in stakeout at Kerry's house, 237–43

top ten favorite quotes from, 231
writing about, 230–31
Trippi, Joe, 48–49, 107, 113–14, 133, 146
  Perfect Storm concept and, 130–31
  replacement of, 156
  scream speech and, 138, 139
Twin Towers:
  1993 attack on, 252
  see also September 11 attacks
Two Americas, 114–15, 117, 188, 190

unilateralism, 11–12
Union Square protests, 259–61, 262–63
United Nations, Iraq policy and, 12
USA Today, 91, 138, 269

Vermont, Dean associated with, 49
VH1, 220
vice president:
  Dean and, 239
  Kerry's selection of, 239, 253–56
Vietnam war, 78, 92, 121, 122, 143–45, 209, 217, 254, 272
  antiwar movement and, 11, 79
  Kerry in, 10, 92, 122, 143–45, 162, 217, 248, 251, 273

Wallace, Chris, 150–53
Wall Street Journal, 121
Warner Bros., 196
"War on Terror," 269
Washington, D.C., 16, 28, 178, 202, 274–79
  Dean's criticism of, 112, 113
  World War II memorial dedication ceremony in, 246–49
Washington, George, 81
Washington Post, 85, 90–91, 124, 227

Washington Times, 87, 218
Watergate, xiii
weapons of mass destruction, 138, 152, 270
Weekend at Bernie's (movie), 107
Weekend Today (TV show), 213
Weekly Standard, 152
Wellstone, Paul, 21
WGBH, 91
White, Theodore, xii
White House, 11, 127
  Congressional Christmas Ball in, 3–6
  press corps of, 21, 210, 277
  television department of, 228
whites:
  in Iowa, 102
  in media, 102, 131, *132,* 176, 226
  in New Hampshire, 102
  poor Southern, 111
Wilgoren Watch, 123
Willkie, Wendell, 78–79
Wilson, Owen, 196
wire services, 227
Wisconsin, 166, 175–76
wives of candidates, role of, 27–31, 154–55, 178
Wolfe, Tom, 54–55
Women's Campaign Fund, 13–15
Woodruff, Judy, 136
Woodward, Bob, xiii, 278
work ethic, 54
World War II memorial dedication ceremony, 246–49

Yago, Gideon, 61, 147
Yarrow, Peter, 121
Young Conservative Movement, 149

zoo planes, 227

About the Author

After six years of toiling in the trenches of television news, Alexandra Pelosi got assigned by NBC to cover George W. Bush in the 2000 election. She brought her camcorder along and made a movie, *Journeys with George.* Then she went back on the road for HBO to make a movie about the 2004 campaign, *Diary of a Political Tourist.*